SHIFTING THE BLAME

LITERATURE, LAW, AND
THE THEORY OF ACCIDENTS IN
NINETEENTH-CENTURY AMERICA

Nan Goodman

Boulder, Colorado
13 May 1999

PRINCETON UNIVERSITY PRESS   PRINCETON, NEW JERSEY

Library of Congress Cataloging-in-Publication Data
Goodman, Nan
Shifting the blame : literature, law, and the theory
of accidents in nineteenth-century America / Nan Goodman
p. cm.
Includes bibliographical references (p.) and Index.
ISBN 0–691–01199–0 (cloth : alk. paper)
1. American literature—19th century—History and criticism.
2. Accidents in literature. 3. Accident law—United States—
History—19th century. 4. Legal stories, American—History
and criticism. 5. Law and literature—History—19th century.
6. Negligence in literature. 7. Responsibility in literature.
8. Blame in literature. I. Title.
PS217.A25G66 1998
810.9'355—dc21   97-44478   CIP

This book has been composed in Sabon

Princeton University Press books are printed
on acid-free paper and meet the guidelines
for permanence and durability of the Committee
on Production Guidelines for Book Longevity
of the Council on Library Resources

http://pup.princeton.edu

1   3   5   7   9   10   8   6   4   2

For Erik Urdang

Contents

Acknowledgments

FOR GUIDING the early drafts of this book when it was a dissertation at Harvard University, and for helping me to imagine and then investigate aspects of the various chapters that would otherwise have remained hidden from me, my thanks go first to Professor Elaine Scarry. While words may never adequately express the gratitude I feel for the direction Professor Scarry provided, I wish here to acknowledge the tremendous influence she has had on me. Her astonishing insights, her intellectual generosity, her deep concern and careful attention to the logic of my thoughts and prose, have marked not only this book but my habit of mind in general and my continuing enthusiasm for the study of literature, language, and history. I also especially want to acknowledge and express my thanks for the guidance of Professor Sacvan Bercovitch, who encouraged and directed my work on this project from the beginning, and who urged me to pursue the field of law and literature in the first place. Professor Bercovitch combines brilliance and compassion in a way that helped to sustain me when I was a graduate student and that continues to inspire me as a teacher and scholar.

I also owe an enormous debt of gratitude to Professor Brook Thomas, who read the manuscript in its penultimate draft and who was especially generous with his reflections on my work. His extensive commentary on and his detailed suggestions for how to make the book more inclusive and more focused on the subject of agency and responsibility were crucial in my reshaping of it. The book benefited from the careful readings of many friends and colleagues. In particular I wish to thank Professors David Simpson, Margaret Ferguson, Anne Janowitz, and Richard Halpern. Without their helpful suggestions and encouragement, the manuscript would never have survived to see a better day. Special thanks are due to Professor Nancy Ruttenburg, in whose class I was first given the forum, as a graduate teaching assistant, to try out my ideas for the book. Her extraordinary kindness, critical intelligence, rib-tickling humor, and friendship have kept me going me throughout this project and have allowed me to test many of my wildest ideas without fear of humiliation or reprisal. I want too to thank Professor Lee Krauth for his invaluable contributions as a Twain scholar to chapter 4, and Edie Rosenberg, who helped me get that first and crucial chapter on James Fenimore Cooper right. Also my friends Bradley Alpert, Silva Chang, Betty Symington, Dan and Ann Donoghue, and Roland Greene, perhaps without knowing it, helped me get through periods when the work would have otherwise seemed endless. I would also like to thank Professor John Stilgoe at Harvard University for sharing his wealth of knowledge about railroads and railroad films and in helping me flesh out some of the particulars of chapter 6.

Many members of the library staff at Harvard and at the University of Colorado have been crucial in helping me find my way through vast source materials. But two in particular stand out. Lee Ann Walther, a reference librarian at the University of Colorado Law Library helped me hunt down obscure cases and treatises at a moment's notice and did so with a cheerfulness and expertise that floored me. Lynnette Westerlund, a library technician in the Interlibrary Loan Office at the University of Colorado Libraries also went beyond the call of duty in managing the many requests I made over the years. For providing me with crucial research time, I wish to thank the National Endowment of the Humanities for the year-long fellowship during which I wrote much of this book, as well as the University of Colorado and its English Department for a semester's research leave.

In its final stages, this book also benefited from the help of many people. I am grateful to my editor at Princeton University Press, Deborah Malmud, who helped me to rethink many aspects of the law and literature connection and who has handled it with a wisdom, courtesy, and friendliness that have put me at ease. Bill Laznovsky at Princeton University Press also did a wonderfully sensible and thorough job of copyediting the manuscript. Thanks also go to Professor Wai Chee Dimock, one of the Press's readers, for her marvellously helpful comments and close reading of the manuscript, as well as to Professor Maxwell Bloomfield whose comments on the legal narratives of the book made it much tighter.

The members of my family also deserve mention here, not only for their inspiration and support, but for their interest and resourcefulness. My sister, Susan Goodman, who was always ready with examples of books containing accidents that often found their way into the manuscript, also proved enthusiastic about the project when I could no longer conjure up any enthusiasm on my own. She has been the most supportive and encouraging of sisters. I would also like to thank my mother, Ruth Goodman, for making up the rule when I was a child that while I might not always get the toy I demanded, I could always get a book, and for instilling in me the love of literature that underwrote such a rule; and especially my father, Norman Goodman, for helping me to track down a source for several of the photographs that appear in these pages, but more important, for showing me, through his own enlightened practice of it, that the law was a fertile area for thought and interpretation. Thanks too to my sister-in-law, Gwen Urdang-Brown, for expressing interest in the manuscript in its various incarnations and for doing much legwork to get me otherwise unavailable books, and to my mother-in-law, Esther Urdang, for her moral support and encouragement. Finally, my sincere thanks to my father-in-law, Elliott Urdang, M.D., whose interest and aid went beyond the bounds of family and without whose keen critical eye and meticulous research—research that included trips to nautical museums in New England and to many libraries—I would not have been able to write chapter 3. The research he did for chapter 3 and the countless conversations we had about the logic of that chapter and of the book as a whole were invaluable to me in rewriting much of the manuscript.

My most comprehensive and personal thanks, however, go to my husband and son. I wish to thank my four-year-old son, Sam Goodman Urdang, for proving the most delightful of distractions and for demonstrating from the moment he could talk an uncanny interest in and sympathy for my own obsession with vehicles that blow up, crash, and go boom. And finally, thank you, Erik, for being my first and last reader and advisor, my constant source of inspiration and most ardent supporter, my cover artist, and my loving husband. Our non-accidental meeting has been the happiest of my life.

✳   ✳   ✳

I would gratefully like to acknowledge permission to publish chapter 2 of this book, which was previously published in altered form in *Arizona Quarterly*, vol. 49, no. 2, Summer 1993.

SHIFTING THE BLAME

CHAPTER ONE

Introduction

And if one man's ox hurt another's, that he die;
then they shall sell the live ox, and divide the
money of it; and the dead ox also they shall divide.
Or if it be known that the ox hath used to push
in time past, and his owner hath not kept him
in; he shall surely pay ox for ox; and the dead
shall be his own.
(*Exodus* 21:35–36)

THE PRINCIPAL ARCHITECT of American railroad law,[1] Chief Justice Lemuel Shaw (1781–1861), of the Supreme Judicial Court of Massachusetts,[2] was known for handing down landmark decisions. The case of *Brown v. Kendall*,[3] however, decided by Shaw in 1850, did not, at first glance, appear to be among them. In fact, far from providing him with an opportunity to review public policy and to forge new legal doctrine, it called attention to an unambiguously *private* dispute between two dog owners. In trying to part the fighting dogs by beating them with a stick, one dog owner accidentally hit the other in the eye and in this caused an actionable injury. In deciding the case, Shaw was called upon to rule on the question of liability, which until that time had not been a controversial area of the law. Indeed, it was a tribute to Shaw's ingenuity as a jurist that from facts as seemingly dull and incontrovertible as these, he was able to articulate the influential and revolutionary new doctrine of negligence that altered the legal resolution and the literary representation of accidents in nineteenth-century America.

An emphasis on blameworthiness was at the heart of the new doctrine. "[F]or if the injury was unavoidable," Shaw wrote, "and the conduct of the defendant [Kendall] was free from blame, he will not be liable."[4] Of course, to readers and litigants in our own time, Shaw's formulation may seem almost commonplace, for it is now customary to associate legal liability for injury with certain standards of care and blameworthiness. But in the first half of the nineteenth century, this connection was far from obvious. Under the doctrine of strict liability which had prevailed in accident cases for centuries, the law imposed liability even on perpetrators whose conduct was unblameworthy. This outcome, jurists and legal scholars believed, furthered the "dominant idea of Anglo-Saxon law . . . that man acts at his peril,"[5] and thus must suffer the consequences that issue from his acts. For Shaw, however, the fact that the accident in *Brown v. Kendall* was "such as the defendant could not have avoided by the use of the kind and degree of care necessary to the exigency, and in the circumstances" greatly problematized the inquiry into liability. For if the defendant was in fact "using the kind and degree of care that prudent and cautious men use," Shaw wrote, there was no logical basis on which to assign liability to him. Rather, for Shaw and his colleagues, the appropriate standard for adjudicating accidents involved an inquiry into fault, where "fault" was construed as the failure to use "ordinary care." Thus, fault was defined as a form of carelessness or negligence, making negligence the comprehensive standard by which all future accident cases were to be judged.

Although by no means immediate, the implications of the transformation ushered in by the doctrine of negligence were enormous. As a legal doctrine, negligence was undoubtedly most transformative for the litigants who went to court to get compensation for their injuries. In addition to the changes wrought by negligence in the law were the changes it precipitated for industrialization and for America's understanding of individual agency[6] and responsibility for risk as a whole. In fact, so pervasive was the impact of negligence that virtually no aspect of nineteenth-century culture escaped its influence. *Shifting the Blame*, however, focuses on one particular aspect of that cultural reformation—the narrative manifestations and implications of accidents that emerged not in scientific tables and charts that correlated risk with other variables or even in the histories of industrial risk and danger, but in the literary telling and retelling of accidents. In turning my attention to literature, moreover, I conclude that nowhere was the significance of the new doctrine of accidents more visible than in the pages of the accident narratives that began in this period (a period that roughly coincides with the heyday of American industrialization) to permeate the literary marketplace. For in these stories of accidents, the features of accidental risk that might otherwise escape our attention—the suddenness of impact, the encounter between strangers, and most important, the changing nature of liability and human agency under negligence—were painstakingly reconstructed, taking a particular, and culturally significant, shape.

THE ORIGINS OF NEGLIGENCE

The modern doctrine of negligence is crucial to an understanding of the nineteenth century because it altered the story that the culture told itself about blame and responsibility. Specifically, the doctrine altered the story of blame that was associated with the legal doctrine of strict liability for accidents—the doctrine that had prevailed in Anglo-American culture for centuries before modern negligence took hold. Under strict liability—the general principle governing cases that came under the heading of torts or "wrongs" not arising from contract—responsibility for compensating someone for an accident fell absolutely or strictly to the individual who caused the injury. There was no inquiry under the doctrine of strict liability into whether the agent who had caused the injury had done so in a blameworthy manner. As one legal theorist put it: "The early law asked simply, 'Did the defendant do the physical act which damaged the plaintiff?'"[7]

Indeed, in some instances in early accident law, the law inquired only into the status relations between the injurer and injured party, thus making an inquiry into the physical act itself superfluous. Liability, that is, was often attributed on the theory that those in certain status relations with others, like that of parent and child or master and servant, should assume responsibility for those less capable of doing so. In the early stages of industrial organization, when factories were small and employees were few, relationships in the workplace were likened to those in a family where there had always been a basic presumption of compensation: family members were in the habit of taking care of each other in time of injury. On this theory, the law typically held masters liable for their servants' actions. A similar argument, based on status, applied to the liability of parents for their children and employers for their employees, extending even to the liability of doctors and lawyers for their patients and clients.[8]

Curiously, in many of these status cases the courts spoke of the "action" involved as negligent. But this early use of the term had little or nothing to do with the concept as we now know it. In fact, in these cases, without exception, negligence did not signify a *careless* performance but rather the *failure* to perform a task that had been assigned. In all of these cases, in short, negligence was tied to the absence to specify a preexisting duty or to the breach of a duty imposed by contract, statute, or by clearly defined status relations. This understanding of negligence, then, diverged only slightly from the concept of strict liability that attributed liability on the basis of causation alone, without inquiry into fault or carelessness. Thus, in a typical invocation of negligence in an escape case dating from 1795, the court attributed liability to a sheriff on the basis of this older, stricter notion of liability even in the face of evidence that the "escape was occasioned by circumstances not to be foreseen, and which could not be prevented by even more than ordinary exertions and caution."[9] For, as the court reasoned, "every escape not happening by the act of God, or the public enemies was, in the eye of the law, considered a negligent escape. The law admits no other excuse."[10]

As events became more complex, however, the strict causal emphasis of strict liability as well as the status orientation of early "negligence" became increasingly irrelevant. Indeed, in America as early as the late eighteenth century,[11] in certain accidents,[12] a new defense emerged that absolved the defendant of liability where the accident itself appeared to be inevitable, the result, for instance, not of the defendant's act directly but of a natural disaster. A very common confusion, for example, arose in cases where a sea captain allowed his ship to become disabled when a storm then forced it to collide with and cause damage to another, for in these instances it was never clear whether the accident would have occurred even in the absence of the captain's contribution.[13] In these cases, defendants often argued that not only was the accident unavoidable but that their action was lawful or unblameworthy, at the very least the result of the best efforts that could have been taken at the time and in the circumstances. Thus, in the place of strict liability, a new standard of ordinary care began to creep into the standard for adjudicating accidents long before Shaw wrote his landmark decision which was based upon it.[14] Indeed, *Brown v. Kendall* echoed an emphasis that had been placed as early as the first quarter of the nineteenth century by a small number of judges in Massachusetts and elsewhere[15] on the unavoidable and unblameworthy nature of certain injuries.

Distinguishing between blameworthy and unblameworthy behavior on the basis of the kind of care taken during the act that resulted in injury introduced a much broader notion of responsibility. It assumed, in fact, that a certain level of care was owed to each and every individual, not just to specific individuals in specific status relations. And once the notion of ordinary care replaced status and causation as an arbiter of liability, liability depended on a definition of duties which, having been violated, would lead to a finding of fault. Indeed, in larger factories, and in more densely populated urban centers that were made possible in large part by steamship and railroad travel (which were themselves prime sources of accidental injury), accidents increasingly took place between people who had never met before and between whom there was no preexisting sense of obligation. In this new, highly industrialized and technologized climate, where the causes of accidents were uncertain, and the perpetrators and victims of accidents unknown, decisions about liability for accidental injury required both a new theory of liability, and a new calculus for distinguishing between a primary cause and a potential host of others.

The concept of duty—the duty to exercise ordinary care when engaged in potentially hazardous activity—proved a paradox. Insofar as it assumed a duty that was in Oliver Wendell Holmes's words, "of all the world to all the world,"[16] it turned liability from a standard that applied to certain individuals because of their status either as actors or in certain occupations into a concept that applied to everyone indiscriminately. In short, liability went from being a specific designation for certain acts or actors to a universal standard, a shift that in America coincided with a turn from status-based notions of government to more democratic ones. Under negligence, for the first time, liability for accidents was based not on the status of the victim and perpetrator or on the fact of injury alone but on the question of fault or blameworthiness. Thus, we recall from Shaw's decision, negligence was defined as the absence of "ordinary care," or the "kind of care prudent and cautious men would use . . . in the circumstances." But if the concept of ordinary care and the invocation of the average, prudent, and cautious man paralleled a rise in democratic social relations, it did so in part by imposing a model of universal liability. In the early nineteenth century, universal liability was especially problematic for it threatened to put an end to the taking of risks necessary to an expanding industry.

The paradox of universal liability, then, was that it led to a limited liability. Indeed, almost as soon as the universal duty of taking ordinary care was introduced in America, it was curtailed by four important legal doctrines. The first and most important of these was the doctrine of negligence under which the courts defined fault and assigned liability only in the absence of ordinary care which was, generally speaking, construed quite loosely in favor of the risk-taking entrepreneur. The second of these doctrines was known as the fellow-servant rule.[17] The brainchild of Lemuel Shaw, whose influence on the negligence doctrine has already been noted, the fellow-servant rule paved the way for employer dereliction of all kinds. Under this rule, the courts explicitly reversed the earlier, status-based presumption in favor of employer liability by forbidding workers to sue their employers for injuries inflicted by their fellow employees. Because few injuries were inflicted by employers themselves, although many were the product of their negligence, this rule seriously limited suits for work-related accidents. Hand in hand with the fellow-servant rule was the third restrictive legal doctrine, the doctrine of the assumption of risk which absolved the employer of responsibility for risks the employee had assumed voluntarily. (A variation on this theme emerged in the doctrine of the scope of the employment which held all acts that endangered the employee to be, quite literally "outside the scope of employment," and thus nonactionable under the law.) Thus, employees who, in Holmes's words, "appreciated the danger"[18] of their jobs—an attribute no employee could afford to be without—had no legal right to sue employers for injuries that arose in the course of their employment.[19]

The fourth and last of these doctrines had to do with limiting the liability not of capitalists but of spectators, yet it reflected the general climate of the new restrictions on liability for all. Under the doctrine of the good Samaritan, as it came ironically to be known, the law defined the duties of all to all as negative ones and thus did not expect and even actively prohibited bystanders from acting affirmatively as good Samaritans unless a relation of status required them to do so.

Central to all of these limitations on liability were assumptions about how liability and responsibility should work. But perhaps the most important of these assumptions was a theory of causation that was drastically different from the one that underwrote the doctrine of strict liability. As Morton Horwitz has observed, the theory of causation relied on two metaphors: a chain of causation and the distinction between remote and proximate cause.[20] Thus, someone could be held responsible for causing harm to another only when a chain of proximate rather than remote causes could be established from that person's act to the effect of damage on the other. These metaphors helped to construct a narrative of very limited liability, of very limited duties that all owed to all.

Horwitz locates these metaphors in an instrumentalist view of the rise of negligence. In his view the legal doctrine of negligence was the inevitable result of the changes in economic conditions that accompanied industrialization. In keeping with his instrumentalist conception of the law, Horwitz argues that negligence was primarily a result of the law's interest in promoting policies of industrial expansion. Specifically, he points to a series of influential court decisions in the middle of the nineteenth century in which negligence became a tool designed specifically for encouraging entrepreneurial risk. By altering the already vague and variable standard of care central to the negligence calculus, the courts were able almost imperceptibly to remove certain barriers to the capitalist risk-taking they saw as necessary to the well-being of society. In short, a pattern of practice emerged in which the courts increasingly found the behavior of industrialists—factory, steamship, and railroad owners, primarily—to be within the parameters of "ordinary care," even when the facts clearly suggested an absence of care or an adequate attention to safety. While my own view benefits tremendously from that of Horwitz, it has a different emphasis. That is, while I too point to the influence of economic conditions on the rise of negligence, I do not argue for the exclusivity or inevitability of their effect. Rather, in turning my attention to the many literary narratives of accidents, narratives that compete with each other and that tell multiple and varied tales, I hope to identify the contingencies rather than the exigencies of legal history—the possibility, in short, that legal history in general, and the notion of liability under negligence in particular, need not have taken the path it did.

LITERATURE, LAW: A MODEL

In comparing and contrasting legal and literary narratives, *Shifting the Blame* both builds on and diverges from the general trend in legal and literary studies. Insofar as it assumes literary and legal texts to be equally rich and illuminating, for example, it is indebted to many of the assumptions made by some of the earliest and most influential of law and literature scholars. In particular, it draws upon the insights of James Boyd White who has emphasized the extent to which both law and literature are narrative and interpretive institutions comprised largely if not exclusively of what he refers to as "compositional activities."[21] In White's terms, both kinds of texts interpret, legitimate, and even regulate empirical data through narrative descriptions—in the one case a novel or a poem, in the other, a trial transcript or a judicial opinion. Similarly, in investigating the constructedness of both law and literature, *Shifting the Blame* borrows from the invaluable work of the legal scholars Owen Fiss and Ronald Dworkin, both of whom have helped to break down the barriers between the legal and literary disciplines. For Fiss, for example, the judicial act reveals the extent to which the law is, like literature, "neither a wholly discretionary nor a wholly mechanical activity . . . . [but rather] a dynamic interaction between reader and text."[22] Such a recognition, Fiss writes, "build[s] bridges between law and the humanities." Similarly for Dworkin, literary and legal paradigms are comparable mixtures of critical and creative acts. Indeed, Dworkin offers a notoriously odd but apt metaphor for the legal process, proclaiming that the law is like a chain novel, "each judge . . . a novelist in the chain."[23]

But if Dworkin, Fiss, and White inform the present study and even make possible some of its assumptions about the interrelated nature of legal and literary narratives, they alone cannot account for the particular version of legal and literary scholarship it provides. For far more central than the rhetorical relationship between law and literature emphasized by these theorists is the claim made here for a historical relationship or reciprocity between law and literature. In making this claim, I diverge from the emphasis that has most recently characterized the law and literature enterprise and in large part confined it to the analysis of the compositional process. Most significant, perhaps, my historical perspective is indebted to the insights of the legal scholar Robert Cover, whose work consistently articulates new possibilities for the cultural and historical pairing of law and literature. In one of his most influential essays, Cover describes law and literature as coequal narratives in a normative world. "No set of legal institutions or prescriptions," Cover writes, "exists apart from the narratives that locate it and give it meaning."[24] Specifically, by elevating both legal and literary narratives to an equal stature in the creation of what Cover calls a normative world, Cover sets the ground for a new kind of interdisciplinary study. In the first place, he ascribes to literary narratives the same kind of normative potential that we typically ascribe only to the law. The law alone, Cover suggests, is only part of a larger world of narrative myths, a lexicon of normative action that surrounds it in the form of critique, utopian aspirations, apologies, and fictions. But these fictions, Cover explains, cannot easily be distinguished from the rules that constitute the law itself for even these incorporate and cannot exist without the expression of their own alternatives. Thus, as Cover explains, "[l]aw may be viewed as a system of tension or a bridge linking a concept of a reality to an imagined alternative."[25]

The present study takes seriously Cover's vision of the law as a bridge between one version of reality and an imagined alternative to it, for it argues that neither literary nor legal narratives in nineteenth-century America can be understood without the other. More important, it follows the implication of Cover's argument about the normative world in holding both literary and legal narratives up as equally important components for an understanding of the culture as a whole. For it is only in combination with each other that the whole story a culture tells itself about how to act and which patterns of behavior to pursue can be discerned. Specifically, *Shifting the Blame* argues that for any given legal or literary narrative a complex relationship with the culture may exist. As Brook Thomas explains in *Cross-Examinations*, his invaluable study of the law and literature of mid-nineteenth-century America, a *literary* narrative may either reflect or subvert an existing or dominant culture[26] or, I might add, do both simultaneously. Similarly, although perhaps somewhat counterintuitively, a *legal* narrative may not only reflect but project or anticipate changes in the culture before they actually occur. Nor do the fields of law and literature have to be seen as temporally or even topically related in order to profit from a comparison between them. Thus, as Wai Chee Dimock explains in her insightful book, *Residues of Justice*, law and literature at times developed unevenly, "as institutionally and historically oblique to each other, marked by a historical noncoincidence of boundaries. . . ."[27] But whether complementary, subversive, or reflective of each other, taken together, legal and literary narratives can illuminate the way the culture constructs itself through narrative without privileging either the ostensibly real or the imaginary, the ostensibly true or the morally ambiguous.

Of course, to interrogate the culture through its literary and legal narratives is not to suggest that these are the only narratives available for doing so or that they interact exclusively with each other. On the contrary, this study assumes and makes explicit the existence of multiple narratives within the nineteenth-century American culture it examines, be they social, economic, legal, or literary. Indeed, at every turn there is an insistence on contextualizing both legal and literary narratives within a larger culture of social and economic change. To reinforce the sense of cultural and industrial change in this period, for example, I have turned to the insights of several important historians of change in the century, including Alan Trachtenberg, Walter Benn Michaels, and Howard Horwitz.[28] The work of these literary and social historians has been central to my own in that they have managed, while emphasizing the importance of economic change, to demonstrate the simultaneous importance and development of other social and cultural phenomena. I hold with them the view that nineteenth-century America was not a monolithic culture, but one of competing cultures and of competing classes and class concerns.

Indeed, it is partly to destabilize the exclusivity of the economic model and the instrumentalism that so often accompanies it in descriptions of nineteenth-century American culture that I invoke the paradigm of accidents and responsibility. For although it was largely in terms of the economic and industrial development in this period that the notion of responsibility came to the fore, the economy was by no means the only area that affected or registered the changes occurring in the notion of responsibility. For if responsibility took on a new meaning in the context of corporate expansion, for example, it underwent significant changes and took on new meanings in social, legal, and moral contexts as well. Indeed, my use of legal scholars as diverse as Morton Horwitz, Robert Rabin, and G. Edward White,[29] who have quite different views of how negligence arose and operated, to explicate changes in the legal context alone reveals how conflicted and varied the understanding of responsibility had become. As *Shifting the Blame* reveals, changes in the notion of responsibility had implications for a nineteenth-century revisioning of individual and collective agency as a whole.

LITERARY EXAMPLES

Although it is not possible to trace all of the different nineteenth-century permutations in the concept of responsibility, *Shifting the Blame* concentrates on the two fields—law and literature—that represent the greatest number of them insofar as they seek at all times to respond to and to resolve social conflicts. Thus, each chapter of this book not only sheds light on a different moment in the evolution of the legal and literary concept of negligence and responsibility, but also represents a different version, a different balance between prevailing and alternative or residual and emergent narratives.

Chapters 2 and 3 deal with literary works that anticipate the doctrine of negligence as Shaw articulates it in *Brown,* and thus show possible alternatives to it. Chapter 2, which revolves around James Fenimore Cooper's first Leatherstocking tale, *The Pioneers* (1823), reveals the competing narratives of responsibility that arose in the wake of the earliest articulations of careful use and universal obligation. Moreover, this chapter focuses on the development of the negligence paradigm in the context of the taming of the wilderness, an exercise itself fraught with risks and accidents. Chapter 2 argues that in the first tentative manifestations of the transition to modern negligence from strict liability lay the seeds of a strategy both for forming a consensus in a community remarkably divided by ethnic, national, and religious differences, and for coping with the scarce resources of the wilderness. Thus, in this chapter, I situate the discourse of *personal* injury within and against the discourse of *property* damage that the Anglo-American and European conquest of the Native-American wilderness represented. Although we think of negligence as pertaining only to bodily injuries (which constitute the bulk of all tort actions), it had an early and surprisingly large impact on the resolution of claims of injury to property which ultimately paved the way for the vexed transition from a wilderness to an industrial society.

Continuing my analysis of Cooper's leading role in examining the implications of negligence for the culture as a whole, chapter 3 explores his effort to rewrite the nautical novel in their light, and again focuses on competing narratives that arose alongside early revisions of strict liability. In this chapter I argue that Cooper, who popularized the genre of the nautical novel in America with his first sea tale, *The Pilot* (1827), made it possible for the first time to imagine a hero who was more attuned to the challenge of accident prevention than to that of last-minute, dramatic escapes. Indeed, in highlighting the attitude of caution and the use of "due care" in so many of his nautical protagonists (he wrote eleven novels of the sea, many of which incorporate this notion), Cooper fashioned the first fictional character of the American negligence regime: the prudent and reasonable man. In developing his new hero, moreover, Cooper began the process of wresting the concept of heroism away from the portrait of the swashbuckling, pirate-adventurer that had dominated the examples of nautical literature before him. Furthermore, Cooper's choice of the maritime context for the emergence of the first negligence-minded character proved especially fitting, for the very first legal applications of negligence in its modern sense—as a standard of due care—occurred in the context of ship collisions. As a way of calling a halt to the frequency of these collisions and to the catastrophic loss that typically resulted from them, negligence targeted seamen and urged them to be vigilant and careful. Due no doubt in large part to the communal nature of the shipping enterprise—an enterprise in which everyone had a vested interest in making the ship run smoothly—both the law and literature in this period began to focus on the responsibilities and heroism of even the common sailor. On the strength of Cooper's work and of the law's injunctions, in fact, a powerful and immensely popular type of nautical tale, authored by Richard Henry Dana Jr., John Sherburne Sleeper, and T. S. Arthur, among others, emerged in mid-century to champion the quiet and common hero of negligence law. After analyzing Cooper, then, chapter 3 turns to these authors whose unexpected elaborations illustrate how important negligence was to the development of the mid-century nautical hero and to examples of prudence and victimization that did not necessarily make it into the law.

The alternatives to the legal narrative imagined in the work of Cooper became even more finely honed as the accident paradigm moved into the second half of the nineteenth century. Thus, in chapter 4, I locate the first sustained indictment of the problems with the law in the work of Mark Twain whose own experience with and reflections on the accidents endemic to technology, and in particular to steamship technology, permeate his work from *The Gilded Age* (1873) to *Life on the Mississippi* (1883) to *A Connecticut Yankee in King Arthur's Court* (1889). What Twain found most infuriating about negligence law in his day was its abdication of the intended inquiry into fault. Rather than characterizing the behavior in question as blameworthy or blameless, in other words, more and more investigations into negligence found that the question of fault was undecidable. Indeed, the concept of undecidable or "inscrutable fault" became a common fallback position in those cases in which a technical and causal complexity seemed to preclude any clear finding of liability. For Twain, whose own brother was killed in a steamboat explosion, the absence of causal attribution was both personally dissatisfying and socially destabilizing for in his view it indicated an erosion of social responsibility as a whole. Curiously, however, Twain's frustration signals his own inability to devise a convincing alternative to the legal narrative he condemns.

Chapter 5 takes up the culturally undesirable effects of that aspect of negligence law that pertained to the duties of bystanders. Here my examples include Stephen Crane's novella, *The Monster* (1899), and Charles Chesnutt's novels *The Marrow of Tradition* (1901) and *The Colonel's Dream* (1905), as well as several of Chesnutt's short stories, which situate the problems generated by the law of the good Samaritan in the context of a racially divided post-Reconstructionist America. Chapter 4 moves beyond the binary framework of the accident proper in which someone inflicts injury and someone else receives it to examine the role of a lateral figure—of the witness and potential rescuer. According to the letter of the law, this figure, the potential rescuer, has no affirmative duty to rescue. In this, the law followed the classical liberal view of individual responsibility, as defined by C. B. Macpherson,[30] and not the classical republican view, as defined by J.G.A. Pocock,[31] in which each citizen has positive duties and obligations to all fellow citizens. Moreover, in adhering to the negative, liberal articulation, the law maintained a crucial neutrality, requiring no one individual to do more than any other. But what an analysis of Crane's fiction reveals is that an apparently neutral legal doctrine does not necessarily have a neutral application in a society in which a hierarchy of racial status persists. Thus, this chapter puts the implications of negligence in direct dialogue not only with the legal discourse but with a philosophical and moral discourse about altruism that was a crucial feature of the fin-de-siècle intellectual landscape.

An aspect of the new advances in technology, specifically in railroad technology, signs and signals began to proliferate in a pulp railroad fiction that dominated the literature of accidents in the period after Crane and Chesnutt. Indeed, signs and signals functioned in literature as they did in real life to clarify the trajectory of the accident's often inscrutable fault by contributing a system of visible and audible milestones that ultimately transformed it from an apparently unique and frequently incomprehensible event to a commonly understood and reiterable one. But they also raised questions about the abilities and responsibilities of the human agents behind them. Chapter 6, then, traces in this fiction the threatened subordination of individual agency and its alternative, the boundless opportunity for human heroism and sentiment.

Ultimately, however, the accident narrative of individual responsibility that I identify did come to an end with the close of the nineteenth century. Indeed, with the exception of the railroad narratives that appeared in the first decade or two of the twentieth century, the latter saw very little, if anything at all, of the kind of accident narrative that raised questions about individual responsibility. Rather, the twentieth century witnessed the rise of an accident narrative that, with the decline of traditional inquiries into causality, addressed problems inherent in new kinds of accidents—toxic accidents, for the most part—and new, collective kinds of responsibility. In the Epilogue, the seventh and final chapter of the book, I follow the accident narrative into this phase of development through the imaginary accidents of Stephen King and Don DeLillo as well as those of actual toxic tort cases. And it is here that I speculate about the transformations undergone by the accident novel in the postindustrial period—a period in which negligence declines and strict liability returns, in which many accidents, such as toxic accidents, have become peculiarly collectivized, and in which the story of products-liability, not human liability, tends to prevail.

CHAPTER TWO

A Clear Showing

THE PROBLEM OF FAULT IN
JAMES FENIMORE COOPER'S THE PIONEERS

> . . . . even a dog distinguishes between being
> stumbled over and being kicked.
> (Oliver Wendell Holmes Jr., *The Common Law*)[1]

IN the opening scene of James Fenimore Cooper's *The Pioneers* (1823), Judge Temple is returning with his daughter, Elizabeth, to Templeton, the wilderness settlement named after him, when he hears the sound of dogs chasing game through the woods. Impulsively and with no other thought than to give his daughter "a saddle for [her] Christmas dinner,"[2] he stops his sleigh, checks the priming of his gun, aims, and shoots at a buck that darts suddenly into view. Several shots later, the buck falls dead and two "unseen marksmen," one of whom turns out to be the legendary Natty Bumppo, come out from behind some trees. Though Cooper acknowledges only that the shot was accomplished "with a rapidity that confused the female," its rapidity appears to have confused the males as well. In the midst of an argument over who actually killed the deer, and by tracing the trajectory of all the bullets, Natty demonstrates that all but one of the judge's bullets hit a tree while the last lodged in the shoulder of the other marksman who, shrouded in mystery for most of the novel, is eventually revealed to be Oliver Effingham, the son of one of Temple's long lost friends. Aiming at a buck, the judge shot a man, by accident. This accident remains central to the development of the novel's form, language, and ideas.

Suffused with accidents and near-accidents, *The Pioneers* is obsessed with the idea of danger and unintentional harm. Immediately following the initial shooting scene, we witness the accident in which Effingham rescues several of Temple's Christmas guests from the precipice where they are perched in their sleigh. Later in the novel, during a fishing expedition and after a lengthy discussion about the safety of canoes, we see the servant Benjamin Pump knocked overboard, only to be "speared" to safety by Natty. The job-related death of the minor character, Jotham

Riddel, who has been hired by Temple's unscrupulous cousin, Richard Jones, to mine for silver in the hills provides an instance of a quasi-industrial accident. Finally there are three near-accidents involving Elizabeth, in which she is, on three different occasions, attacked by panthers, engulfed by a forest fire, and almost crushed on horseback by a falling tree. While far from significant in terms of the novel's plot, the last of these accidents seems to have been on Cooper's mind when he started writing *The Pioneers* and may have served as an inspiration for the novel. In a footnote in the 1832 edition of the novel, Cooper writes: "More than thirty years since, a very near and dear relative of the writer, an elder sister and a second mother, was killed by a fall from a horse, in a ride among the very mountains mentioned in this tale" (233). Though in the 1851 preface to the novel, Cooper explicitly denies any resemblance between his sister and his heroine lest it be believed that a "sister who was singularly dear to the author" had been "converted by him into the heroine of a work of fiction" (11), it seems clear that the incident continued to haunt him and formed the basis if not for the novel's heroine herself then for the plot's concern with those who fell "victim to the chances of the wilderness" (233).

In broad outline, the "chances" to which Cooper here refers are those attendant on the formation of the American nation, a subject which in one form or another occupied the author in almost every one of his numerous novels. The first of the Leatherstocking tales, a distinct series of five novels about the American wilderness that established Cooper's reputation in his own time and for which he is best remembered today, *The Pioneers* narrates the adventures of the intrepid Natty Bumppo and describes his hesitant and ambiguous interactions with the settlers whom he inevitably precedes and who, in each of the Leatherstocking tales, threaten his way of life. Through the story of Natty's encounter with Temple and with the other inhabitants of Templeton, the novel describes the process of socialization by which New York and by extension America turned from a wilderness society into an industrial one—a process that, as Cooper explains, increased the population and productivity through settlements and "conduced to effect . . . [a] magical change in the power and condition of the state" (16). That Cooper was especially interested in the effects of industrialization on the "state" and country becomes apparent in the novel's abiding concern with contemporary politics and law. Through Temple, in particular, who is not only a *de facto* patriarch of the community but its first officially appointed judge, as well as through a variety of other characters, including lawyers, sheriffs, and scofflaws, the novel touches on several of the legal controversies that were central to the early settlement of the country both in the 1790s—the period covered in the novel—as well as in the 1820s when

Cooper wrote *The Pioneers* and began to consolidate his skills as a professional novelist.

Capitalizing on his obvious interest in political and judicial matters, many critics have read Cooper's novels in the context of legal history. For example, Brook Thomas provides a rich account of *The Pioneers* against the backdrop of debates over property and an independent judiciary at the New York State Constitutional convention in 1821.[3] In addition, Charles Swann uncovers a new depth to the novel by juxtaposing it with an interpretation of contemporary game laws.[4] But no critic, to my knowledge, has examined the novel in the context evoked by its preoccupation with accidents, a context dominated by a rapidly changing law of accidents that took on more and more importance as the country entered an industrial and accident-laden age. Specifically, from the burgeoning body of accident law emerges the concept of negligence, a newly fashioned fault-related doctrine of liability that eventually displaced the concept of strict liability and that altered not only the *legal* adjudication of accidental injuries, but also *social* and *individual* notions of responsibility and blame. Needless to say, the implications of this change for the legal, social, and literary landscape were enormous, both generating and reflecting increased attention to accidents and the issues raised by them. To read the novel in terms of the legal history of accidents, then, is in part to emphasize the centrality of accidents in the culture at this time and to highlight an important and previously neglected aspect of Cooper's representation of them.

More important, to view the novel through the prism of tort or accident law is also to see, as Cooper clearly did, how interrelated were the concerns of accident law and property law and how relevant both developing bodies of law were to ideas about responsibility in the new nation. Crucial to the association between property and tort is the salience in this early period of legal change (roughly the first quarter of the nineteenth century) of cases in which accidental injury referred exclusively to property. Indeed, it was in the context of injury to property that the growing debate over the nature of responsibility, agency, and blame was first played out. Thus, in terms that echo their opening argument, Natty and Temple continue to bicker throughout the novel over who should shoulder the blame not only for killing the deer, but also for inflicting injury on the land, the individual, and the community. These notions of responsibility rely in part on the idea of custom or experience. Thus, Natty, in blaming the judge for treating the wilderness carelessly, links his views on property with the newly emergent standard of care peculiar to the negligence doctrine, while Temple, by contrast, clings to the resolution provided by his superior title to the land and to social class, echoing principles central to the residual doctrine of strict liability. But what emerges,

finally, from Cooper's depiction of the conditions preceding and surrounding the transformation from strict liability to negligence is not the
discrete association of one or the other doctrine with any given character,
but their combination and interrelation. Indeed, the complex relationship
between the two doctrines is transmitted largely through the complexities
of Cooper's characters who are, like their historical counterparts, full of
contradictory ideas and emotions. If at first I link Natty with the doctrine
of negligence and Temple with that of strict liability, it is only to point out
a dialectical interplay between them that results by the novel's end in a
model of mutual influence and gradual displacement. *The Pioneers*
proves essential to this interdisciplinary reading in depicting the moment
at which these opposing legal doctrines existed side by side—a moment of
ideological overlap in which new definitions of property, agency, and
responsibility were slowly being sorted out.

TORTS AND PROPERTY

Unlike other areas of private law, such as contract and property law
which, according to the liberal legal theory first formulated by men like
John Locke and Jean-Jacques Rousseau, exist to define and enforce the
positive rights of individuals, tort law is composed of a negative calculus;
it predicates liability on the infringement of already specified rights. In
particular, tort assesses physical harms which are necessarily understood
as an interference with property.[5] This is true even in cases of bodily
harm. Only by designating the body or certain portions of it as property
with ascertainable and compensable value has tort law been able to secure the protection of the injured person. From a theoretical standpoint
alone, then, it should be clear how intimately associated tort law is with
valuations of property. But the theory alone need not suffice, for the first
struggle over the measure of tort liability manifested itself in the context
of disputes over property.

Property cases were of particular interest to Cooper for two reasons.
Because his father was a large landowner in upstate New York whose title
to certain holdings was occasionally contested in the courts, Cooper had
a personal interest in the debate over the rights and liabilities of property
owners. So pervasive, in fact, was the family's involvement in these
disputes that property became something of a dominant metaphor for
Cooper's own creative work. He was famously proprietary about his
ideas for books and explicitly linked his literary output with land ownership: "The sale of the Prairie [a novel from 1824]," he wrote, "shall be
a leasehold for fourteen years."[6] But insofar as Cooper's subject in *The
Pioneers*, as in all the Leatherstocking tales, is the industrial transfor-

mation of the wilderness—of land previously unclaimed and undeveloped (by white settlers)—it is clear that his interest in property went beyond the merely personal. For at stake in the resolution of disputes over property and accidents was nothing less than the future of the American economy.

Cooper's dramatization of the intimate links between the concept of accidental injury and property is first evident in the opening scene of *The Pioneers* in which a debate takes place over who killed and can legitimately claim the body of the deer. Both Natty and Temple assert a property right in the animal. Natty believes that the one who actually killed the deer has a "title to the venison" (25). To this end he insists on tracing the accident back to its point of origin, arguing that any confusion about who can claim responsibility for shooting the deer is the direct result of the judge's carelessness; specifically, Natty claims that the accident could have been prevented had Temple used a different type of gun. At first his criticism is good-natured: " 'Did ye think to stop a full grown buck . . . within sound, with that pop-gun in your hand? . . . if you're for a buck, or a little bear's meat, Judge, you'll have to take the long rifle, with a greased wadding, or you'll waste more powder than you'll fill stomachs, I'm thinking' " (21). Temple naturally defends himself and his gun: " 'The gun scatters well, Natty, and it has killed a deer before now . . . ' " he says. " 'Here are two hurts; one through the neck, and the other directly through the heart. It is by no means certain, Natty, but I gave him one of the two' " (21). But the judge's language, despite its pretension to certainty, is full of the very imprecision Natty reviles, and he counters angrily that the smooth-bore rifle the judge used was obviously dangerous. " 'A body never knows where his lead will fly, when he pulls the trigger of one of them uncertain fire-arms' " (25).

In claiming that the judge acted carelessly and therefore faultily, Natty speaks a language that has less to do with the residual doctrine of strict liability than with the emergent doctrine of negligence. Negligence law is written in the language of this circumstantial propriety. It is a use-based legal standard grounded in the primacy of our relationships to objects, made and natural. Indeed, in his emphasis on the judge's mistakes and injurious uncertainty, Natty invokes the new standard of "ordinary care" that negligence introduced to replace the doctrine of strict but unparticularized liability. Thus, Natty argues the primacy of rights of those who do not own the land but respect it: " 'There's them living who say, that Nathaniel Bumppo's right to shoot on these hills, is of older date than Marmaduke Temple's right to forbid him' " (25). In urging Effingham to sue Temple for the injury, Squire Lippet, one of Templeton's two lawyers, rephrases Natty's argument when he asks " 'whether a man who owns, or says he owns, a hundred thousand acres of land, has any more right to shoot a body, than another' " (151). For Natty, then, the question of who owns a particular piece of property depends on finding its appropriate use. In short, for Natty who owns no land and believes the wilderness is indivisible, the question of ownership continues to devolve on each and every deer and how it is used or acquired.

In responding to this argument, Temple pursues several different tacks. He first asserts that he killed the deer, but then finding himself "out-voted—overruled," he backs down and offers to buy the meat instead. When finally confronted with the harm he has done to Natty's friend, he not only admits the other's title to the deer but also showers him with favors. " 'Admit it!' repeated the agitated Judge [in the accents of a Quaker]; 'I here give thee a right to shoot deer, or bears, or anything thou pleasest in my woods, forever' " (25). Without conceding what is most dear to him—that he alone killed the deer—with this statement, Temple decisively shifts the focus of the debate away from the perpetrator to the victim. As soon as the injury is brought to his attention, he admits with horror that a " 'fellow creature [is] suffering from my hands,' " and offers to compensate him for the injury; indeed, he commands the accident vic-tim, an utter stranger to him, to live under his roof, not only " 'until thy wound is healed,' " but " 'for ever afterwards' " (25). In offering eter-nal protection for the accident victim, Temple's response provides a key to understanding the peculiar nature of his sense of responsibility; he feels sympathetic, even apologetic, but he does not feel wrong. That he sees himself as the absolute owner of the property on which the deer was killed simultaneously immunizes him from and defines his liability. He is responsible because the injury happened on his land, not because he used his firearm carelessly, and his open-ended offer to Effingham—to house, feed, clothe, and, incidentally, to employ him as his scribe—becomes merely the prerogative of a good landlord. Temple's offer to care for Ef-fingham, then, stems not from a legally compelled form of compensation, but from an older, increasingly obsolete sense of *noblesse oblige*.[7] For the judge, in short, the question of who owns a specific deer is subsumed by the question of who owns the land and who therefore owns the right to hunt there in the first place.

That the judge admits the suffering of the person he shot and yet fails to admit that he did not take the proper precautions to avoid shooting him—fails to admit, that is, that he was at fault—links him for the time being to the residual standard of strict liability. According to Oliver Wen-dell Holmes Jr., a strict liability case is one "in which the cause of action (the legal basis for liability) is determined by certain overt acts, or events alone, *'irrespective of culpability.'* "[8] This emphasis on the patent visibil-ity of the act dovetails, as we shall see, with Temple's own personal preference for dealing in generalities and for avoiding the specificity required by an inquiry into carelessness and fault. More important, it betokens his generalized sense of responsibility, one that pervades his interactions with Natty and that continues to set the tone for his adjudication of property and accident disputes even as it comes under the influence of the negligence doctrine. In ceding his claim to the deer, the judge may have successfully defused the situation and forestalled a suit against him, but his logic—his reliance on the primacy of landownership—remains a constant source of conflict.

USE RIGHT AND EXCLUSIVE RIGHT

In the language of political philosophy, Natty and Temple exemplify the conflict between the use-right and exclusive-right theories of property. At the heart of Natty's argument is a conception of property as a contingent or limited possession which extends only to use and falls short of absolute ownership. C. B. Macpherson identifies this theory as belonging to a pre-capitalist society. "Until the emergence of a capitalist economy," he writes, "property had in fact mainly been a right to a revenue rather than a right to a thing. In the first place the great bulk of property was then property in land, and a man's property was generally limited to certain uses of it and was not freely disposable."[9] Temple, on the other hand, articulates a theory that MacPherson associates with a capitalist market economy "which brought the replacement of the old limited rights in land by virtually unlimited rights, and the replacement of the old privileged rights to commercial revenues by more marketable properties in actual capital, however accumulated."[10]

If there is an exclusivity to Temple's view of the land as MacPherson defines it, however, it is not yet the exclusivity of a full-fledged capitalist economy. Cooper's novel, we recall, is concerned with the *transition* from a feudal to a capitalist economy, not with its final incarnation. The kind of right Temple's argument with Natty exemplifies at this point, therefore, might more accurately be described as a right of first ownership,[11] a criterion commonly invoked by the courts in the eighteenth century for adjudicating land disputes. According to this view, rights over a given parcel of land were conferred on the property owner who could claim prior land use and possession. In some cases, courts even evicted first owners in favor of those who could prove an older title despite the fact that they had not been in residence on the land. (This is of particular relevance to *The Pioneers* since Temple's title to the land, seemingly so secure at the start, gradually comes under attack not only by Natty but also by Oliver Effingham whose family, Tories ousted in the Revolution, once owned a part of Temple's estate.) The owner who was first in time, Blackstone, the great legal commentator, wrote, could assert a "despotic dominion in total exclusion of the right of any other individual in the universe."[12]

The stridency and absoluteness of Blackstone's language begins to suggest the political culture in which such a rule might prevail, for the right of prior possession was well suited to a society that gave priority to an original class of settlers over those who preceded or followed them. Thus, in enforcing this right, the courts routinely ordered that relative newcomers compensate existing neighbors for nuisances caused, for example, by the stables, blacksmith shops, and drains they erected on their land, regardless of the community's economic need for such improvements. Indeed, the rule of first ownership enforced a status quo with respect to land development that strongly favored the first generation—in this case the generation of revolutionary colonists—and that furthered the goals of a society that was, in the eighteenth century, still predominantly agrarian and given to relatively stable and simple land use.

In order to promote strictly agrarian use, in fact, courts in pre- and postrevolutionary America frequently relied on an additional principle for deciding land disputes that set limits even on the first owner's use. The principle invoked was that of "quiet enjoyment," also known by the Latin maxim "*sic utere tuo, ut alienum non laedas.*"[13] Borrowed from the English common law, the notion of quiet enjoyment had always had an explicitly antidevelopmental bias, serving to legitimate the English gentry's concept of land as a private estate that existed purely for its own pleasure. In depicting Temple as a sportsman who hunts deer not out of any necessity but on a whim to please his daughter, Cooper associates Temple, at least provisionally, with this notion of landownership. Indeed, the sense is reinforced much later in the novel when Temple effectively equates the ownership of land, an ostensibly permanent possession, and game, a traditionally transient one. " 'I hope to live to see the day,' " Temple tells Natty, " 'when a man's rights in his game shall be as much respected as his title to his farm' " (160).

Under the rubric of quiet enjoyment, the law threw all of its protection behind predictable land use where "predictable," as the language of the judicial decisions suggest, was synonymous with "natural" and where "natural" was synonymous with "agrarian." Only uses that promoted husbandry, as opposed to industry, in other words, met with the court's approval. But while land disputes were often settled in favor of those whose land use was least injurious to others, the most common venue for the invocation of quiet enjoyment was in that subset of land cases dealing specifically with water rights. Given the increased construction of dams and mills in the last years of the eighteenth century, more and more cases arose in which natural uses of water had to be adjudicated. The dominant line of cases assigned damages to owners of land in which the "natural" flow of water had been obstructed. A late eighteenth-century New Jersey case articulates the legal standard in this way: "In general it may be observed, when a man purchases a piece of land through which a natural water-course flows, he has a right to make use of it in its natural state, but not to stop or divert it to the prejudice of another."[14] Thus, as Morton Horwitz reports, the typical water-rights case involved a suit by a downstream riparian landowner against his upstream neighbor for diverting the natural flow of water to raise an upstream mill dam.[15]

Well into the first quarter of the nineteenth century, courts continued to rule in favor of first owners who were using their land in ostensibly natural ways. [16] But as the century wore on, the old doctrine of exclusivity which authorized the "quiet enjoyment" of one's land and which encouraged only the most traditional land uses was found to limit capitalist expansion. It thus gave way to a standard that permitted more land development. Indeed, there were several noteworthy cases early in the century that paved the way for a new standard whose pro-development bias seems to have figured in the gradual transformation of Temple's views, for Temple ultimately comes to see the inevitability if not the logic of developing Templeton. As early as 1805, in the case of *Palmer v. Mulligan*, the New York Supreme Court first accepted the idea that a landowner could obstruct the natural flow of water for mill purposes even if that obstruction interfered with a landowner downstream.[17] The rationale depended heavily on the court's recognition that the law as it stood conferred a quasi-exclusive right to the land and to its water on downstream owners, thus disadvantaging all newcomers or upper riparian owners. This result, the judge reasoned, was unacceptable for the inconvenience it inflicted not on individual landowners but on the community. The upshot, he wrote, would be that "the public, whose advantage is always to be regarded, would be deprived of the benefit which always attends competition and rivalry."[18]

Supporting the interests of the community over those of the individual continued to inform the outcome of decisions in subsequent cases. In *Platt v. Johnson* (1818), for example, the court began to chisel away at the singularity of the right implicit in first ownership in favor of a right that was more evenly distributed across the population. "Although some conflict may be produced in the use and enjoyment of such rights," the court wrote of the use by an upstream mill owner whose dam occasionally obstructed the natural flow of water for those downstream, "it cannot be considered, in judgment of law, an infringement of right. If it becomes less useful to one, in consequence of the enjoyment by another, it is by accident, and because it is dependent on the exercise of the equal rights of others."[19] In *Panton v. Holland* (1819), the court extended this sanction to other profitable land developments. Here it found that the "maxim [of 'quiet enjoyment'] does not apply so as to prevent the owner of a lot of ground contiguous to another, from using his ground to the best advantage."[20] Thus, a new understanding of property—one that supported the needs of a growing community over those of the privileged individual—began to accommodate a new economic imperative by enlarging the range of permissible land uses and of noncompensable injuries at the same time.[21]

As the negligence doctrine begins to exempt more and more risk-taking from its prohibitions it loses touch with Natty's formulation of it and grows more conducive to Temple's nascent interest in development. Indeed, just as the negligence doctrine falls prey to a burgeoning economic imperative, so too does Temple slowly merge his belief in the primacy of the individual with his concern for the needs of the emerging industrial community. Without abandoning entirely his allegiance to private property, he begins not long after the shooting scene with Natty to reveal his interest in promoting the interests of the group. Temple's initial solution is to make laws that regulate the uses of the wilderness. To this end he is instrumental in drawing up and lobbying for several new pieces of legislation which include laws prohibiting "the drawing of seines, at any other than proper seasons," and "the killing of deer in the teeming months." " 'These are laws that were loudly called for by judicious men,'" says the judge. " 'Nor do I despair of getting an act, to make the unlawful felling of timber a criminal offence'" (160). But if these laws seem genuinely "judicious" to the environmentally conscious modern reader, however, it is best to bear in mind the judge's underlying motive in enforcing them, for in the absence of these controls, the natural resources targeted by them could never be exploited. Indeed, the judge believes that Natty's way of life is a threat to the exploitation of resources on behalf of the community. He thus turns his attention to clearing and controlling the land in a way that interferes directly with Natty's ability to fend for himself in the wilderness; and he is particularly angered when Natty's credo of self-sufficiency brings him into conflict with the settlement's newly implemented game laws. " 'You may make your laws, Judge' [Natty] cried, 'but who will you find to watch the mountains through the long summer days, or the lakes at night? Game is game, and he who finds may kill; that has been the law in these mountains for forty years, to my sartain knowledge; and I think one old law is worth two new ones'" (160).

THE ROLE OF CUSTOM

Natty's sentiment—that "one old law is worth two new ones"—reveals a lot about the underlying composition of the legal process at the time, for it was to the new customs and needs of the community over those long established by individuals like Natty that the law now turned to legitimate its shifting sense of acceptable behavior. Determining what was customary behavior for the group became most compelling in the context of accident law as the courts struggled to find ways to justify their failure to compensate for injuries that had been compensable under strict liability in the past. Of course, some sense of human custom had long been associated with the common law. "General customs," John Adams wrote in 1770, "form the common law . . . they have been used time out of mind, or for a time whereof the memory of man runneth not to the contrary."[22] But a closer look at the history of the law reveals that Adams's understanding of custom was quite different from the notion that began to pervade the judicial temperament in the first quarter of the nineteenth century. For what Adams understood by custom was a fixed and unchanging standard that was to govern common law decisions for eternity. Having discovered and enshrined some aspect of customary behavior in the law, in short, Adams and his contemporaries seemed incapable of imagining a future in which such behavior would no longer be the norm—would no longer, in fact, be customary.

Had the common law responded to every fluctuation in customary patterns of human behavior, the judiciary—a putatively fixed and stable institution—would have quickly lost its authority. But centuries of judicial innovation since Adams indicate that the courts would have lost credibility just as quickly had they remained as resistant to change as Adams might have liked. Indeed, the history of the common law suggests that it derives its vitality and authority from observing and reflecting the things ordinary people do while engaged in ordinary activities. Lon Fuller, a moral philosopher and legal theorist describes legal systems comprised entirely of customary laws that were common to many archaic societies and that historically preceded systems of "made" or enacted law, as a set of rules reached "by a kind of inarticulate collective preference."[23] That the rules are "inarticulate" suggests what certain scholars have described as an inevitable rift between institutionalized law—whose essence lies in its articulation—and social custom. "[C]ustomary behavior comprises precisely those aspects of social behavior which are traditional, moral, and religious, which are, in short, conventional and nonlegal" writes the legal anthropologist, Stanley Diamond.[24] Nevertheless, a combination of the purely customary and the purely institutional, however illusory, has been the explicit goal of the common law since it began to consider itself responsive to the group as well as to the individual.

Indeed, it was on the basis of just such an understanding of patterned action and expectation that tort law devised its notion of "ordinary care"—the standard by which it was to distinguish between injurious and noninjurious behavior. In its ideal form, the standard of ordinary care was, as has already been discussed, far more democratic than that of strict liability since it was based on an appeal to community custom and not dependent for its enforcement on the determination of rank or status. In theory, that is, negligence insisted on behavior that conformed to a standard of ordinary care because it was required of everyone without distinction. No longer determined by the nature of one's relationship to another—for example, the relationship of master to servant or of parent to child—negligence required a "universal duty of all to all," as Holmes once put it. Not long after it was first invoked in court cases, however, negligence began to resist the implications of this universality, increasing the category of acceptable and responsible customs and practices so as to diminish the category of potentially blameworthy ones.

The need to seek guidance from prevailing custom in deciding questions of responsibility and blame is given voice in *The Pioneers* by Natty and Temple's contradictory experiences of scarcity and abundance in the wilderness. Natty's views stem directly from his perception of nature as a limited resource. Natty inveighs against Temple's "wastey" ways, "'as if the least thing was not made for use, and not to destroy'" (248). Natty, who has watched the deterioration of the wilderness at the hands of those, like Temple, who have come to settle it, chastises the judge, "'Ah! the game is becoming hard to find, indeed, Judge, with your clearings and betterments'" (22). Sounding the same theme later in the novel, he scolds: "'It's the farmers that makes the game scearce, and not the hunters'" (161). Natty, who clearly believes that nature will provide for each individual so long as that individual uses the resource wisely, understandably clings to the tenets of a subsistence economy—the only economic model he has ever known. "'Use, but don't waste,'" he cautions repeatedly (248). Temple's experience, however, has deafened him, at least partially, to Natty's advice. He recalls the time, only five years before the novel begins, when the settlement of Templeton was still in its infancy, and "'the tenants of these woods were compelled to eat the scanty fruits of the forest to sustain life'" (233). In identifying the cause of the famine he assigns the blame to the forces of a market economy. "'The necessities of life commanded a high price in Europe,'" he explains, "'and were greedily sought after by the speculators'" (234). He thus reminds his daughter, Elizabeth, that relying on nature without making provisions for the future can lead to famine for the group. But as far as Natty and the Indians are concerned, in laying claim to the available land, in supporting mills, grain, roads, and clearings—in protecting things of "increase" (234)—these laws are themselves to blame.

Establishing that Natty and Temple have differing views of the land and differing customs based on those views is only the beginning, however. For the law, having once acknowledged them, needs to choose between them. Cooper foregrounds this interpretive problem throughout *The Pioneers* which repeatedly asks whose version of America will take hold. His adoption of a seeming neutrality in the subtitle of the novel—*A Descriptive Tale*—cannot veil the constant struggle for hermeneutic superiority between Temple and Natty and among the members of Templeton's eclectic group of European inhabitants. The problem most troubling to Cooper in this struggle seems to be the potential disparity between any one interpretation of custom and its translation into law. The problem is, perhaps, most evident in the novel's trial scene in which Natty, who has been arrested for shooting a deer out of season as defined by Temple's new game laws, is also being tried for "resisting the execution of a search-warrant by force of arms" (365). It is clear from the testimony of both Natty and Billy Kirby, the woodsman who had been temporarily deputized to execute the search warrant, that while the law has pitted them against each other, they parted from their hostile encounter as friends and " 'would never have thought of bringing the business up before a court' " (368). Kirby admits that Natty pointed a rifle at him, but it was precisely what he expected Natty to do. In convicting Natty regardless of Kirby's testimony, however, the jury ignores the weight of the two men's habits or customs in favor of their own, firmly establishing in law, much to the consternation of the parties involved, that the act of pointing a gun is always to be construed as hostile.

Indeed, central to the task of choosing between differing interpretations of custom is the problem of how to identify one custom as more representative and thus more legally binding in the first place. For Fuller, "the central problem of 'interpretation' in customary law is that of knowing how to read into an act, or a pattern of repetitive acts, an obligatory sense like that which may attach to a promise explicitly spelled out in words."[25] In using the example of a promise, Fuller picks a relatively accessible model for choosing between competing versions of customary behavior—a model based on contract where the issue of customary behavior is typically agreed upon beforehand by the parties in question. The more perplexing and relevant example, however, is that of tort law where the compensatory mechanism differs from that of contract in that it cannot rely on an explicit obligation (written or oral) and therefore cannot administer justice in conformity with it. If, as Elaine Scarry explains, consent can be measured in terms of degrees, a tort would be relatively nonconsensual.[26] Indeed, for Oliver Wendell Holmes Jr. the law of negligence was explicitly unlike contract in that its rules were derived exclusively from the patterns of human behavior it was intended to regulate. "... [w]hen A assaults or slanders his neighbor, or converts his neighbor's property," he wrote, "he does a harm which he has never consented to bear, and if the law makes him pay for it, the reason for doing so must be found in some general view of the conduct which every one may fairly expect and demand from every other, whether that other has agreed to it or not."[27] Lon Fuller puts it a slightly different way when he writes that customary behavior is "a language of interaction" in which a sense of obligation must stem from the action or repetition of action and not from previously agreed upon categories.[28] He explains: "Where by his actions toward B, A has ... given B reasonably to understand that he (A) will in the future in similar situations act in a similar manner, ... then A is bound to follow the pattern set by his past actions toward B."[29]

PROBABILITY

The most noticeable thing about Fuller's formulation is its essential ambiguity. For regardless of how hard it tries, such a principle reduces the law to a guessing game. If as Holmes suggests, the "business" of tort law is to identify those cases in which a person will be liable for the harm he or she has done, it cannot do so without guessing. Tort law, he writes, cannot "predict with certainty whether a given act under given circumstances will make [a person] liable, because an act will rarely have that effect unless followed by damage, and for the most part, if not always, the consequences of an act are not known, but only guessed at as more or less probable."[30] Moreover, as society increased its reliance on mechanization, the greater was the need for this kind of guesswork which, although it often verged on the precisely calculable as the science of mechanization advanced, was nevertheless a product of an increasingly chancey universe. In short, probability, not certainty, was the logical currency of negligence because harm was always speculative.

Although it was not until later in the century, with the explosion of statistical thinking,[31] that probability became a set piece in tort law decisions, it emerges in Cooper's novel as one of several ways to measure and regulate the issue of personal agency and responsibility at the heart of the negligence doctrine. Indeed, Cooper's novel abounds with instances in which the attenuation and uncertainty of accidental action figure prominently. The original and most elaborate instance of this is in the initial argument over who killed the deer. But the problem resurfaces in other contexts as well, usually at the instigation of Temple's despicable cousin, Richard Jones. Like Temple, Jones himself claims that on at least one occasion he killed a deer that Natty said he killed (53); he also wonders whether credit is due him for the death of a memorable partridge. " 'I never could tell yet,' " he remarks, " 'whether it was I or Natty, who killed that bird' " (88). Jones also insists that he, for example, and not Hiram Doolittle (a fellow artisan in Templeton), was responsible for the design of a certain church steeple (54), and that he, not Effingham, saved their sleigh from plunging down a snowy cliff. A final, humorous instance of this preoccupation with agency and responsibility can be found in the scene in which Templeton's doctor, Elnathan, is extracting the bullet from Effingham's shoulder. The doctor here takes advantage of the dim lighting with his own sleight of hand. "Elnathan took a pair of glittering forceps, and was in the act of applying them to the wound, when a sudden motion of the patient, caused the shot to fall out of itself. The long arm and broad hand of the operator . . . caught the lead, while at the same time, an extremely ambiguous motion was made, by its brother, so as to leave it doubtful to the spectators, how great was its agency in releasing the shot" (82).

Not surprisingly, in all of these examples it is the settlers, not Natty, who find the social and mechanical confusion about agency and causation to be self-serving. In each case, that is, the settlers claim responsibility for what they perceive to be worthy actions despite the ambiguity of their own role in bringing them about. Natty singlehandedly struggles to bring the confusion to their attention and, more important, to scold them for contributing to it, since for Natty the confusion is directly related to their carelessness. Most important, as we have seen, Natty argues that using the wrong instrumentality can contribute to the confusion as when he accuses the judge of using the wrong rifle to shoot the deer, misusing both rifle and deer in the process. But the conflict between Natty and the judge—embodied in the conflict between the emergent and residual accident doctrines—is not confined to the opening scene or to the issue of the ownership of the deer. Rather, it emerges very plainly in the scenes concerning Temple's daughter Elizabeth. Like her real-life counterpart, Elizabeth plays a pivotal role in Cooper's novelistic discourse about the culture's sense of responsibility and blame. Physically at risk several times, including from a near-accident on horseback that, as suggested earlier, precisely recalls that involving Cooper's sister, Elizabeth is in mortal danger on two memorable occasions: first from an attack by panthers and then from a raging fire in the hills. In each case Natty rescues her and, in each case, Elizabeth is a pawn in the debate between Natty and Temple about how to assess responsibility and how to assign blame. It is, for example, clear in both instances of rescue that it is Natty, not Temple, who is capable of acting responsibly in the presence of danger. Of course, as one of the founding fathers of Templeton, Temple himself promotes the idea of his own leadership and responsibility for events in the town. But his assumption of this role is directly challenged in these scenes by Natty's greater capability in the wilderness. When it comes to the "chances of the wilderness," it seems, Natty remains the superior agent and leader.

In the case of the panther attack, Natty's rescue efforts are so instinctive and immediate that they are taken as a given. Just when Elizabeth has resigned herself to an early death—". . . [t]he beautiful figure of Elizabeth was bowing meekly to the stroke," Cooper writes—Natty sneaks up on her from behind, almost completely camouflaged by the natural surroundings. "[A] rustling of leaves behind seemed rather to mock the organs," Cooper explains, "than to meet the air" (309). Nor does it escape notice that just as in the deer killing scene, Natty saves the day by knowing precisely how and when to deploy his gun, demonstrating once again how carefully and responsibly he treats dangerous instrumentalities. Taking aim from behind Elizabeth as he crouches in the forest growth, Natty acts swiftly and urgently before he offers her any consolation or comfort: " 'Hist! Hist!' said a low voice—'Stoop lower, gall; Your bunnet hides the creater's head' " (309). In the second instance, as Elizabeth is on the verge of being engulfed by flames, the point is made more explicit that it is Natty and not Temple who has come to Elizabeth's rescue. In this case, for example, Natty does not appear magically on the scene, but suspects Elizabeth is in danger after he sees the fire and dutifully inquires after her. As soon as he gets confirmation of his suspicion, he starts to run up the mountain, risking his own life in the process. Temple, of course, has not remained oblivious to the fire, which threatens to consume nearly all of the surrounding forest and can be observed from any point in town, but only to his daughter's presence in the midst of it. But if his inferior instincts and knowledge make him seem less of a father figure in this scene, his role as Elizabeth's protector is even further diminished by her superior devotion to Natty. For as Cooper soon reveals, Elizabeth would not have been on the mountain in the first place had she not promised secretly to meet Natty there and to deliver some gunpowder to him against her father's express wishes. Moreover, the contrast between Natty's ability, energy, and ingenuity and Temple's powerlessness, even superfluity, is tracked meticulously by Cooper who now describes the town as it looks from the summit through Natty's eyes. "The distance was not so great but the figure of Judge Temple could be seen, standing in his own grounds, and apparently contemplating, in perfect unconsciousness of the danger of his child, the mountain in flames" (413).

Although it is clear to the reader that Natty has behaved more responsibly than any other character in both rescue operations, the issue of how to evaluate responsibility and blame for the fire, panther attack, and rescue is the subject of some debate for the citizens of Templeton. As the direct beneficiary of Natty's responsible agency, Elizabeth, of course, is grateful to him. Indeed, with respect to the panther attack, she embarrasses Natty by thanking him too profusely. "Natty received her vehement protestation of gratitude, with a simple expression of good will, and with indulgence for her present excitement, but with a carelessness that showed how little he thought of the service he had rendered" (310). But even Elizabeth, who acknowledges the debt she owes Natty in this first instance, seems a bit confused about whom to thank for the fire rescue. An embodiment of the raging interpretive crisis within the community over these issues, she seems less indebted to Natty than to her father, to God, and finally to Oliver Effingham who, while he promises to die with her rather than abandon her to the flames alone, is conspicuously inept in the face of real danger. Unlike Natty who dramatizes the carefulness and action-orientation of the negligence doctrine in its ideal state, Effingham only despairs. " 'If Natty were here,' " he cries to Elizabeth as he desperately tries to think of ways of escape, " '. . . [his] ingenuity and long practice would easily devise methods to do it; but I am a child, at this moment, in everything but daring' " (408). Given this admission, Elizabeth's sentiment—" 'I am grateful, Oliver, for this miraculous escape; and next to my God, to you' " (417)—is puzzling; yet in the final analysis, it is explicable not only in terms of Elizabeth's emotional attachment to Oliver but also in terms of the increasing trend toward the dissociation of agency and liability that became characteristic of the negligence doctrine as it diverged from its idealistic beginnings in the hands of land developers like Judge Temple.

Subsequent chapters take up the story of this dissociation within the negligence doctrine, but the examination of *The Pioneers* serves in this chapter to reveal its early stages. As Brook Thomas makes clear, the struggle over how to accommodate and acknowledge Natty's contribution to Elizabeth's safety within the parameters of the law essentially recapitulates the conflict between the head and the heart that characterized the nascent culture of New England.[32] But nowhere is this age-old conflict so clearly expressed as in the context of the critical concepts of responsibility and blame. For what lies at the center of this conflict in *The Pioneers* is precisely how to register Natty's crucial skills and contributions to the society as a whole while punishing him for violating certain of its prohibitions. That Temple recognizes the conflict is obvious after Elizabeth is saved from the panther attack and returned to his custody. "While the agitated parent was listening to the avid description that his daughter gave of her recent danger and her unexpected escape," Cooper writes, "all thoughts of mines, vested rights, and examinations, were absorbed in emotion; and when the image of Natty again crossed his recollection, it was not as a lawless and depredating squatter, but as the preserver of his child" (325).

When the scene switches to the legal deliberations over Natty's most recent offense—shooting deer out of season—Natty naturally hopes to capitalize on the judge's new vision of him. He thus refers Temple to the fact that he has repeatedly rescued his daughter, Elizabeth, from life-threatening danger and asks him to take this into consideration both in judging his character and in adjudicating the dispute. But Temple's image of Natty as preserver does not endure. The judge quickly reverts to his role as lawmaker and refuses to admit his gratitude or the evidence of Natty's good behavior into the legal proceedings. Convinced that no ties are stronger than blood ties, Natty cannot believe that Temple would betray his sense of indebtedness to him for rescuing his daughter by issuing the warrant for his arrest in the first place. " 'Well, well,' " Natty says, " 'that man loves the new ways, and his betterments, and his lands, afore his own flesh and blood' " (336). Natty, in other words, believes the matter to be a personal one, determined in the final analysis by the history he and Temple have shared and, specifically, by the give and take of debt and responsibility. Natty's solution, however, ignores the institutionalizing force of the law—the same institutionalizing force that turned individual customs into established standards. Temple, on the other hand, embodies this institutionalization. For Temple, the impartiality of the law requires that he put all thought of his daughter aside. Natty's punishment, he says, " 'shall be whatever the law demands, notwithstanding any momentary weakness I may have exhibited, because the luckless man has been of such eminent service to my daughter' " (344). Temple's solution dilutes the concept of personal responsibility into the generality of the law. Indeed, it could be argued that Temple's allegiance to the law's impartiality is of a piece ideologically with his refusal to look more closely into the causes and particularities of the accident he himself perpetrates in the novel's opening scene.

But Temple's preference for the rule of law cannot be taken at face value. If Temple believes, as one Cooper critic has written, that "the civil law is the only guarantee of liberty,"[33] it is undoubtedly a one-sided, ahistorical, guarantee. As was the case with his offer of compensation in the accidental shooting of Effingham, Temple's sense of justice is here again informed by the "justice" already carried out by the distribution of property. Lecturing Natty on this justice, Temple calls his attention to what he believes is the impartiality of property laws. That the novel's plot is in part concerned with the complicated and contested nature of the judge's own title to property underscores the irony of his position.[34]

Lest it be forgotten in the details of Natty's particular circumstance, it should be noted that at issue in the struggle over the land in the novel is the ownership of nothing less than Temple's estate (deeded under mysterious circumstances), the town of Templeton, and by extension the fate of the nation which is alternately claimed by Chingachgook (Natty's Native-American friend), Natty, Temple, and Effingham. Extending this conflict to the novel's end, Cooper is forced to conclude it summarily, concocting a preposterous ending that not only strains credibility but shifts the burden of resolution away from the larger issues of responsibility and blame. In rapid and somewhat haphazard succession, it is revealed that the Native-American claim to the land is dismissed not because of some deficiency in that ethnic group's theory of responsibility for injury or respect for property but because the Native-Americans had given the land to Effingham's grandfather as a gift. He, in turn, bequeathed it to his son who was Effingham's father and Temple's friend. When the elder Effingham, a Tory, left the colonies during the Revolution, he entrusted his fortune to Temple. When his land was sold after the war, Temple purchased it, legally. As many critics have pointed out, the fictional resolution of this conflict is both improbable and dissatisfying.[35]

The legal, negligence-related, resolution to the conflict is by contrast more credible and more faithful to the questions Cooper raises in the body of the novel. Indeed, the American transition from wilderness to frontier, and the property conflicts that accompanied it were in many ways indistinguishable from the conflicts over responsibility and blame that surfaced most clearly in the shift from strict liability to negligence in the standard of tort liability. Negligence mediated the legal and literary conflict over property by introducing into the question of priority of ownership the question of use. In theory, negligence identified fault as the misuse, or abuse, of property, and assigned liability on the basis of it, but it soon developed a tendency to exempt those most responsible for injury in order to promote economic development. In Cooper's novel, this shift begins to occur when Natty's emphasis on *careful* use becomes Temple's emphasis on *utmost* use, where "use" is defined by economic efficiency. That the novel begins with an accident by means of which Effingham's ancestry and the truth about Temple's property is revealed is no coincidence. It is precisely through this literary circuit that we come to see how the theory of liability introduced in the initial accident helps to justify and determine the disposition of property in the novel's final scenes. The conveyance of Temple's estate to Effingham and Elizabeth, and through Elizabeth back to Temple again, is both enabled by and indicative of the new consensus about responsibility embodied by negligence.

If this disposition of property accommodates Effingham's and Temple's needs, however, it is not universally satisfactory. Though he is encouraged to stay in Templeton, Natty is, by the novel's end, effectively dispossessed; he introduces the people of Templeton to a concept of liability based on fault at his own expense. But as if in recognition of Natty's original contribution to the discourse of fault and circumstantial propriety—to the theory of negligence if not to its practice—*The Pioneers* makes room for one final iteration of his theory of use and, by extension, liability. " 'The meanest of God's creaters be made for some use,' " he says, " 'and I'm form'd for the wilderness' " (454). Always the consummate individual, Natty departs for the wilderness with his individualized version of negligence not only intact but raised to the level of a personal ontology.

CHAPTER THREE

Negligence before the Mast

SHIP COLLISIONS AND THE NAUTICAL LITERATURE
OF THE MID-NINETEENTH CENTURY

> But the chief causes of collision are to be found
> in negligence, or in ignorance of, or inattention
> to the rules of law, which are but a repetition
> of the rules of the sea.
> (Henry Flanders, *A Treatise on Maritime Law*)[1]

No SOONER had Cooper put the finishing touches on *The Pioneers* than he began to wrestle with the transformations brought about by accidents in yet another wilderness, the sea. The subject of negligence and of accidents makes an appearance in the nautical memoir,[2] and in virtually all of the eleven nautical novels[3] Cooper wrote. Inspired by his own experience as a sailor in the merchant marine in 1806 to 1807, an experience that was marked by storms, fogs, and near-collisions,[4] Cooper set about trying to create a new type of fiction—a fiction that would, among other things, represent the threats posed by accidents at sea. Indeed, the representation of accidents in Cooper's sea novels reflects a cultural preoccupation with ship collisions that was at the heart of the development of accident law. More specifically, this chapter argues that in focusing on accidents, and on ship collisions in particular, Cooper, together with other writers of nautical literature in the mid-nineteenth century, created a nautical hero who shared many of the qualities endorsed by the emerging doctrine of negligence. Like Natty and Temple in *The Pioneers*, Cooper's sailors and sea captains prove in part to be vehicles for the new notions of responsibility and blame that were central to the legal doctrine and to the culture's changing self-definition. In keeping with the attention paid by the negligence doctrine to preventative measures and to prudence in general, Cooper's narratives portray accidents less as opportunities for bravery and courage than for vigilance and caution. More important, they associate the responsible nautical hero with behavior marked not by confrontation but by circumvention, warnings, and avoidance.

Of course, the nautical novel was not entirely without precedent. There had been several attempts at nautical fiction before Cooper by such English authors as Tobias Smollett and Sir Walter Scott,[5] but Cooper had found them wanting. In the first place, these novels were nautical only in the sense that they occasionally made use of material relating to ships and to events at sea; the sea, in short, provided a colorful but highly elusive backdrop to plots that took place almost exclusively on land, and in no case was the nautical material thematically central. More important to Cooper's way of thinking, however, was the fact that when they did speak of nautical matters, the novels of his English predecessors were marred by serious inaccuracies. On the one hand, Cooper felt that an author like Scott, whose novel *The Pirate* (1820) was very popular on both sides of the Atlantic, had misrepresented the details of nautical life in his effort to convey its romantic and sublime nature. Not surprisingly, Scott's characters, who possessed the dramatic individualism of the Byronic hero, were given not to cautious action but to last-minute rescues and escapes, to the swashbuckling actions of the heroes of old. On the other hand, the model that Smollett offered in novels like *Roderick Random* (1748) and *Peregrine Pickle* (1751), though far more realistic, lacked the nobility and adventurousness that was an essential part of almost every sailor's experience. Smollett's characters, in short, tended to be simple, loyal, but in the end completely unheroic. Thus, Cooper aimed at and achieved a fiction of compromise—a fiction that like his Leatherstocking tales proved to be transitional, vacillating in each novel as well as over the course of the more than twenty years he devoted to them, between the newly emergent pole of nautical realism and the well-established pole of nautical romanticism. Moreover, in his characterization of the prudent sea hero, Cooper may have borrowed from an even older tradition of prudent heroes in fiction. Indeed, Jane Austen's *Persuasion* (1818), which served as a source for Cooper's first novel, *Precaution* (1821), offers a sterling example of a prudent sea captain several years before Cooper's time, giving rise to speculations about a tradition of literary nautical negligence that preceded Cooper and on which he may have relied.

But in raising the possibility of a literary tradition of prudent heroes, we need also to acknowledge another vital tradition that existed alongside it, replete with reckless and passionate heroes who roamed the seas looking for high adventure. Indeed, the works of both Edgar Allan Poe and Herman Melville articulate a model of seamanship that gives life to both prudent and reckless heroes. If Melville's Ahab is an example of the latter, for example, Captain Vere, the complex and superbly restrained character from *Billy Budd* (1888–91) is a definite though vexed example of the former. Indeed, Vere derives in part from models of responsibility and foreseeability that were emerging at the time in a series of mutiny cases, among them the notorious *Somers* affair which, as many have long noted, served as a source for Melville's story.

As Vere and his historical counterparts gained more credibility for their restrained behavior, literature turned more conspicuously to a representation of them. The work of Richard Henry Dana Jr., the author whose portraits of sea captains in *Two Years Before the Mast* (1840) took the reading public of mid-century by storm, is particularly relevant in this regard. In this work the contours of the risk-averse hero that are visible in Cooper are finally filled in. Here the question of accident prevention and the competence required to insure it take center stage in a series of narrative anecdotes whose realism allows for a sustained explanation of how the character bent on accident prevention becomes a hero and how the character whose inability to prevent accidents wallows in a nonheroic fate. It is in this same vein that we can also view the work of Dana's numerous imitators and successors. For just as Cooper inspired Dana to new heights of realism in his quest to represent the seafaring life more accurately, so too did Dana inspire a new generation of nautical authors who felt compelled to make their own adjustments to his model. Specifically, what these mid-century imitators contributed to the genre was a popularization of the prudent hero and an application of the precepts of vigilance and caution to the common sailor. Indeed, it was the prudent actions of everyone on board ship, regardless of station or rank, that came to the fore in the context of ship collisions since the ship itself was a uniquely communal enterprise in which the negligence or vigilance of any one of its members could determine the fate of everyone on board. It is inevitable, then, that as more common sailors themselves began to contribute their own tales to the growing numbers of nautical memoirs and short stories—authors such as T. S. Arthur and John Sherburne Sleeper (alias Hawser Martingale)—they would bring an emphasis on the common seaman's capacity for heroism under negligence law with them.

NEGLIGENCE AND COLLISIONS AT SEA

The modern concept of negligence—the concept that determines liability for accidents on the basis of an understanding of fault and carelessness—owes its existence in large part to the specific problems posed by collisions, both at sea and on land. According to Morton Horwitz, it was the unprecedented number of collision cases between ships and between horse-drawn carriages in the late eighteenth and early nineteenth centuries that was largely responsible for the emergence of negligence as we know it today.[6] Of the two groups, however, the latter seemed to have had a certain priority in time and number and thus in the formation of negligence law.[7] Horwitz refers to a claim based on a notion of negligence in a collision case between ships as early as 1770;[8] while Nathan Dane, the legal scholar whose treatise, *The General Abridgement and Digest of American Law* (1824) was the first to recognize negligence as an independent legal action, used the example of a ship collision to illustrate it. "If the owner of a ship, in the care of a pilot, through negligence and want of skill, sinks the ship of another," Dane observed, "this owner is liable."[9] Of course, accidents at sea had long been a familiar part of military life in America, but in the first half of the nineteenth century, the country's commercial uses for the sea increased dramatically. Packet ships loaded with cargo began regular runs from New York to Liverpool and whalers and sealers plied the waters in increasing numbers. In addition, a new demand for speed bore fruit in the design of unusually large vessels like the clipper ship which were, though fast, often hard to steer and prone to accidents, especially on crowded seas and in small harbors.

Of course, as we saw in the last chapter, some of the earliest invocations of negligence involved claims by land owners, or by characters like Natty, who aimed to prevent others from owning the land at all. But in most of these cases, negligence determined the responsibilities of individuals in preexisting relationships, typically that of neighbors. In this sense, it bore traces of the kind of determination at the heart of strict liability which was heavily informed by the rules about preexisting status and contractual relationships. In the context of the sea, by contrast, negligence took on the new and more recognizably modern shape of a negotiation of responsibilities between individuals in differing circumstances. Specifically, collision cases altered[10] earlier uses of negligence in two significant ways.[11] First, collisions involved strangers—people who, by definition, had no preexisting duties toward or contractual relations with each other. Thus, the determination of liability for an accident between them could no longer focus on the question of a failure to perform a given task or to treat a given person in a certain way since, typically, there was no prior history between the parties. In order to assess whether liability should be attributed to one or another stranger, in other words, a new understanding of responsibility had to come into being—an understanding that specifically addressed the anomic relations of individuals within an increasingly industrialized society. Under this understanding of negligence, in short, even strangers owed a duty to each other—a duty to take the necessary and reasonable precautions available to them to avoid unnecessary harm.

The second way in which collisions altered the understanding and application of negligence was in offering examples of accidents that were potentially the responsibility of *both* parties involved, without a distinct victim or victimizer. This alteration worked hand in hand with the first, which challenged lawmakers to establish an independent obligation between noncontracting strangers, and yet had less to do directly with the notion of responsibility per se and more to do with causation. In the context of collisions, that is, courts for the first time were faced with the problem of deciding liability between joint actors, both of whom were in motion at the time the accident occurred, and each of whom might have caused it. Before collisions became so prevalent, the typical accident case involved only one perpetrator, the accident victim being a passive recipient of injury and pain. In determining responsibility for injuries to land, for example, it was clear from circumstance and topography that one landowner—typically, the upper riparian owner—had injured the land of his neighbor downstream, not the other way around. In collisions, however, a more complicated inquiry into causation was required—an inquiry that turned on fault and that came inevitably to rest on the question of carelessness. In fact, as one early commentator pointed out, without a fault-related notion of causation, the typical collision case would have been a logical absurdity. "It seems reasonable," wrote the legal scholar Benjamin Oliver in 1828, "that, if two vessels run foul of each other in a dark night, one can maintain no action against the other; for, if otherwise, then if both were injured, each might maintain an action against the other; which would be absurd; and so for the same reason, if both parties are to blame, neither should be allowed to bring an action against the other."[12] Obviously, what was needed to resolve Oliver's paradox was a notion of negligence that was able to distinguish the relevant contributions and responsibilities of each party to the accident's cause.

Given the narrowness of so many harbors and channels, a disproportionate number of accidents and accident cases in which the determination of responsibility became an issue involved the negligent action of a harbor pilot hired specifically for the purpose of guiding a vessel from its berth to safety in the open sea. Typically, pilots either collided with neighboring ships, or with the rocks and shoals that lay hidden along the coast. Indeed, the first legal reference to negligence in Dane's *General Abridgement of American Law* refers not just to a ship collision but to the actions of a pilot. So too does the majority of cases reported in the most popular maritime newspaper of the nineteenth century, *The Whaleman's Shipping List and Merchant Transcript*. Of course, in the many cases where the pilot was named in the lawsuit simply because he was an easy target, the court refused to attribute negligence to him. Thus, in the case of *Henry Taber and als. Newell, Sturtevant and als.* (1847), as reported in *The Whaleman's Shipping List*, "[t]he Court decided that upon the evidence, no blame would be rightfully imputed to the pilot; that the ship was managed as prudently and skillfully as the exigencies of her situation admitted."[13] Still, in other cases, the pilot revealed obvious incompetence, as in the case of the *Ship Stephania of New Bedford* whose captain was so convinced of the pilot's error and so adamant about avoiding liability himself for the leaks and damage to cargo that resulted from it, that he filed what was known as an official marine Protest,[14] a common pretrial document of the time. "The Ship Stephania struck her bottom on the ground at Gage's Roads, Freemantle, in the month of March 1855," this Protest reads, "through the negligence of the Government Pilot, who anchored her in an improper place."[15] Considering the prominence of pilots in the legal cases and complaints about ship collisions, moreover, it should come as no surprise that the literary texts about negligence also testify to their importance. Thus, in much of the literature I examine below, it is the assessment of the pilot's competence that serves as the main impetus for the investigation into the safety measures necessary to determine liability under negligence law.

THE PRUDENT SAILOR

If the collision-laden sea became the birthplace of a new emphasis on prudence in the law, it also served a similar function in contemporary literature, especially in the nautical novels of James Fenimore Cooper where the character of the cautious sailor finds its most frequent expression. Of course, the association between the sea and the prudent hero was neither necessary nor sufficient as both setting and character found their way into literary works without the other. Thus, there were, as we shall see, works about the sea in this period that continued to feature reckless sea captains as well as works about prudent and reasonable men that had little or nothing to do with the sea. It bears repeating then that Cooper's fashioning of the prudent sea hero was not new precisely, but derived in part from a rich tradition not only of nautical novels, as noted at the start of this chapter, but of domestic novels that featured the thoughtful and prudent hero long before negligence appeared on the scene.[16] Indeed, even Cooper's interest in this character, as chapter 2 illustrates in detail, predates his interest in the nautical life. Nor was *The Pioneers* his only prenautical expression of interest in prudence. His first novel, *Precaution* (1821), also deals with the subject, although in ways less revealing than its title might suggest. A novel of manners and morals about star-crossed lovers and family name,[17] *Precaution* does not take up the idea of carelessness or prudence in the same detailed way that some of Cooper's later novels do. But it does include an accident scene that bears a striking resemblance to the accident with which *The Pioneers* begins and which reveals his early interest in the negligence-related issues of responsibility and blame. A veritable prototype for the later novel's accident, the accident in *Precaution* also involves the misuse of a gun. In *Precaution*, John Moseley, the heroine's brother, playfully brandishes a gun he thinks is unloaded at his sister, Emily, pulling the trigger only to find that the gun was loaded after all. Horrified, George Denbigh, a family friend and the hero of the tale, hurls himself into the path of the bullet, protecting Emily but wounding himself (although not fatally) in the process. As Emily's gratitude turns to love during the period of Denbigh's convalescence, however, the importance of the accident quickly fades. Indeed, Cooper refers to it once more only to write that Jarvis, the neighbor whose gun had been used in the prank, "felt something like a consciousness that but for his folly [he failed to discharge the gun fully before entering the house] the accident would not have happened."[18]

But even if *Precaution* does not elaborate on the accident scene as *The Pioneers* does, it remains an important example of Cooper's prenautical interest in the subject of carelessness and prudence as well as a telling precursor to his nautical tales. For as scholars have conclusively shown,[19] *Precaution* was consciously modeled on Jane Austen's *Persuasion* (1818). Borrowing much from Austen's masterpiece, including characters, plot (in both cases the novel revolves around the marriageability of the three daughters of an English baronet), and even the idea of a near-fatal accident,[20] Cooper did only one obvious thing to disguise his source; he changed the occupation of the hero. In *Precaution*, the hero, Denbigh, is something of a drifter who turns out, in the end, to be the heir to an estate, while in *Persuasion*, the hero, Wentworth, is a sea captain. More important, in Austen's novel, Wentworth's occupation plays a significant role. In fact, guided by the well-intentioned but bigoted advice of her best friend and neighbor, Anne Elliot, the heroine of Austen's tale, initially rejects Wentworth as a suitor because of what his profession suggests about his family's standing. Years later, however, when she and Wentworth meet again, she resolves to defy society's class bias against the navy and its meritocratic rather than aristocratic tradition. Although Wentworth has by this time accrued a sizeable fortune and a reputation to match, it is less these things than the prospect of life on board ship that attracts Anne to him. Indeed, the nautical life holds out the only promise in the novel of a prominent place for a married woman in a man's world. "She gloried in being a sailor's wife," Austen writes of Anne at the end of the novel, "but must pay the tax of quick alarm for belonging to a profession which is, if possible, more distinguished in its domestic virtues, than in its national importance."[21] In speaking of the navy as a profession distinguished in its *domestic* virtues, Austen underscores the paradox of the nautical life. For it is at sea, in the face of the often agonizing conflict of war and away from the burdens and customs of conventional domestic life, that a new domestic order can be created. It comes as no surprise, then, that Wentworth and the other sea captains in the novel, including Captain Benwick, Captain Harville, and Admiral Croft, whose wife has accompanied him on almost every voyage, prove to be the most reasonable male characters in the book. Indeed, for a man inured to the unpredictability and hazardousness of the nautical life, Wentworth's pursuit of Anne Elliot throughout the novel—a courtship that takes place over several years in many different cities—is nothing if not a model of restraint and caution.

Without drawing too conclusive a connection between the nautical novel and the prudent hero who seems to dominate its pages, it is, especially given Austen's pairing of the two, possible to speculate on a more than coincidental relationship between them. More important, to view Cooper's contribution to the characterization of the prudent sea captain in light of Austen's novel allows us to see the diversity and richness of the literary traditions he drew on while also noting the singular importance of negligence-related concepts to his work. Indeed, the subsequent development of Cooper's work shows a strong preference for the pairing of these novelistic elements—the sea and prudence—confirming rather than dispelling suspicions of its shared concerns with negligence law. In *The Pilot* (1824), Cooper's fourth book and the first of his many nautical novels—novels that are rarely read today but that proved immensely popular and influential in his day—Cooper once again created a character who, like Natty Bumppo, embodied the most important principles of negligence law—the principles of due care and vigilance. As the novel opens, the title character, known either as "the pilot," or by the pseudonym "Mr. Gray," has been engaged by an American captain in the Revolutionary War to guide his frigate away from the rocky English coast. Needless to say, the situation is fraught with danger; moreover, because of the volatile tides and an approaching storm, the departure of the ship cannot be delayed. Thus, when the order is finally given to cast off, the officers and crew respond with urgency. "Human beings sprung out from between the guns," Cooper writes, "rushed up the hatches, threw themselves with *careless activity* from the booms. . . ."[22] But in the midst of this "tumult of preparation and general bustle," the pilot seems strangely detached. In fact, to the great consternation of the crew, and especially of the proud and skeptical Lieutenant Griffith, one of the ship's ranking officers, Mr. Gray seems to have made no move to alleviate the crisis other than to confer secretly with the captain. "The captain and the pilot alone remained passive in this scene of general exertion" (40), Cooper remarks. Indeed, even when reminded by the captain that the entire safety of the ship has been placed in his hands—"'I leave all to the pilot,' said the captain"—the pilot remains unmoved, exhibiting a "calmness bordering on the supernatural, considering his station and responsibility" (41).

Far from being indifferent, however, the pilot proves to be intensely active in his own unobtrusively vigilant way. Pacing the quarterdeck in what appears to be a "trance," he devotes himself to quiet study, reading the signs on the ocean's surface, and taking careful account of the ship's position until he "had seized, with a perception almost intuitive, the only method that promised to extricate the vessel from her situation" (55). Indeed, in this perceptiveness, the pilot argues, lies the future safety of the ship, for no charts or navigational aids could possibly disclose the hidden perils that surround them. "'And how shall I find my way,'" grumbles one sailor. "'[Y]ou will let me trust to neither time, lead, nor log.'" "'You must trust to a quick eye and a ready hand,'" returns the pilot. "'The breakers only will show you the dangers, when you are not able to make out the bearings of the land'" (42). With this advice the pilot articulates the very essence of negligence law, for he urges the sailor to obey its two most central precepts: to maintain a constant watchfulness and to trust to common sense and experience in the absence of more specific or relevant information. By taking the time to survey a situation rather than acting precipitously, the doctrine of negligence suggests, people can reduce the risk of accident if not avoid it altogether.

But along with vigilance, negligence demands action, and the pilot of Cooper's novel rises to the occasion. "The pilot turned from his contemplative posture, and moved slowly across the deck," Cooper writes ". . . like a man who not only felt that every thing depended on himself, but that he was equal to the emergency" (49). In fact, as the tide turns and the tempest increases, the pilot proves as adept at practical action as he was at quiet preparation. Instructing the men with "a startling quickness," to adjust their sails and tack "whenever prudence or skill required any change in the management of the ship" (55–56), he convinces even Griffith to trust him. For having assessed the crisis long before it occurred, Griffith notes, the pilot can now devote all of his energies to preventing it. Yet even in the process of "thundering orders," the pilot never loses his sense of calm, but rather speaks in "those cool tones that are most appalling in critical moments, because they seem to denote most preparation and care" (54). Until all threat of danger has passed, the pilot combines vigilance and action to focus exclusively on accident prevention. "Again and again," Cooper notes, "the frigate appeared to be rushing blindly on shoals, where the sea was covered with foam, and where destruction would have been as sudden as it was certain, when the clear voice of the stranger [the pilot] was heard warning them of the danger, and inciting them to their duty" (56).

But if the pilot's prudence reveals itself most clearly in these early scenes as he negotiates the narrow channel and prevents a shipwreck, it is, as Cooper makes amply clear, essential to the novel's central action as well. For the overall purpose of the frigate's voyage is to land near a certain section of the English coast without being detected to facilitate the kidnapping of several English hostages who are themselves members of the military elite. For this action, undertaken in order to retaliate for English brutalities in the war and to use as a bargaining chip in the peace negotiations in Paris, the pilot's skills are crucial. After discussing the many necessary preparations for anchoring near the coast, Barnstable, one of the officers on board, explains the centrality of the pilot's role in no uncertain terms: " 'Mr. Pilot, you will accompany me,' " he says, " 'for you carry as true a map of the bottom of these seas, in your head, as ever was made of dry ground' " (77). Nor is the pilot's prudence relevant only on the sea. While he plays a relatively small role in that part of the plot that involves the sneak attack on the English officers, his quiet forbearance figures prominently in the rescue of his own comrades who have been taken captive by the English in turn. " 'If sir, he has but a moiety of the skill on land that he possess on the water,' " Lieutenant Griffith explains, " 'I will answer for his success' " (77).

Moreover, after the hostages are taken in the novel's final scenes and the pilot and his comrades depart for calmer waters, the requisite sea battle breaks out and the pilot's prudence is once again paramount. Indeed, his prudence in the midst even of battle marks him as an unusual kind of naval hero—the kind of hero Cooper had discovered in his readings on the legendary naval hero John Paul Jones. Contemporary readers and more recent scholars have long noted that the pilot's character is modeled on that of John Paul Jones,[23] the English renegade who aided the Americans and the French in their revolutions. Tarnished by accusations of treason in England, Jones's reputation was also troubled by American reports of his brutal and piratical acts. But intrigued by the little that was known of him and convinced that too many naval heroes were drifting into obscurity, Cooper set about to recover information about him and to rehabilitate him in the public's eye. In an effort to balance accounts of his uncontrollable temper, Cooper provides an image of a man who was careful, calm, and above all, a flawless seaman—an image for which he had documentation of his own.[24] Thus, in Cooper's account, even as the guns fired all around him, the pilot remains remarkably wary and cautious, "straining his eyes to pierce the fog" (389) to discern the shape of the English cutter, and speaking "coolly, though like a man sensible of the existence of approaching danger" (395). Here then is the figure of the

reasonable and prudent nautical hero epitomized by the negligence regime—a hero who is anticipatory rather than reactive, thoughtful rather
than rash, and subdued rather than dramatic.

BETWEEN NEGLIGENCE AND PRUDENCE: COOPER,
POE, AND MELVILLE

In Cooper's work, the pilot has many successors, although none, admittedly, as cautious or as vigilant as he. Indeed, the balance of Cooper's
nautical *ouevre*, like *The Pioneers*, his fullest investigation of negligence-
related issues, better demonstrates the mid-nineteenth-century *conflict*
over notions of liability than its ultimate *resolution*. In subsequent novels,
that is, Cooper struggled to find a voice for the prudent hero amid the
general romanticism of the times and the particular romanticization of
the sea. Torn by an attraction to the Byronic and the sublime, Cooper
and others like him who sought to give the sea its own literary genre,
vacillated between the creation of heroes who found recklessness a more
natural response to crisis, and those who, like the pilot, were more restrained and cautious. Thus, in almost every nautical novel he wrote
from *The Pilot* to *The Sea Lions* (1849), there is a hero who alternates
between reasonableness and uncontrollable passion. The alternation is
especially striking in his early nautical novels, novels that were written
after *The Pilot*, but before Cooper turned his attention more consciously
to a literary realism that was gaining prominence in mid-century. In novels like *The Red Rover* (1827) and *The Water-Witch* (1830), for example,
Cooper does not hide the wild nature of his heroes; both books revolve
around the exploits of a pirate or renegade who has broken with society
to live on its margins and to fight his own war with even fewer institutional loyalties than the Pilot. Yet in each case, the character who fits this
description exhibits a surprising prudence. In one scene in *The Red
Rover*, one of the two main outlaws, not the Rover himself, but his companion, Wilder, whose divided personality is perfectly expressed by his
epithet, "watchful adventurer," engages in an act of accident prevention
that Cooper characterizes in explicitly legal terms. Having just dismissed
his pilot for incompetently and carelessly steering the ship toward a near
collision with another, Wilder takes over the challenge of piloting himself. "In dismissing the Pilot," Cooper writes, "Wilder had assumed a
responsibility from which a seaman usually shrinks; since, in the case of
any untoward accident in leaving port, it would involve a loss of insurance, and his own probable punishment."[25] Yet, Wilder approaches the
task with a serenity and vigilance that may not equal Mr. Gray's but is a
close rival to it. Moreover, even when he is at his most visibly "wild,"

Wilder is able to call on an unusual reserve of calm and caution. In the midst of a sudden storm, for example, in a scene that almost perfectly recalls in miniature the opening scene of *The Pilot*, Wilder contemplates the ocean, and waits calmly for the most propitious moment to act. But just as Griffith misunderstands the pilot's actions, Wilder's crew misconstrues his hesitation. ". . . the meanest seamen among them," Cooper writes, "had long thought that his unknown commander had been heedlessly trifling with the safety of the vessel, by the hardy manner in which he disregarded the wild symptoms of the weather. But they," like their counterparts in *The Pilot*, "undervalued the keen-eyed vigilance of [their commander] . . ." (641).

Similarly, in *The Water-Witch*, an even more excessively romantic book than *The Red Rover*, and one in which the characters, as the Cooper scholar Thomas Philbrick notes, are even more removed from the normal constraints of reality, Cooper creates a hero whose actions are in part if not in whole in harmony with the standards of negligence law. In one of the novel's most memorable scenes, which takes us once again to the site of a difficult harbor passage and recalls the importance of pilots to the drama of negligence law, the captain of the *Water-Witch*, who is himself known for his navigational skills, finds that his pilot has abandoned him. It is thus incumbent upon him to guide his ship through Hell Gate, the notoriously treacherous channel between the New York harbor and the open sea. Not surprisingly, he performs the task in a manner worthy of Mr. Gray. "The Skimmer of the Seas [this captain's epithet] was deeply practiced in all the intricacies and dangers of shoals and rocks," Cooper writes. "Most of his life had been passed in threading the one or in avoiding the other. So keen and quick had his eye become, in detecting the presence of any of those signs which forewarn the mariner of danger, that a ripple on the surface, or a deeper shade in the color of the water, rarely escaped his vigilance."[26] Untutored and unconventional in his navigation and occasionally even foolhardy, the Skimmer, as this passage explains, could be prudent when he wanted or needed to be.

But if Cooper's characters seem divided in their response to emergencies, they are not alone. A reflection of the contemporary struggle over notions of responsibility, Cooper's works are representative of similar divisions in other nautical works of the day. In particular, the work of Edgar Allan Poe and Herman Melville, both of whom were interested in nautical themes, vacillates like Cooper's between the prudent and reckless sea hero revealing a complicated picture of how the culture began to revise its ideas about responsibility and blame. In Poe's work, the antipodes of recklessness and prudence are best represented by two of his most famous sea stories, "MS. Found in a Bottle" (1836) and *The Narrative of Arthur Gordon Pym* (1838). "MS. Found in a Bottle" revolves around the strange fate of a passenger who is traveling from Java to the Archipelago Islands on a beautiful but ill-fated ship. Several days out from shore the passenger observes a singular cloud whose changing color and shape he tracks assiduously for hours. As it spreads across the sky, he notes a strange calm overtaking the ship which is now drifting toward shore. Confessing that "every appearance warranted me in apprehending a simoon," he nervously but dutifully alerts the captain. "I told the captain of my fears," he remarks, "but he paid no attention to what I said, and left me without deigning to give a reply."[27] Predictably, only moments after he issues his warning, the ship is caught in a terrible storm which "swept the entire decks from stem to stern" (119). The passenger who is, of course, the lone survivor, is ultimately rescued by a vessel that seems to appear out of nowhere and bears mysteriously down on him. Scrambling aboard this strange ship, the passenger, who is grateful at first for its appearance, soon realizes that his experience on board this second ship rivals the nightmare of the first. Indeed, if on the first ship the passenger's warning about the imminent accident was ignored, here he himself goes undetected; he is as invisible to the other members of the crew as if he were a ghost. "Concealment is utter folly on my part," he writes, "for the people *will not* see" (123).

In raising questions about the reality of the narrator's existence on the second ship, of course, Poe casts doubt on what had originally appeared as reasonable behavior on the first, for now, in the terrifying fashion that is so characteristic of his prose, the reader is set adrift without knowing which, if any, version of events to believe. Nevertheless in tying the issue of the narrator's reasonableness to the practice of storytelling, "MS." tends ultimately to reinforce our initial impression for at the very least the narrator has been reasonable enough to generate a viable fantasy. Thus, the rest of the story concerns the narrator's efforts to insure not his own survival, an effort he now knows is futile, but the survival of his narrative. To this end, he steals writing implements from the captain's cabin and commits his tale to paper. "I have seen the captain face to face," he writes, "and in his own cabin—but, as I expected, he paid me no attention" (124). Indeed, so thoroughly shut out is the narrator from communication with anyone on board ship that he is forced to entrust the evaluation of his own reasonableness to the ocean's drift—as a manuscript in a bottle. With this symbol of desperation, Poe turns the threat posed by recklessness to prudence into a threat to the narrative of negligence itself. More important, by metaphorically tossing the story out in a bottle he, more obviously than any other author, throws the burden of devising an appropriate standard for determining responsibility and blame for otherwise preventable catastrophes back on his readers and on the culture at large.

Far from washing his hands of it himself, however, Poe returns to the issue of assessing responsibility and blame for catastrophes at sea from a somewhat different perspective in *The Narrative of Arthur Gordon Pym*. Like "MS.," this narrative represents the alternatives of reasonableness and recklessness but weighs in more obviously on the side of recklessness, holding it out not as a virtue necessarily but as a more powerful and naturally compelling response to the possibility of disaster. Briefly, *Pym* tells the story of the eponymous Pym, a boy who with the help of his friend Augustus Barnard manages to sail as a stowaway on Barnard's father's ship merely to satisfy his craving for a sea adventure. From the start the boys plan to disclose Pym's presence on board the ship once the vessel is far enough from land to make a return to shore impossible, a period that they expect will last about three days. But when some members of the crew decide to mutiny, holding the captain and everyone else hostage, things go awry. Naturally, during the period of the takeover, Barnard is prevented from furnishing Pym with the food and drink he requires, and he consequently languishes in the hold, feverish, far from lucid, and near starvation.

Without detailing the story's many interesting twists and turns which follow Pym and one other survivor of the mutiny on an extended adventure that leads ultimately to the South Pole and possibly even to another dimension, it remains only to be said that like "MS." *Pym* connects the idea of negligence on board ship with the writing of a nautical narrative. Unlike "MS.," however, *Pym* serves to reinforce a connection between recklessness, not prudence, and the process of storytelling. Indeed, while the narrator can at times appear to be quite rational, discoursing at length in the beginning of the novel about the likelihood of an accident resulting from Captain Barnard's "negligence" in diverging from accepted methods of stowing partial cargo, these moments are few and far between. After the brief opening incident of the novel, for example, in which Pym and Barnard almost die in Pym's small boat as a result of some seriously reckless sailing, we learn that Pym is more eager than ever to go to sea. "It is strange, too," Pym relates, "that he [Barnard] most strongly enlisted my feeling in behalf of the life of a seaman, when he depicted his more terrible moments of suffering and despair. For the bright side of the painting I had a limited sympathy. My visions were of shipwreck and famine; of death or captivity among barbarian hordes; of a lifetime dragged out in sorrow and tears upon some gray and desolate rock, in an ocean unapproachable and unknown."[28] Surrounded by a meta-narrative by Poe that comments on the authenticity of Pym's authorship and the novelty of his gruesome tale, the manuscript itself seems to attest to the importance of imprudence for a certain kind of writing.

Of course, that kind of writing—that is to say, Poe's writing—is often considered anomalous in literary histories of his time. Yet if it is justifiable at times to treat Poe's writing separately from that of his contemporaries, it is also a mistake to ignore many of the typicalities it embodies. I invoke him here to emphasize the representativeness not only of his concerns about negligence and reasonableness, but about madness and recklessness as well, and further to place the strain of recklessness in his characterizations within a larger literary tradition of romanticism in writings about the sea. As many scholars have pointed out, it was Cooper who first brought a romantic notion of the sea to American nautical fiction, imbuing the sea with the awe and sublimity with which we still often view it today. And while Cooper himself ultimately turned away from a purely romantic aesthetic in his later nautical novels, the romanticism he introduced in these early works finds echoes in many later fictions, including Melville's. For examples of romantic sea characters, one thinks immediately of Melville's Ishmael lost in a reverie atop his masthead on board the doomed *Pequod*. But it is useful to think of Melville's Ahab in this context as well, for the romanticization of the sea contributed to the characterization of the classically mad sea captain whose actions at sea epitomize a certain kind of recklessness.

Alternately characterized as villain and victim,[29] Ahab is undoubtedly one of literature's most complex naval captains, and a complete analysis of his motivations fall outside the scope of my discussion here. But it is worth noting, if only briefly, that his decision to turn the *Pequod*'s mission to hunt whales for commercial reasons into a mission for personal vengeance against one whale alone, reflects a key aspect of his culture's debate over leadership and responsibility. While Ahab is, like Pym, a symbol of imprudent behavior, his behavior is actively critiqued in the novel by a character who figures as his polar opposite, Starbuck. Melville goes to great lengths to describe Starbuck as a "careful" fellow who in the fashion epitomized by negligence law is interested in preventing danger before it happens. In perhaps the most perfect expression of such a negligence-minded sentiment, Starbuck is heard remarking to the men who will make up the crew of his small whaling boat, " 'I will have no man in my boat . . . who is not afraid of a whale.' "[30] But if Starbuck, who is "no crusader after perils" (103), is guided by the precepts of negligence, Ahab, as we have already noted, is not. Indeed, the conflict between these two approaches[31] to accidents figures prominently in one of the most famous scenes in all of American literature, the scene on the quarterdeck when Ahab inspires the crew to join him in his mad endeavor. Reproaching Ahab for wanting "vengeance on a dumb brute" (144), Starbuck attempts to convince the crew of Ahab's folly. But here, as in the rest of the novel, Ahab has the upper hand rhetorically, turning Starbuck's relatively mild reproach into an act of rebellion which Starbuck himself would be the first to denounce. Thus, at the end of his long monologue daring Starbuck to defy him, Ahab announces with characteristic aplomb, " 'Starbuck now is mine; cannot oppose me now, without rebellion' " (144). Under Ahab's rules, in short, leadership and responsibility are embodied in the person of the captain regardless of his actions. And without assuming that position by rebellion or mutiny, he implies—the very kind of action Starbuck condemns in Ahab—Starbuck's challenge is doomed.

But if these scenes in *Moby Dick* are not alone sufficient signs of Melville's concern with the question of responsibility and leadership, additional evidence can be found in other texts and in his relationship with his father-in-law, Lemuel Shaw, the Chief Justice of the Massachusetts Supreme Court and one of the authors of the negligence doctrine. Indeed, as many scholars have pointed out, Shaw may very well have served as a model for Captain Vere, the complex naval captain of Melville's last work, *Billy Budd* (1888–91). In this work Melville, like Poe, does an about-face, turning his attentions to the characteristic intricacies and tensions inherent in the seemingly prudent and reasonable character rather than in the reckless one. In fact, in *Billy Budd*, there are two prudent protagonists, Billy and Vere. Intent on preserving his image as the Handsome Sailor and peacemaker on board the *Indomitable*, Billy is ultimately foiled in his attempts. Interestingly, Billy falls out of favor with his superior, Claggart, as a result of two accidents, one more disastrous than the other. Indeed, the whole story of *Billy Budd*, one could argue, is a sustained investigation of the consequences of accidents as well as a debate on the possibility or impossibility of prudent behavior to prevent them. In the first accident, Billy spills a bowl of soup, a trivial mishap which nonetheless secretly irritates Claggart as Billy reveals that he has been privy to malicious gossip about Claggart in using the pejorative nickname, "Jemmy Legs," for him. The second incident, a fatal one for both Billy and Claggart, is the defining moment in which Billy, confronted with Claggart's assertion that he has conspired to mutiny, resorts to physical, although involuntary, violence instead of speaking out on his own behalf. In killing Claggart with an accidental blow, Billy is himself condemned to death by hanging. Of course, many have argued that in condemning Billy to death for killing the evil Claggart accidentally, Vere demonstrates an extreme, even maddening logic, but there can be no doubt that he *intends* to deal reasonably with him. Indeed, Vere's judgment is marked throughout the text by his fastidious attention to the precepts of the law. What is interesting about this attention, moreover, is that it reveals not only the priority of legal rules over individual rights, as many scholars have pointed out,[32] but also the importance of a particular kind of legal rule, namely, that of preventative action. For what is often overlooked in discussions of *Billy Budd* is the historical justification of death sentences for individuals like Billy who were accused, as Billy was by Claggart, of conspiring to mutiny. Indeed, most readers probably assume that in adhering to the Mutiny Act, Vere's punishment of Billy is dictated by the logic of retribution or deterrence—that Billy's execution serves either a punishment for his deed or as a lesson to others contemplating mutiny in the future. But while these goals are surely part of Vere's decision, they do not encompass the desire to prevent further misconduct that figures in it as well.

RICHARD HENRY DANA JR. AND THE U.S.S. *SOMERS*

Indeed, so compelling was the logic of preventative and prudent behavior in this period that it affected the legal and literary characterizations of accidental and criminal actions alike. In addition to its appearance in the many accident cases that were flooding the court dockets, it also figured in criminal cases of all sorts, including an important mutiny case that has also been cited as a model for *Billy Budd*. The *Somers* case (1843) involved the court-martial of Commander Alexander Slidell Mackenzie of the U.S.S. *Somers* for summarily executing three sailors at sea for conspiracy to mutiny. Apart from the controversy over whether there was sufficient evidence of the mutineers' guilt, the case became a cause célèbre because one of those hanged, Phillip Spencer, the alleged ringleader, was the son of the then Secretary of War, John Spencer. Among other things, John Spencer was furious that instead of hanging the suspects himself without trial, Mackenzie did not wait the four days it would have taken for the *Somers* to reach the island of Saint Thomas, where it was bound, or for that matter any one of a number of closer islands, where the mutineers would have been tried by duly appointed officers of the law. Spencer led the charge to have Mackenzie tried for murder in a civil rather than a military court where he thought justice would be better served, but sentiment in favor of a court-martial prevailed. Mackenzie, of course, was not free from attack in the naval court or in the press. In fact, Cooper, whose recently published book on naval history had been publicly criticized by Mackenzie, was among his most voluble detractors. But public opinion was largely in his favor, and testimony both inside and outside the courtroom from several other prominent figures[33] helped to acquit him of all charges and return him to active duty.

Significantly, those who justified Mackenzie's actions believed not only in the guilt of the mutineers but in the necessity of the drastic and immediate action Mackenzie took against them. This action, they argued, was justified because it was preventative and the prevention of crime, like the prevention of accidents, was of the utmost importance. Even Cooper, who argued vociferously against Mackenzie's actions and whose long review of the case was appended to the court proceedings, invoked the concept of prevention and of foreseeability. For Cooper, however, the available evidence suggested that neither Mackenzie nor his officers were in any danger from the mutineers. "Now nothing can be more just," he writes, "than to say that Captain Mackenzie was not obliged to risk his own life, or that of his officers. . . ."[34] But, he continued, "We conceive the only way in which this point can fairly tell in favor of Captain Mackenzie, is to say that he had no other means of saving his vessel, himself, or his officers, than to hang those he did hang" (272). That Cooper devoted the bulk of his argument in a review over eighty pages long to this point helps us to appreciate the gravity not only of Mackenzie's actions but of the idea of prudence for his defenders, for it was in the face of relatively weak evidence of danger, from Cooper's point of view at least, that they justified Mackenzie's safety measures.

Of the prominent figures who spoke out on Mackenzie's behalf, the one who urged this justification most consistently[35] and is for this and other reasons most telling for our purposes was the nautical memoirist and lawyer Richard Henry Dana Jr. In a long letter published in 1843 in at least four major newspapers in New York and Boston, Dana focuses on the importance of acting quickly, even summarily, to prevent the otherwise dire consequences of a mutiny itself. "Must they [the captains of sailing vessels] then wait the onset and its chances?" he asks. "Perhaps, so far as personal danger to themselves was concerned, Mr. Mackenzie and his officers would have been willing to run the risk of the contest . . . but they had also a solemn duty as public officers, at all hazards to prevent this vessel's becoming a pirate."[36] In short, Dana suggests that a mutiny is unforeseen and unpredictable in precisely the same way an accident is and requires action that is prudent and preemptive.

To this end Dana stresses the reasonableness of Mackenzie's actions under the circumstances. He argues that though the exercise of summary execution would certainly be considered unreasonable on land, it is understandable at sea. "On shore," he writes, "life is rarely taken to prevent the commission of a capital crime (although the law allows it when necessary) because there can be usually other precautions and means of defence [sic]. Not so at sea, in a case like this" (57). More to the point, he spends a good deal of time describing the layout of the *Somers* itself. Apparently Dana found the *Somers* to be surprisingly small and thus incapable of housing the three mutineers in a way that was consistent with proper safety precautions.

From the North Carolina I went to the Somers, and here I must say that no one ought to form an opinion upon the issue of this conspiracy without first seeing the Somers. You have been on board a man-of-war, and you have, doubtless (as I find others have), formed your notions of the state of things in the Somers by what you have seen before. . . . But you must make a revolution in all your ideas upon these particulars to judge of the Somers. You would hardly believe your eyes if you were here to see, as the scene of this dreadful conspiracy, a little brig, with low bulwarks, a single narrow deck flush fore and aft, and nothing to make the officers' quarters but a long trunk-house . . . such as you may have seen in our smaller packets which ply along the seaboard. You feel as though half a dozen resolute conspirators could have swept the decks and thrown overboard all that opposed them before aid could come from below. . . . In short, no one at all acquainted with nautical matters can see the Somers without being made feelingly aware of the defenceless [sic] situation of those few officers dealing with a crew of ninety persons, of whom some were known to be conspirators, while of the rest they hardly knew upon whom to rely for active and efficient aid in time of danger (53).

Like any good lawyer, Dana clearly argues from the specific case, making a lasting exception for the *Somers* based on his own observation of it, and carving out a new understanding of what was reasonable under the circumstances. Indeed, it is the circumstantial reasonableness of Mackenzie's otherwise unreasonable "precautions," as Dana puts it, that links him with the portrait of Captain Vere in *Billy Budd*, for Vere's order to execute Billy is, like Mackenzie's order to execute the *Somers*'s mutineers, ultimately condoned as a necessarily evil.[37] As Vere remarks to his fellow officers: "Our vowed responsibility is in this: That however pitilessly that law may operate, we nevertheless adhere to it and administer it."[38]

The reasonable behavior of which negligence speaks is linked to a prudence that is determined largely by circumstance. When later in the century, around the time Melville was writing *Billy Budd*, Oliver Wendell Holmes Jr. turned to the formulation of these rules, he emphasized the importance of context for theories of responsibility and blameworthiness. The reasonable man, he argued, guarded against harmful consequences that he could reasonably foresee given the circumstances. Nor was Holmes content to let the idea of context itself remain vague. "It is equally clear," he writes, "that the featureless generality, that the defendant was bound to use such care as a prudent man would do under the circumstances, ought to be continually giving place to the specific one, that he was bound to use this or that precaution under these or those circumstances."[39]

TWO YEARS BEFORE THE MAST

This emphasis on precautions deemed appropriate by circumstance remained central to the writings of Richard Henry Dana Jr. whose vision of the executions aboard the *Somers* as a preventative act was both vehement and persuasive. Indeed, three years before voicing his concerns about the *Somers* mutiny, Dana recorded similar views in a journal he published of the two years he spent as a cabin boy sailing around Cape Horn from Boston to California, entitled *Two Years Before the Mast* (1840). In this journal, which changed the nature of nautical literature in America, Dana regales the reader with the requisite number of high seas adventures, but the book's most persistent theme is that of safety and its violations. Indeed, what was so revolutionary about Dana's work was the attention it paid to the mundane but nevertheless perilous incidents in a sailor's life. Of course, like the *Somers* mutiny, many of Dana's complaints about preventable maritime disasters involved criminal actions by sailors or captains. In one of the most noted passages in the book, in fact, Dana focuses on a gruesome flogging inflicted by the captain of his ship on a reliable and well-liked sailor for an unwitnessed act of impudence. "A man—a human being, made in God's likeness—" Dana writes, "fastened up and flogged like a beast!"[40] But if he finds himself disgusted by the captains's tyranny, interestingly, Dana does not endorse retaliatory measures. Indeed, he remains an advocate for the kind of preventative action that will avoid further catastrophe. "But beside the numbers," he writes, "what is there for sailors to do? If they resist, it is mutiny; and if they succeed, and take the vessel, it is piracy. . . . Bad as it was they saw it must be borne" (97–98). It is at this point in the narrative, in fact, that Dana vows that in his later life as a lawyer he will take up the cause of sailors who have been brutalized by despotic captains and help put an end to the reign of criminal impressments and floggings on board ship not by encouraging mutinies but by enforcing legal measures designed to prevent otherwise lawless actions at sea.

To this end, in fact, only months after *Two Years* was published, Dana compiled a para-legal manual, *A Seaman's Friend* (1841), that, together with *Two Years*, served to identify criminal and civil abuses at sea and to raise the public's awareness of them. Intended primarily "for sea-faring persons," and for "judges and practitioners in maratime [*sic*] law,"[41] the manual's plan is quite simple; it spells out the minimum requirements for preventing crimes and accidents, and emphasizes, above all, the need for each and every member of the crew, no matter how elevated or inferior, to be vigilant and calm. Underscoring the need for every sailor to act as circumstances dictate, Dana provides a rigorous classification of all the positions, ranks, and duties for insuring safety on board ship among a ship's personnel. It is to the "ordinary and every-day duties of . . . office, and the customs which long usage has made almost as binding as laws" (131), to which Dana turns his attention in this book. Much later, in a case[42] argued before a Federal District Court in Massachusetts, Dana continued his commitment to the task begun in *Two Years* and *A Seaman's Friend* by singlehandedly rewriting some of the rules for avoiding ship collisions between steamships and sailing vessels.[43]

Although it is more representative of a manual than of a literary memoir, the specification of duties and rank that characterizes *A Seaman's Friend* has an almost exact counterpart in *Two Years* which focuses on the routine rather than romantic aspects of the sailor's life. Indeed, in *Two Years* Dana's critique is directed less at sensationalized criminal abuses like flogging than at the frequency of collisions and shipwrecks brought on by the negligence of those in a position of responsibility. The image of the sea as a place fraught with accidents becomes the dominant image of his memoir. Specifically, he targets certain individuals for their failure to perform at a level appropriate to their station and task. It is not surprising, then, that like *A Seaman's Friend*, the book begins with a "description of the duties, regulations, and customs of an American merchantman, of which ours was a fair specimen" (17). More important, in explaining the work assignments of every seaman, from the captain to the mates to the steward and cook, Dana provides the reader with the information necessary to evaluate the carelessness of the various individuals he encounters along the way.

Specifically, *Two Years* offers several cautionary tales of the common incompetence and unusual competence of various sea captains. Indeed, the most memorable description of negligent action is based on Dana's observations of his own captain, Thompson, the very same man who earlier was seen flogging an undeserving member of his crew. Far more than the flogging, Thompson's display of negligence shows how truly illegitimate his authority over others proves to be as he proceeds to endanger the entire crew. Indeed, in this vignette, Thompson has trouble with the simplest navigational maneuver. The scene opens as Thompson, at the helm of Dana's ship, the *Pilgrim*, is approaching the San Diego harbor. The harbor, according to Dana's report, is small but welcoming, and though populated at the time of their arrival by three other ships— the *Loriotte*, the *Lagoda*, and the *Ayacucho*—it has berths to spare. Given this, the process of anchoring the *Pilgrim* should be easy, but due to Thompson's utter incompetence, it turns into a dangerous series of collisions with one after another of the neighboring vessels. Dana's account is worth quoting at length for its merciless and detailed depiction of negligence in action. He writes:

As we drew near, carried rapidly along by the current, we overhauled our chain, and clewed up the topsails. "Let go the anchor!" said the captain; but either there was not chain enough forward of the windlass, or the anchor went down foul, or we had too much headway on, for it did not bring us up. "Pay out chain!" shouted the captain; and we gave it to her; but it would not do. Before the other anchor could be let go, we drifted down broadside on, and went smash into the *Lagoda*. . . .

Fortunately, no great harm was done. Her jib boom passed between our fore- and mainmasts, carrying away some of our rigging, and breaking down the rail. She lost her martingale. This brought us up, and, as they paid out chain, we swung clear of them, and let go the other anchor; but this had as bad luck as the first, for, before anyone perceived it, we were drifting down upon the *Loriotte*. The captain now gave out his orders rapidly and fiercely, sheeting home the topsails, and backing and filling the sails, in hope of starting or clearing the anchors; but it was all in vain, and he sat down on the rail, taking it very leisurely, and calling out to Captain Nye that he was coming to pay him a visit. We drifted fairly into the *Loriotte*, her larboard bow into our starboard quarter, carrying away a part of our starboard-quarter railing, and breaking off her larboard bumpkin, and one or two stanchions above the deck. . . . After paying out chain, we swung clear, but our anchors were, no doubt, afoul of hers. We manned the windlass, and hove, and hove away, but to no purpose. Sometimes we got a little upon the cable, but a good surge would take it all back again (106).

Comical, even farcical, in its portrayal of an alternately panicked and resigned Captain Thompson caught in a seemingly endless and destructive pattern of negligent collision, this passage is also a brutal examination of the kinds of improprieties that typically resulted in the accidents adjudicated by negligence. And while the consequences of Thompson's glaring display of incompetence are never very serious—there is no loss of life and only minor property damage—the scene provides a serious critique of the problems of negligent behavior for the maritime industry.

Lest the lesson to be learned from Thompson's careless and misguided maneuverings be overshadowed by the humor of the scene, however, Dana follows it with a portrait of Wilson, the captain of the *Ayacucho*, who not only prevents Thompson from colliding with his ship, the only other vessel in close proximity, but defines the calm, collected, and commonsensical action we saw earlier in Cooper's pilot. Having witnessed Thompson's collisions with the *Lagoda* and the *Loriotte*, Captain Wilson of the *Ayacucho* resolves not to become his next victim. He boards the *Pilgrim* and takes command of the ship to the great relief of Dana and his fellow sailors. What is striking to Dana, however, is not simply Wilson's superior navigational skills, but the effortlessness and serenity which characterize his actions. In stark contrast to Thompson, that is, whose panic in the moment of crisis gives way all too rapidly to utter resignation, Wilson remains calm, quiet, and controlled. Since his primary concern is the safety of the ship, its crew, and its property, moreover, Wilson spends little or no time establishing his authority. It follows directly from his assumption of responsibility. Dana writes: "He did not hesitate to give advice, and from giving advice, he gradually came to taking the command; ordering us when to heave and when to pawl, and backing and filling the topsails, setting and taking in jib and trysail, whenever he thought best" (106). Indeed, as his manner throughout is exacting and precise, his authority is never questioned. "Our captain gave a few orders," Dana notes, "but as Wilson generally countermanded them, saying, in *an easy, fatherly kind of way*, 'Oh no, Captain Thompson, you don't want the jib on her,' or 'It isn't time yet to heave!' he soon gave it up" (106–7, my emphasis).

So deft and careful is the action of Captain Wilson and so different is the model of action he provides from that of Captain Thompson, in fact, that it remains a powerful memory for Dana long after the voyage is over. It even reappears in the sequel he wrote to *Two Years Before the Mast*, entitled *Twenty Four Years After* (which was not published with the original text until 1869). In this memoir, Dana encounters the now elderly Captain Wilson, and after exchanging pleasantries, they revisit the incident involving Captain Thompson in the San Diego harbor. Wilson's own recollection of Thompson's behavior reinforces Dana's insinuations about his negligence. "Thompson, he said, hadn't the sailor in him; and he never could laugh enough at his *fiasco* in San Diego" (349). More important, however, Wilson is delighted by the high esteem in which Dana obviously held his own accomplishments. "I found he had been very much flattered by the praise I had bestowed in my book on his seamanship," Dana notes, "especially in bringing the *Pilgrim* to her berth in San Diego harbor, after she had drifted successively into the *Lagoda* and the *Loriotte*, and was coming into him" (349). Indeed, both for his kind and fatherly ways and for his safety-consciousness, Wilson remains Dana's most cherished example of careful and responsible seamanship.

Other examples of safety-conscious behavior in the book reveal a similar endorsement of the masterful, almost paternal authority Wilson displays, but one more is worth singling out for the way it underlines the importance of prudent "seamanship"[44]—that nautical synonym for the kind of competence required by negligence law. Seen in comparison with Captain Thompson, Captain Faucon, who takes over the command of the *Pilgrim* after Thompson's tour ends, comes across as a natural-born seaman whose skill seems effortless and is consistently aimed at avoiding accidents. The *Pilgrim*, Dana writes, "got under way with no fuss, and came so near us [at this point Dana is on another vessel] as to throw a letter on board, Captain Faucon standing at the tiller himself and steering her as he would a mackerel smack. When Captain Thompson was in command of the *Pilgrim*, there was as much preparation and ceremony as there would be in getting a seventy-four [a much larger ship] under way" (178). Moreover, the quality for which Faucon is selected as a superior seaman is precisely what sets Captain Wilson apart: his natural, almost personal embodiment of prudence. "Captain Faucon," Dana writes, "was a sailor, every inch of him. He knew what a ship was, and was as much at home in one as a cobbler in his stall" (178). Of course, the comparison between captain and cobbler suggests how important it was to internalize the kind of prudence required by the doctrine of negligence. But it is telling for another reason as well, for while Dana happens to focus on the skills of those in positions of acknowledged authority, his analysis applies equally well to the examination of all skilled workers whose actions and efforts at accident prevention became equally subject to scrutiny under negligence law.

THE COMMON SAILOR AND THE POPULAR SEA TALE

The story of nautical literature after Dana is largely the story of the popularization and dissemination of plots and characters involving concerns shared by negligence law. More particularly, it is the story of the embodiment of those concerns by authors and characters from different social ranks, manifesting differing skill levels and differing assumptions of responsibility. But what it reveals on the whole is the overall assumption and redefinition of responsibility for everyone on board ship. Indeed, most authors who wrote nautical tales in the 1840s and 1850s had been common sailors themselves who, though they recognized the significance of Dana's book, felt that Dana had not yet applied the lessons of nautical vigilance to them or to men in their position. With titles that suggest their admiration of Dana—titles like Isaac's *Twenty Years Before the Mast* (1843), Nevens's *Forty Years At Sea* (1850), Hazen's *Five Years Before the Mast* (1853), and Cleveland's *In the Forecastle, or, Twenty-Five Years a Sailor* (1846)—the books these authors wrote speak of the impact of newly defined hazards and the skills required to avoid them more frequently from the perspective of the cabin than from that of the quarterdeck.

Cooper himself contributed to this popularization, falling under the sway of Dana's nautical realism even as he was partly responsible for it. Although Cooper had turned away from the romantic excesses of his early nautical novels when he returned to the genre after a relatively long hiatus in *Homeward Bound* (1838), he showed a marked affinity for Dana's journalistic method in a memoir he wrote in 1843—a memoir not of his own experience at sea but of that of a fellow sailor, entitled *Ned Myers, or A Life Before the Mast*. Like the work of a majority of Dana's successors, however, Cooper's book focused more on the common sailor than Dana's had. Based on a series of lengthy conversations with Myers who served for a time with Cooper in the Navy, this work is replete with information about routine duties and schedules, interactions between the crew, and examples of responsible action on the part of common sailors.

From Ned's perspective as a common sailor often assigned to the most dangerous tasks, the sea is fraught with accidents that affect him a disproportionate number of times and that only he can handle. Time after time he is caught in the midst of a disaster and finds himself scrambling to avoid injury from a falling masthead, leaky boat, or fierce gale. Admittedly, in most cases the injuries Myers suffers are the results of faulty equipment—of negligent acts, in short, committed not by pilots, sailors, or officers, but by the owners and shipmasters whose job it was to outfit the ship properly before it left the port. Thus, as one particularly violent storm begins to wash over his ship, he writes: "We now discovered the defects of old canvass and old rigging, splitting the foretopsail, foresail, and fore-topmost-staysail, besides carrying away sheets, & c." (146). But in other cases, Myers seems to find fault with those around him. Indeed, after years of suffering the bumps and bruises of his "perilous calling," Myers seems to have developed a permanent habit of watchfulness. Especially in its second half, his narrative reveals a striking attention to safety, and relates, in the style of a manual or guide, how to avoid the disastrous consequences of certain known perils. Thus, as he and his fellow sailors struggle with yet another storm, Ned relates his "plan of getting the fore-top mast otayoail loooo . . . which did blow out in a way greatly to help uo, as I think" (224). Not only does Ned do what he can to prevent disasters, but he asserts his own ability to do so more and more as the book and his voyages wear on. In commenting on a particularly difficult passage along the coast which is made, not coincidentally, without the benefit of a pilot, Ned goes so far as to second-guess his captain. "I suppose we passed the Eddystone at a safe distance, or the captain would not have attempted going to windward of it," he notes, "but to me, it appeared that we were fearfully near" (232). Given that he is unable to take command of the ship, Ned becomes vigilant about the actions of others, expressing a view of negligence that emphasizes the diffusion of responsibility.

As we learn from Cooper and his more obscure colleagues, it was often the common seaman who was most acutely aware of imminent dangers, either because he was by nature more alert or because he was less distracted by the arrogance and pretension that often made those in command take unnecessary risks. Moreover, in stressing the potential for everyone, regardless of rank, to exercise the proper caution, the law of negligence spoke in terms that were especially relevant to the communal nature of risk on board a ship. In its emphasis on the common man, then, this popular nautical literature, which was characterized by repetition and stock formulas, tells the story of the common man's warning and his superior's dismissal of it over and over again. In issuing the first warning about a nautical peril, the common man, who was often barred from taking direct action to prevent an accident, was able to take advantage of that aspect of negligence law that rewarded all dimensions of preventative action and all gestures of admonition. But the formula was revealing in a second way as well, for in the dynamic between superior and subordinate, these narratives not only celebrate the prudence of the common man for itself, but show how favorably it compares with the negligence or recklessness of those with greater authority and power. To be sure, there could be no clearer evidence of negligence than in the behavior of one who was explicitly warned to avoid a given accident and yet failed to heed the advice, for the prudent and reasonable course of behavior was undeniably available to him.

The dramatization of a responsibility far superior to that of the one nominally in charge, although not himself a common seaman exactly, is the theme of a story in this genre of popular nautical tales by the prolific author T. S. Arthur.[45] In Arthur's story "The Shipwreck," we get a detailed portrait of the reasonable hero who, in obedience to the precepts of negligence is both quietly vigilant, responsible, and yet perilously ignored. Indeed, like so many of Arthur's temperance tales for which he was more famous, this story, more than any other in the canon of nautical tales, celebrates the virtues of restraint and caution. The story opens on a young lieutenant in the English infantry, named Stewart, who together with two hundred soldiers in his charge, forty-eight other passengers, and a full complement of sailors and naval officers, is traveling on "a large, strongly built ship"[46] from Quebec to Halifax. As a lieutenant, of course, Stewart has a duty to provide for the welfare of his men, and to this end he has taken up a post on deck from which he can supervise their activities. His duties, however, do not extend to the maintenance and management of the ship. Taking the universal injunction implied by negligence seriously, Stewart nevertheless assumes a posture of profound vigilance, limiting "his own hours of rest to the smallest possible number" (151), so that he can watch for accidents at sea. With a storm in the offing, the lieutenant refuses sleep altogether, keeping his eyes fixed on the horizon. Eventually, his efforts are rewarded as he perceives a strange light in the fog, but when he relays the information to the pilot he "receive[s] a very short uncourteous reply, together with a command from the captain who was by, to go back to his post" (152). Becoming convinced that the presence of the light signifies that the ship is too close to the shore, however, the lieutenant approaches the captain and pilot again. This time, of course, he is repulsed even more strongly. " 'Sir, I have been a royal pilot on this coast for twenty-five years,' the pilot replies, 'and I ought to know where I am' " (152).

Rejecting the kind of mechanical and blind assumption of knowledge that this pilot implies and that flouts the emphasis on circumstance that we associate with the standard of care dictated by negligence law, Stewart turns his attention to mitigating the effects of the disaster after it occurs. In this effort, he combines an ability both to perceive danger and, like Cooper's pilot, to take appropriate and concrete action to insure safety. Indeed, in attributing a self-centeredness and cowardice to almost every character in the story except the young lieutenant, Arthur, ever the moralist, strongly implies that one's ability to foresee and to prevent danger is intimately tied to one's concern for others even after injury occurs. Thus, of all the soldiers, crew members, and passengers, the lieutenant alone remains sufficiently calm to negotiate a transfer of all on board to some nearby rocks after the ship begins to founder. Everyone else, by contrast, even those with families, abandons all semblance of responsibility. "The men forsook their wives in the endeavour to save their own lives; . . . and an officer who had heretofore been considered not only as a most courageous soldier, but had showed himself a kind and affectionate husband, now turned a deaf ear to the prayers of his wife . . . intent only on his own deliverance. . . ." (153). More important, once it is determined that the rock they now inhabit will soon be engulfed by the rising tide, the captain and pilot prove the most self-centered of all as they abandon the soldiers for a taller rock that will hold but a few lucky survivors. The lieutenant meanwhile remains focused on the collective survival of those who are stranded with him. Even as the soldiers are being rescued from their rock by a passing ship that has sighted them, Stewart makes sure that "the shipwrecked embark quietly, and not rush in such numbers as to peril their own safety" (164). Thus, Stewart displays a leadership and a sense of responsibility that, in accordance with the spirit of negligence (if not its letter), views danger as a threat to the collectivity, not as an opportunity for self-aggrandizement.

Written in the same vein as Arthur's story but to a slightly more didactic end are two stories—"The Unlucky Ship, or Ned Spanker's Story" (1857), and "The Drunken Captain, or Ned Rollins's Story" (1857)—by perhaps the most popular nautical writer of this period, John Sherburne Sleeper. Sleeper's stories were published as part of a short story and essay collection whose stated purpose was both to "impress upon the mind of the reader the duties of a seaman," and to "promote the welfare of seamen" themselves. This dual purpose is significant for two reasons: it links a consciousness of duty to a sailor's welfare and assumes an association between the common reader and the common seaman that characterized and motivated much of the popular fiction about negligence. Indeed, in Sleeper's versions of the negligence drama, the stories themselves are conceived in protest against the negligence of officers as a group, and serve to solidify bonds between the common sailors on watch for whom they were intended.

Given this emphasis, it is not surprising to find that Sleeper's stories are more clearly focused than Arthur's on the refusal to heed the common sailor's warnings than on the lingering effects of the sailor's heroism after the accident has occurred. Divided into three parts, with one told on each of three successive night watches, the story of the *Hope*, the "unlucky ship" of the first story's title, includes three different incidents of negligence involving warnings and premonitions of danger that are prematurely dismissed. The villain in this case is not the captain but the mate whose authority, although it is not supreme, nevertheless invests him with an arrogance that results in negligence and injury to both the ship and the crew. The hero, of course, is Spanker himself, the old sailor whose yarns are entertaining, instructive, and self-congratulatory. Thus, in the first part of the story, the young Spanker establishes himself as an exemplary hand on deck. He first sees an iceberg, which the ship manages to avoid, and later notes a strange calm that overtakes them. "I noticed that the sea became very smooth," he remarks, "and some other circumstances, or perhaps some mysterious presentiment caused me to think that we were getting too near the land."[47] Before alerting the mate on watch, however, Spanker conveys the information to another sailor who urges him to keep the information to himself. "I mentioned this to Dick Grummet," Spanker says, "who shrugged his shoulders, and said that it was none of our business if we were" (202–3). Manifesting a deep understanding of the rigid nature of the hierarchy on board ship, Grummet clearly chooses short-term self-preservation over the dictates of duty and propriety. Spanker, however, is undeterred. "I then walked up to the mate," he continues, "who, I verily believe, was snoozing at his post. 'Mr. Tileston,' said I respectfully, 'I am afraid we are getting too near the land, don't you think we had better get a cast of the lead?'" (200). But Tileston is inflexible. "Tileston was one of those self-sufficient men, who think they know everything, and that other persons know nothing," Spanker observes: "Accordingly my proposal did not meet his approbation. 'Heave a cast of the lead,' said he, with a laugh of derision, 'here in the middle of the English channel? My good fellow, attend to your own duty, and I'll take care of mine'" (203).

Needless to say, the mate's notion of "duty" is a flawed one. By the end of Part 1, it is discovered that the ship is indeed dangerously close to the coast, and Ned's vigilance is vindicated. But as the ship emerges relatively unscathed from its brush with the rocks, the mate remains unrepentant. Thus, Parts 2 and 3, which continue the narrative of the ship's mishaps, serve to reiterate and reeducate both reader and mate as to the duties required by negligence. In Part 2, for example, Spanker tries to alert the mate to an approaching squall, but the mate shrugs off the warning again until after the ship has suffered irremediable damage; in Part 3, the ship finally meets with its demise after the officers fall asleep during their watch and thus fail to see that another ship is on a collision course with them. Assigned the task of warning others of possible perils—a task normally carried out by the common man, as we have seen—the officers fail miserably, which makes the common man's actions in this regard all the more admirable. Thus, in his heavy-handed conclusion to the story, Sleeper simultaneously underscores the importance of the common man's role as a herald of danger and denigrates the officers for their failure to do the same by elevating the act of warning to the level of a general, commonsensical philosophy keyed to the precepts of negligence law. The sinking of the ship was "owing to a neglect of keeping a good look-out ahead" (231), one of Spanker's shipmates remarks. "'No doubt of it,'" echoes another shipmate who has the last word, "'for after all, the great secret of success in life, whether on sea or on shore, is to KEEP A GOOD LOOK-OUT AHEAD'" (231).

If the inability of the officers to live up to the standards set by their subordinates serves to fuel the vision of the common man's sense of responsibility in the first of Sleeper's stories, the second of his stories is even more forceful in this regard. For in this tale, "The Drunken Captain, or Ned Rollins's Story," the captain in question is not simply forgetful, arrogant, or indolent, but rather knowingly reckless, putting himself in a position that leads to incompetence and negligence by getting drunk. "But you will always find it the case," he remarks to his fellow sailors, "that a captain who is fond of a good stiffener of grog will be sure to get half seas over during a heavy gale of wind, or when approaching a dangerous coast, where the navigation is difficult, and when, if ever a navigator ought to have a clear head and all his wits about him."[48] Indeed, in this story, the captain repeatedly gets drunk when he is most needed, and like the mate in "The Unlucky Ship" is deaf to all admonitions. Thus, Rollins's attempt to prevent a shipwreck is, like Spanker's, ignored. ". . . [A]s I had been through the South Channel several times," Rollins remarks, "I told the captain that it [the land in sight] must be Fishing Rip, which we had just passed over, as there was always a heavy tide-rip upon it, which in a fresh gale could be heard some miles." "'Do you think I don't know where we are?'" he screamed. "'Things have come to a pretty pass, indeed, if such ragamuffins as you are to teach me my duty'" (110–11).

Having narrowly averted disaster in this instance, however, the ship meets its doom at the end of the story when the captain fatally mistakes a light seen on the coast for one further off, thus failing to perceive how dangerously close they really are to shore. "The captain," Rollins notes, "although he could talk as fast, swear as heartily, and shout as loud as ever, could hardly stand, and certainly was not able to judge whether the light before us was single, double, revolving or fixed. . . ." (112). Having determined, after his first warning, never to interfere again—". . . I inwardly resolved to interfere no more, if I saw the ship going to destruction head foremost," (111)—neither Rollins nor anyone else on board alerts the captain to the danger, and like the unlucky ship in Sleeper's first story, this ship is lost due to the negligence of a superior.

It is worth remembering, however, that this *story* of prudence and precaution, like Poe's "MS. in a Bottle," is successfully rescued by Ned Rollins and other sailors like him who used the precepts of negligence law to critique the habit of carelessness at sea. Indeed, from its somewhat marginal position in much of Cooper's fiction, to its central place in Dana's maritime vision, to its even more popular incarnation in the years following Dana, the characterization of the negligence-minded hero achieved a lasting place in American nautical literature and lore. So common a figure did the quiet, vigilant hero become in narratives about the sea that even when the popularity of nautical stories began to wane after mid-century, he lingered on. In fact, later in the century in Mark Twain's representations not of life at sea but on the Mississippi and other American rivers, the image of the safety-conscious hero is reinvoked as an invaluable standard by which to judge the navigation not of sailing vessels but of steamships—a type of navigation that had become so complex as to prevent a clear view of how accidents and collisions could be avoided at all. Despite this confusion and the increasing carelessness of river navigation, however, Twain, as we shall see in the next chapter, keeps the memory of careful and cautionary piloting alive.

CHAPTER FOUR

"Nobody to Blame"

STEAMBOAT ACCIDENTS AND RESPONSIBILITY IN TWAIN

> The [novel is a] liner with hastily constructed boil-
> ers [which] will flounder when she comes to essay
> the storm; and no stoking however vigorous, no
> oiling however eager, if delayed till then, will avail
> to aid her to ride through successfully.
> (Frank Norris, "The Mechanics of Fiction")[1]

EARLY in Mark Twain's and Charles Dudley Warner's *The Gilded Age* (1873), a terrible steamboat accident occurs on the Mississippi River. Initially, the two boats involved, the *Boreas* and the *Amaranth*, engage in a harmless rivalry to determine which is faster. Not long after the race gets underway, however, the boats find themselves precariously close; at first "the *Amaranth*'s head was almost abreast the *Boreas*'s stern," then "the *Amaranth* drew steadily up till her jack-staff breasted the *Boreas*'s wheel-house—climbed along further and further till the boats were wheel to wheel—and then they closed up with a heavy jolt and locked together tight and fast in the middle of the river. . . ."[2] Disaster for both boats seemed imminent, Twain writes, until "there was a booming roar, a thundering crash, and the riddled *Amaranth* dropped loose from her hold and drifted helplessly away!" (47). The amount of steam needed to gain the advantage in speed caused the *Amaranth*'s boilers to explode. "The whole forward half of the boat was a shapeless ruin," Twain notes, "with the great chimneys lying crossed on top of it, and underneath were a dozen victims imprisoned alive and wailing for help" (47). Although the crew members of the *Boreas* were busy tending their own boilers, which were themselves on the verge of exploding, they also did what they could to rescue victims on board the *Amaranth*; their efforts, however, were soon thwarted, for not long after the *Amaranth*'s explosion, the "wreck took fire from the dismantled furnaces," and the boat was engulfed in flames. Although some were saved, dozens more died, scalded by steam, burned by fire, or drowned trying to escape. In the end all anyone could do was to sit idly by as the *Amaranth* drifted downriver, "an island of wreathing and climbing flame that vomited clouds of smoke from time to time, and glared more fiercely and sent its luminous tongues higher and higher after each emission" (47).

In the scenes that follow this wrenching account of the disaster, an attempt is made to identify what caused the accident and who was responsible for it. Some accusations are made in the heat of the moment; for example, the head engineer of the *Amaranth*, a "ghastly spectacle" suffering from fatal wounds, blames his brother, the second engineer who, as fate would have it, emerges from the accident uninjured.

> "You were on watch. You were boss. You would not listen to me when I begged you to reduce your steam. Take that!—take it to my wife and tell her it comes from me by the hand of my murderer! Take it—and take my curse with it to blister your heart a hundred years—and may you live so long."
>
> And he tore a ring from his finger, stripping flesh and skin with it, threw it down, and fell dead! (48).

Apart from those named in such highly personal recriminations, however, no one person or event is, in the end, held accountable for the accident. In fact, the suddenness of the accident and the confusion that ensues precludes a clearsighted reconstruction of it. Even an official investigation into the matter ends inconclusively. "A jury of inquest was impaneled," writes Twain, "and after due deliberation and inquiry they returned the inevitable American verdict which has been so familiar to our ears all the days of our lives—'NOBODY TO BLAME' " (48).[3]

In this chapter I analyze the implications of this verdict—of this finding of blamelessness—and argue for its centrality not only to Twain's and Warner's novel but to the late nineteenth century as a whole. For in this period the idea of blamelessness that concludes the investigation into the steamboat accident in *The Gilded Age* is characteristic of numerous legal and nonlegal investigations. Indeed, the late nineteenth century was typified by the proliferation of an epistemological uncertainty—an epistemology that often failed not only to identify a given individual as blameworthy but to associate a given individual with a given act. Made possible by the advent of negligence in the law, the finding of blamelessness in the context of accidents was at once both a cause and a symptom of a widespread erosion of responsibility.

Scholars of the period often point to the growth of corporate trusts and global money markets as obvious indices of this phenomenon. To be sure, the highly collective and contingent nature of these business and financial innovations made actions less localized and the individual, acting singly, less capable of bringing them about. But even more significant than the growth of trusts and global capitalism for their impact on contemporary constructions of responsibility were transformations in the nineteenth century's industrial and machine technology, for it was the changes in this aspect of the culture that made the economic innovations possible in the first place. Dominated by the development of the steamship and the railroad, which linked vast distances for the first time, the century also saw the birth of such revolutionary devices as the telephone, telegraph, and typewriter which, although not directly related to transportation, were as capable in their own way of producing temporal and spatial dislocations. All of these new mechanical devices contributed to the condensation and disarticulation of agency; with the introduction of electrical and mechanical relays, for example, the simple pulling of a switch might set off a chain of diverse and yet sequentially interlinked actions whose effect nevertheless appeared to be singular and immediate. More powerfully than the trust or global markets, then, these technological changes provided a paradigm of the kind of multiple and attenuated action—a kind of action-at-a-distance—that tended to shift the exercise of agency from the individual to the machine, upsetting traditional notions of personal responsibility in the process.

Novelists and social critics on both sides of the Atlantic registered the disassociative effects of industrial automation. Most notably, in his critique of mechanization, Karl Marx indicted the extent to which machines not only diminished the quality of human labor, but seemingly replaced the element of human agency as a whole. For Marx, labor conditions deteriorated sharply as the worker was first reduced to the status of the machine's "motive power," which coincided with the conversion of tools from manual into mechanical implements, and then erased entirely from it when machines themselves became complex. With the advent of this mechanical complexity, Marx notes, the motive mechanism itself "acquired an independent form, entirely emancipated from the restraints of human strength."[4] Interestingly, of all the mechanically self-powering machines, Marx took special note of the steam engine which was, he observes, initially introduced "not as an invention for a specific purpose, but as an *agent* universally applicable in Mechanical Industry."[5] In England, the debilitating effects of this mechanical surrogacy are clearly described in novels like Charles Dickens's *Hard Times* where Coketown's factory consumes its inhabitants, and Thomas Hardy's *Tess of the d'Urbervilles* where the steam threshing machine is identified as the "primum mobile of this little world."[6]

Twain is a focal point for the articulation of the problems of individual agency and responsibility in America, although his concerns remain slightly different from those of his English counterparts. To be sure, his interests in the subject were wide-ranging, and his work, as many scholars have pointed out, is replete with anxieties about the shifting bases for evaluating and expressing individuality and identity in this period, including that of racial passing, cross-dressing, fingerprinting, and impersonation (concerns which figure most prominently in *The Adventures of Huckleberry Finn* [1884] and *Pudd'nhead Wilson* [1894]). But what has until now been overlooked is the way in which his interest in individual agency revolved around his culture's changing notions about accidents. Indeed, Twain's and Warner's joint production, as well as Twain's other writings, including *Life on the Mississippi* (1883), *A Connecticut Yankee in King Arthur's Court* (1889), and occasional essays and speeches, testify to the unsettling effects of accidents on individual agency. In these works, as we will see, Twain wrestles with the corrosive effects of mechanization, and the causal confusion that accompanied it, on accident perpetrators' sense of responsibility for the injuries they inflicted. And he examines the corresponding effects of blamelessness on accident victims who were too frequently left without any visible means of compensation for the wounds that they received. In addition, he reflects on and critiques the legal and social mechanisms for reconceiving blame or, in some cases, avoiding it entirely. Finally, Twain offers a complicated critique of the institution of insurance, which was first touted as a solution to the problem of blamelessness and the absence of compensation that accompanied the doctrine of negligence, but ultimately contributed to the culture's erosion of individual agency by diffusing and distributing the burden of responsibility across the population as a whole.

The chapter, then, has as its subject some of the many interrelations between Twain's work and the law. But where others have seen a Twain at peace with the law, I see his frustration. Susan Gillman, for example, has written that "Twain, champion of the subversive, also championed the law as one agent of control that resolves confusions about identity, restoring and enforcing the fundamental distinctions of society."[7] In support of this statement, Gillman recalls Twain's use of the law to solve problems of identity in "Personal Habits of the Siamese Twins," *Tom Sawyer*, and *The Prince and the Pauper*; but while Gillman's assessment powerfully elucidates these texts, this chapter should explain why it does not apply to Twain's accident narratives. For in these works Twain critiques the legal and social understanding of individual agency[8] as hopelessly confused and distorting.

BOILER EXPLOSIONS

The verdict rendered in the investigation of the steamboat accident in *The Gilded Age* is representative of a crisis in causation in the late nineteenth century that can be traced in part to the rise of complex technological innovations. Consider, for example, the complexity of steamboat technology. From the moment it was first harnessed for industrial use, steam power wrought changes in manufacturing and transportation technology that seemed nothing short of miraculous. For many, the notion that steam could power small ships, much less large, lumbering ones, seemed an impossibility. Indeed, the first successful trips made by steamboats were met with widespread incredulity. Even as they became more commonplace, however, the sight of a steamboat with its gigantic sidewheels gliding down the river continued to shock and enthrall the onlooker.

Scientists, moreover, were never in agreement about the reasons steamboat accidents occurred. At first a consensus formed around the inadequacies of the high-pressure engine, but when low-pressure boats began to explode, this hypothesis was discredited. Shortly thereafter, attention centered on the boiler itself. One theory held that explosions were due to the formation within the boiler of certain combustible gases, but an experiment as early as 1836 proved that the small amount of gas produced in the boiler had little if any explosive force. Additional theories pointed to low water levels and excessive pressure in the boiler, but in each case counterfactual explosions—explosions with adequate water supplies and normal pressure—invalidated them. Indeed, there was a growing recognition that boilers seemed to explode under a variety of conditions and as a result of many factors. In his masterful *Steamboats on the Western Rivers*, Louis Hunter explains that a great many things, among them a host of manufacturing and maintenance problems, contributed to steamboat explosions including "a boiler head weakened by blow holes or cracks, a badly made plate, a defective supply pump, a clogged connecting pipe, a corroded safety valve, an accumulation of mud in the boiler or a rag or broom left inside after cleaning, [or] a poorly fastened rivet."[9] Nor did these problems typically exist in isolation, making the task of tracing their origins that much more difficult. And just as no one theory and no one mechanical cause could be held responsible, no one human agent could be identified, for as Hunter points out, the candidates—the engineers, pilots, captains, managers, and owners—were numerous, and the extent of their responsibilities overlapping and diffuse.

Of course, not all of the problems associated with machinery in general or with steamboats in particular were the result of technological complexities. Some were the product of the interaction of new technologies with nature. Not surprisingly, natural impediments figured significantly in the number of steamboat accidents, and like the mechanical complexities of the steamboat itself, helped to obscure the identity of a responsible *human* agent. Given the weight and girth of some of the larger steamboats, the narrow, shallow parts of the Mississippi, for example—one of the routes most heavily trafficked by steamboats—posed particular problems. In fact, parts of the river were so treacherous that the culture of steamboating along the Mississippi and other rivers in the west, where conditions, typically, were more dangerous, assumed an air of derring-do. "'Talk about northern steamers,'" one Mississippi steamboat fire-man remarked, "'it don't need any spunk to navigate them waters. You haint bust a biler for five years. But I tell you, stranger, it takes a man to ride one of these half alligator boats, head on a snag, high pressure, valve sodered down, 600 souls on board & all in danger of going to the devil.'"[10] But if the inherent dangerousness of steamboating gave rise to a certain recklessness on the part of the steamboat's crew, it had a similar effect on its passengers. Passengers often urged the crew to adopt unsafe measures and through their obvious preference for the "faster" boats, created an incentive for speed. A committee of steamboatmen noted their displeasure with "the constant desire which a large portion of those who travel on steamboats, manifest to 'go the fastest' and even to urge an increase of speed. Is it wonderful then that under such circum-stances some commanders would be induced to force their boats beyond the bounds of safety, when greater patronage and applause are the re-wards for the risk incurred?"[11] Indeed, like the captains of the *Amaranth* and the *Boreas*, the captain of the elegant steamboat *Moselle* was induced to let steam build up while detained for loading so as to beat another boat to their destination. The boilers, like those on the *Amaranth* and *Boreas*, exploded, and the destruction was devastating (fig. 1). Steamboat cap-tains often found themselves racing against each other, raising the steam pressure to such a degree that if a snag, sandbar, or rapids didn't cause an accident, chances were that a collision or boiler explosion would.

TWAIN'S SENSE OF BLAME

Twain, who spent two years as an apprentice pilot (1857–59) and two years as a pilot (1859–61), knew the hazards of steamboating, both natu-ral and technological, from personal experience. An otherwise exuberant account of steamboating, *Life on the Mississippi,* for example, is suffused with memories of accidents. In the midst of his nostalgia for his days as a river pilot, for example, Twain reveals a morbid awareness of past trage-dies, noting that "between St. Louis and Cairo the steamboat wrecks av-erage one to the mile;—two hundred wrecks, altogether."[12] But even as Twain turns his attention from his past to his current trip downriver, and *Life* turns from reminiscence to travelogue, he remains obsessed with ac-cidents. Although he applauds the improvements made to steamboating since his days as a pilot, he also notes that the number of accidents has not diminished. He stops to mourn the passing of the *Gold Dust*, for exam-ple, which exploded not long after Twain himself was on board, and which killed a pilot who had apprenticed under him some twenty-five

Fig. 1. "Explosion of the Steamboat Moselle," from S. A. Howland, *Steamboat Disasters and Railroad Accidents in the United States*. Worcester, Mass.: Warren Lazell (1846).

years earlier. Nor does he fail to notice the persistence of steamboat collisions. "We came near killing a steamboat which paid no attention to our whistle and then tried to cross our bows," he writes of his own trip downriver. "By doing some strong backing, we saved him," he adds, "which was a great loss, for he would have made good literature" (190).

In fact, Twain's awareness of the frequency and gravity of accidents affects not just the tone but the purpose of *Life*, embedded as it is in the master narrative of piloting, the text's most consistent concern. Much of the material about piloting, moreover, is geared toward describing and praising the skills of the pilot who successfully avoids the accidents of river navigation. Of course, much has been made of the fact that Twain's description of piloting is heavily romanticized. While for most pilots, piloting was hard work, for Twain it was more a form of leisure, the pilot himself "the only real, independent & genuine gentlemen in the world."[13] Recently, Howard Horwitz has called our attention to the political and social dimensions of Twain's romance of piloting in which "its quality as labor is erased."[14] But while Horwitz's account is right as far as it goes (Twain does tend to mystify the actual skills involved in piloting), it fails to note the conspicuously unromantic effect of accidents in Twain's text. Thus, far from "omit[ting] that accidents and explosions were frequent,"[15] as Horwitz suggests, Twain dwells on them, insisting that piloting is an inherently hazardous activity. His experiences as a cub pilot substantiate this view. Taught to memorize all the unseen obstacles of the river as a student of the inimitable Horace Bixby, Twain was forced to keep accidents in mind at all times. In fact, so tricky were the river's ways, that in order to avoid disaster, Bixby cautioned Twain, the pilot must often seem to court it. Having witnessed Bixby negotiate a particularly difficult passage, Twain writes:

> Fully to realize the marvellous precision required in laying the great steamer in her marks in that murky waste of water, one should know that not only must she pick her intricate way through snags and blind reefs, and then shave the head of the island so closely as to brush the overhanging foliage with her stern, but at one place she must pass almost within arm's reach of a sunken and invisible wreck that would snatch the hull timbers from under her if she should strike it, and destroy a quarter of a million dollars' worth of steamboat and cargo in five minutes, and maybe a hundred and fifty human lives into the bargain (84).

An obvious tribute to Bixby's extraordinary piloting skills, this version of piloting also clearly points to the importance of saving the craft from the many accidents to which it was prone, equating piloting with accident avoidance.

But if Twain's occupation as a steamboat pilot made him accutely aware of the problems of steamboat technology and the perils of piloting, the subject of steamboat accidents took on a peculiarly tragic significance for him in that his own brother, Henry, was killed in one. On 13 June 1858, the steamboat *Pennsylvania* exploded on the Mississippi, killing between 80 and 150 people on board;[16] the nineteen-year old Henry Clemens, a "mud" clerk just beginning his steamboat apprenticeship, was among the casualties. Most strikingly, the accident gave rise to multiple, confusing, and contradictory investigations in which the accident's cause remained elusive. So confused and contradictory were the accounts of the accident, in fact, that although the final investigating commission did name a culprit, the finding was permanently tainted. The actual culprit, an engineer named Dorris who, like his fictional counterpart on board the *Amaranth*, was held accountable by his dying brother, was both an easy target and the victim of a personal vendetta.[17] Through their many heated and conflicting reports, moreover, contemporary newspaper accounts suggest that the verdict was not justified. Some lay the blame directly on the captain: "He has acted the part of a heartless thief," wrote the Memphis *Avalanche*.[18] Others helped to scapegoat the engineer: "I do not and will not employ any man on my boat," a source in the Memphis *Daily Appeal* was quoted as saying of Dorris, "who drinks liquor of any kind."[19] What is more important for my purposes, however, is Twain's reaction to the verdict. In converting the story and the finding of blame in the real-life investigation into one of blamelessness, Twain registered his profound skepticism about the legal mechanisms for finding blame and assigning liability as well as his own profound and personal identification with the causes of his brother's death.

For Twain, in fact, the question of causation and blame for the accident was never resolved, and the inconclusiveness proved personally debilitating. Referring to the incident, Albert Paine, Twain's official biographer, observes, "Samuel Clemens, unsparing in his self-blame, all his days carried the burden of it";[20] while Bernard Devoto, another of Twain's biographers, remarks that "Samuel Clemens held himself responsible for the tragedy," the memory of which "festered throughout his life."[21] Memorialized in *The Gilded Age* as the explosion of the *Amaranth*,[22] and recalled in chapters 19 and 20 of *Life on the Mississippi*, the *Pennsylvania* disaster raised lasting issues for Twain about the assignability of blame. Indeed, in *Life*, Twain adds to the rather abstract version of events in *The Gilded Age* the agonizingly personal story of the part he may have played in encouraging Henry to act recklessly during the disaster. The night before Henry sailed on the doomed *Pennsylvania*, it seems, Twain and Henry discussed a variety of potential responses to a steamboat emergency, concluding "that if a disaster ever fell within our experience we would at least stick to the boat, and give such minor service as chance might throw in the way" (161). That Henry remembered this discussion and acted against his own best interests in attempting to follow its precepts is evident in many accounts of his behavior by eyewitnesses to the accident—accounts that made their way into Twain's own narrative. When after the explosion, Twain writes, "Henry fell in the water [he] struck out for shore, which was only a few hundred yards away; but Henry presently said he believed he was not hurt, (what an unaccountable error!) and therefore would swim back to the boat and help save the wounded" (163).

In addition to this unfortunate incident, Twain also seems to have been plagued by two other circumstances that raised doubts, if only in his own mind, about his part in Henry's death. Firstly, he suffered from extraordinary guilt because of his own narrow escape from his brother's fate, for he too would have been on the *Pennsylvania* at the time of the disaster had he not argued with the pilot (who provoked Twain by insulting Henry) and been ordered off at the nearest port. Indeed, Twain's letters to his sister-in-law after Henry's death make much of this bizarre coincidence.[23] Secondly, it seems that while Twain kept a vigil by Henry's bed, the attending physicians, young interns as it turned out, carelessly administered an overdose of morphine—a procedure which, for complicated reasons, Twain had been asked to oversee. Understandably, Twain felt guilty about these bizarre and disturbing events. Indeed, at least one noted Twain critic, Forrest Robinson, has gone so far as to suggest that these and other related events, including a portentous dream Twain once had about Henry's death before it occurred,[24] indicate Twain's actual ambivalence about his younger brother who had always held a privileged place in his mother's heart. This ambivalence, he writes, "must have been rooted in a sibling jealousy which was born, with Henry, when Mark Twain was just midway in his third year." He continues, "It was not until 1858, when the fatal steamboat accident gave horrifying expression to his repressed resentment and hostility, that the disruptive potential of Mark Twain's fraternal ambivalence began to surface. The psychological result was strikingly similar to an affliction which Freud describes and analyses in his study of *Mourning and Melancholia*."[25] Admittedly, Robinson makes a strong case for the complexity of Twain's feelings about his brother, even if we do not want to buy into his Freudian reading in its entirety. But whether we ultimately see Twain's mourning as normal or abnormal in Freudian terms, we can begin to appreciate the extent to which Twain was tormented by his brother's death and wrestled with the idea of his own responsibility for it based on this strange concatenation of events and his own self-incriminating obsession with them.

CAUSAL CONFUSION

That much of Twain's bewilderment about who caused his brother's accident and who ultimately was responsible for it (which were not necessarily the same things in Twain's mind) was partly self-induced and personal seems clear from reports of his relationship with Henry. But this should not eclipse the problems that ensued from the causal obscurity that characterized the actual events of the accident itself and that surfaced in the legal investigation of it. Indeed, the difficulties of tracing causality in the context of modern technology were of lasting concern to members of the legal establishment whose primary task was to identify responsible parties and assign blame to them. Moreover, in no area of the law was this task more central or more obviously problematic than in cases dealing with industrial accidents where the obfuscating aspects of new technology threw the efforts to identify causal agents into crisis. As accidents themselves grew more complicated and confused, it became more and more difficult to isolate a negligent act or to identify a single causally responsible agent. Indeed, the relativity of causation and the remoteness of so many modern, mechanized injuries made it necessary to distinguish between long-standing conditions and intermittent causes, minor and substantial contributions, and initial and subsequent intervening factors in a myriad of injuries.

Lawyers and judges spent a good deal of time reckoning with the problems of individual agency generated by the causally confusing nature of steam power in particular, and in this the legal debate largely reiterated the scientific one. On the one hand, there were those in the law who, like the scientists before them, believed that when the right theory presented itself, which it surely would in time, everything would be explained. "A steam engine properly constructed," said a lawyer in a famous western case of 1842, "is entirely within man's control. Such is the common sentiment. Did not men think so, they would as soon embark on a floating volcano as on a steamboat. . . .The laws of steam are as well understood as the laws which regulate any other power."[26] According to this position, steam power was no more mystifying than any other technological innovation and steamboat accidents no less the products of negligence than any other kind of industrial accident. In fact, many steamboat accident cases did find that human negligence was involved.[27] Other legal scholars and practitioners, however, found themselves siding with the scientists who remained perplexed by steam power in general and overwhelmed by the number of possible causes involved. At least one notable opinion expresses the belief that the effort to fix blame or assign causality in the case of steamboat accidents was futile. "Whatever natural philosophers may think of this," reads the opinion in a court case of 1845, "the elements which combine to create the power of steam, are as entirely within the reach of accident, and are no more subject to fixed laws than the elements which propel the ship at sea. Whatever may be the theories on the subject, universal experience is that no human skill can entirely guard against accidents, either in the one case or in the other."[28]

The analogy between "the power of steam" and "the elements which propel the ship at sea"—an analogy that links steamboat accidents to natural disasters—has important ramifications for the issue of legal blamelessness. In drawing a comparison between steamboat accidents and natural and uncontrollable phenomena like floods, earthquakes, and lightning, for example (in which, by definition, no one is to blame), the inquiry into human agency and causality automatically becomes irrelevant. To their victims, of course, the experience of steamboat accidents was often indistinguishable from that of natural disasters and the popular discourse about them frequently invoked the comparison. Even Twain makes use of the idiom when he describes the *Amaranth* as "a moving earthquake" (46). This particular reference, in fact, has a significance in Twain's career that marks the beginning of his interest in blameless accidents and that can be traced to his days as an aspiring journalist and to his columns about the San Francisco earthquakes of 1864 and 1865 for the San Francisco *Daily Morning Call*.[29]

More important even than Twain's invocation of the idiom, however, was its circulation within the law where it most clearly registered contemporary uncertainties about steam-driven technology and its obfuscating powers. Originally, the law was quite strict about the definition of a natural disaster or "act of God," calling it "a disaster with which the agency of man has nothing to do."[30] From its earliest usage, the expression applied to events "occasioned exclusively by the violence of nature—by that kind of force of the elements which human ability could not have foreseen or prevented, such as lightning, tornado, sudden squalls of wind, and the like."[31] Over time, however, the definition lost some of its rigidity and the expression became confused with other kinds of accidents—accidents that were traceable to human agency but seemed otherwise unavoidable, such as when boats collided in the dark, or ran into hidden obstacles.[32] Moreover, the accidents that befell common carriers, like steamboats and railroads, were particularly susceptible to redesignation as natural disasters since they so often happened in conjunction with them.[33] But even when they occurred separately, the analogy was still propounded and in this way the paradigm of blamelessness associated with "acts of God" was officially and legally extended to steamboat accidents.

Confronted by the definitional problems brought on by this revolution in causal relations—a revolution that made it possible to see multiple causes and chains of causation where formerly only single causes and effects were visible—lawyers and most particularly judges faced mind-boggling problems. Specifically, they were forced for the first time to acknowledge the insufficiency of the so-called "but for" or "cause in fact" test in which evidence of causation was traditionally found in all cases where the negligent act was a necessary antecedent to injury. If, as this test declared, "but for" or "not for" defendant's act there would have been no injury, liability was duly assigned to the defendant. Or, to put it a slightly different way, defendant's conduct was not considered to be a cause of the event if the event would have occurred without it.

To supplement the "but for" test which was rendered obsolete by the intricacy of mechanical causality, jurists and theorists proposed the concept of "proximate cause," a concept whose goal was to limit liability in an otherwise potentially endless or multiple chain. The proximate cause of an accident, according to the jurists who invoked it, was the cause nearest to it in space and time. In isolating this cause, it was argued, the law could legitimately narrow the field of potential causes and assign blame to the human or mechanical agency that was deemed to be most responsible for it.

In case after case, judges in the late nineteenth century made their liability limiting decisions about accidental injuries based on the theory of proximate cause. The most notorious of these was an 1866 case, *Ryan v. New York Central Railroad*, in which the New York Court of Appeals held that the New York Central Railroad company, while acting negligently in causing a fire, was liable only to the owners of the first house that caught fire and not to the many others who lost their houses because of the fire's spread. Not surprisingly, the court's logic relied heavily on the distinction between proximate and remote causation, as it was only the first house, according to this logic, that could be called a proximate result of the fire. Any other decision, the court reasoned, "would . . . create a liability which would be the destruction of all civilized society."[34] Of course the railroad's negligence in *Ryan* was so devastating and the fire's spread so rampant that even those lawyers most committed to the doctrine of proximate cause had a difficult time trying to justify it.

That difficulty, however, did not stop other courts from invoking the seemingly arbitrary idea of proximate cause as if it were a scientific principle. In *Wood v. Pennsylvania R. Co.* (1896), for example, a passenger was waiting for a train when he was hit by the body of a dead woman who had herself been struck by an oncoming train and thrown from the opposite side of the tracks through the air. The Pennsylvania court asked whether "the injury was the natural and probable consequence of the [railroad's] negligence—such a consequence as, under the surrounding circumstances, might and ought to have been foreseen by the wrongdoer as likely to flow from his act."[35] The court concluded that the injury to Wood was only remotely possible, not sufficiently natural and probable to assign liability to the railroad. A few years before *Wood*, a court found it foreseeable that a speeding car could hit and kill a man but not necessarily bruise him in such a way as to make it possible for cancer to develop.[36] In a more banal version of the same logic, one court held that while two cars might collide foreseeably, it was improbable and therefore unforeseeable that one of those cars would veer out of control and hit a third or fourth car.[37] Similarly unforeseeable was the case of a car that narrowly missed a pregnant woman but caused her to miscarry.[38] More contorted sequences revealed the unforeseeability of a car that hit a powerline, started a fire in the electric wires, and killed a machine operator over two miles away.[39]

In each of these cases, it could be argued, the court's logic was more or less justifiable, but taken together they reveal the essential arbitrariness of the distinction between proximate and remote causes. Indeed, by the first quarter of the twentieth century, as we will see in the next chapter, the jurists who came to be known as legal realists, openly attacked the vacuity of the doctrine. Few jurists in the nineteenth century, however, were able or motivated to identify the socially manipulative aspect of the theory. Only one, a young instructor at Harvard Law School by the name of Nicholas St. John Green, seemed sufficiently struck by the doctrine's false premises to give them voice. In a monograph published in 1870 entitled "Proximate and Remote Cause," Green was the first to raise the specter of a multiple or collective responsibility that later found its way into the pragmatic jurisprudence of his far more influential friend and colleague, Oliver Wendell Holmes, Jr. In time, in Holmes's hands, Green's notion drastically altered the notion of legal liability.[40] Indeed, Green's ideas about multiple causation became one of the main reasons Holmes came to regard the law as a composite of social policies and contingencies rather than as a set of immutable physical conditions.

That it took Holmes approximately twenty-five years to adopt Green's view of causation and disseminate it widely attests to the radical nature of Green's initial argument and to the resistance it met within the legal establishment at the time. For Green's philosophy shook the very foundations of the theory of objective causation on which the law had relied for so long. Under objective causation, the law, like the sciences, could limit liability by holding fast to one cause above all others. But Green observed that such a theory, while it might be appropriate in the sciences, had no real relevance to the law. Indeed, one of Green's major contributions to the theory of causation was his observation that the scientific notion of a "chain of causation" was, for the law, "a dangerous metaphor." "It raises in the mind," he wrote, "an idea of one determinate cause, followed by another determinate cause, created by the first, and that followed by a third, created by the second, and so on, one succeeding another till the effect is reached."[41] Finding "nothing in nature which corresponds to this," Green proposed a pluralistic view of causation. "To every event there are certain antecedents, never a single antecedent, but always a set of antecedents, which being given the effect is sure to follow, unless some new thing intervenes to frustrate such result" (11–12). Zeroing in on the fallacy of the theory of proximate cause, Green spoke in terms of relative causation alone. He wrote:

> There is no settled rule for the application of the maxim [of proximate cause] in determining the damages in actions of tort. In such actions, the damages, which are called proximate, often vary in proportion to the misconduct, recklessness or wantonness of the defendant We cannot add clearness to our reasoning by talking about proximate and remote causes and effects, when we mean only the degree of certainty or uncertainty with which the connection between cause and effect might have been anticipated (16–17).

Not surprisingly, Green's idea about degrees of certainty opened up the law to charges of arbitrariness. For Green, however, there was a method to the apparent madness—a method that relied for guidance on experience and that yielded relatively consistent results. "Our anticipations of the future are founded upon our experience of the past," Green writes. "The experience of the past is the experience of the successions of causes and effects which always surround us. . . . Large classes of such successions can be grouped together, and the order and frequency of their happening can be predicted from past experience with something which approaches to mathematical precision" (16). In his emphasis on the importance of experience, in fact, Green anticipated Holmes's famous formulation that "the life of the law has not been logic: it has been experience."[42]

Many, however, persisted in seeing Green's theories as a threat to the absolutism of the law. Specifically, they believed that his notion of multiple causes put legal decisions about liability at the mercy of arbitrary political factors. Writing in 1874, although not necessarily in direct response to Green, the legal scholar Francis Wharton was perhaps the first to record the fear within the conservative legal community of a discretionary, policy-oriented theory of causation. Wharton begins by taking issue with John Stuart Mill's theory that "the cause of an event is the sum of all its antecedents,"[43] a theory Green himself acknowledged as an inspiration for his own. This theory, Wharton wrote, was "the practical communism which this theory of the causal character of all antecedents promotes."[44] For Wharton it was just a small step from the assumption of an equality among all causes to the decline of capitalism: "Here is a capitalist among these antecedents," he wrote. "He shall be forced to pay. The capitalist, therefore, becomes liable for all the disasters of which he is in any sense the condition. . . ."[45] Interestingly, in his effort to protect the capitalist from what he perceived to be the unfair results of a theory of multiple causation, Wharton clung to an outright contradiction: holding the free agent responsible and yet barring the capitalist from ever being seen as such.

MECHANIZATION AND HUMAN AGENCY

Wharton's fears about a causal communism were shared by other thinkers at the time outside the legal establishment. Indeed, social theorists from both the left and the right of the political spectrum were visibly troubled by the issue of responsibility. For theorists from the right who shared Wharton's preconceptions came complaints about the potentially unlimited liability a theory of multiple causation was seen to embody—

complaints that are still heard among legislators and policy makers today. For William Graham Sumner, for example, the idea of a plurality of causes dangerously led to an assumption of responsibility on the part of institutions which in turn deprived the individual of a crucial sense of responsibility for himself. In his 1887 essay "The Shifting of Responsibility," Sumner raged against what he saw as the immorality of a theory of causation that explicitly violated the ethics of individual responsibility to which he adhered. Indeed, in a passage that clearly reveals his preoccupation with the legal as well as the strictly ethical ramifications of the "socialistic and semi-socialistic propositions" of causation, he writes:

> The new doctrine is that the employer becomes responsible for the welfare of the employees in a number of respects. They do not remain what they were before this contract, independent members of society, each pursuing happiness in his own way according to his own ideas of it. The employee is not held to any new responsibility for the welfare of the employer; the duties are all held to lie on the other side. The employer must assure the employed against the risks of his calling, and even against his own negligence; the employee is not held to assure himself, as a free man with all his own responsibilities, although the scheme may be so devised that the assurance is paid for out of his wages; he is released from responsibility for himself.[46]

Sumner, of course, is something of an extremist in his belief about the supremacy of the individual—a belief informed by a laissez-faire, social Darwinist ideology. Yet his concerns had some basis in fact as the treatment of the theory of multiple causation by advocates of the political left makes clear. Indeed, the widening causal links so visible in models of mechanical agency proved a powerful metaphor for social reformers who aimed to involve members of the formerly distant middle and upper classes in their reform efforts. Thus, the inquiries into the causes of the urban poverty that marked the period tended to implicate individuals who had traditionally expressed ignorance of or apathy toward such conditions; and as scholars of the subject have long pointed out, the explosion of charitable organizations at this time was due in large part to the intervention of middle-class volunteers who not only contributed financially but often gave generously of their own time to various social reform movements.

In addition to its sustained appearance in the works of these political thinkers, moreover, the problem of responsibility emerged in the writings of many novelists contemporary with them.[47] Indeed, it is worth noting that for at least one writer other than Twain, the problem of responsibility, in this case authorial responsibility, centered on the image of a steamboat accident. For Frank Norris, author of *The Octopus*, *McTeague*, and other naturalist novels, the novelist had a responsibility to construct a work that was technologically fool-proof, for novel writing was a "system of fiction mechanics," and the unsuccessful novel a "liner with hastily constructed boilers."[48] In other words, for Norris, the novelist was faced not simply with an artistic problem but with a mechanical one as well which had to be resolved before the product, the novel, could function properly. In discussing the more general concern with responsibility in this period, Wai Chee Dimock connects it to changing notions of rationality and causation, suggesting that the "American novel of the mid-nineteenth century might be called the novel of remote causation."[49] For Dimock the most obvious representative of this phenomenon is the novelist William Dean Howells whose commitment to a realist fiction that was already bent on representing a multiplicity of connections and causalities was particularly concerned with defining the scope of a potentially unlimited responsibility. Of Howells's many novels that deal generally with causality and responsibility, Dimock singles out *The Rise of Silas Lapham* (1885) as the novel in which Howells most explicitly thematizes the dangers of an expanded human responsibility. In brief, in this novel, Howells ponders the question of whether Lapham himself, a prosperous paint manufacturer, has a continuing, possibly eternal, obligation to compensate for the sagging fortunes of his former partner who was booted out of the business when he proved to be a substantial drain on it. For Dimock, Howells wrestles with the idea of responsibility within a "distributive" context—a context, in other words, in which an economy of justice or commensurability struggles to emerge. Or to put it another way, for Dimock the Howellsian approach to the problem of shifting responsibility is to reach a balance between possible causes or responsible agents in a "world of causal infinitude."[50]

In struggling to choose between causal possibilities Howells provides an essential insight into how the problem of responsibility was handled by many authors and thinkers of his day. For Twain, however, an author Dimock does not discuss in this context but whose preoccupation with it is quite clear, the problem of responsibility manifested itself in a slightly different way. Indeed, what seems to have concerned Twain about responsibility was not so much the political arbitrariness of choosing between a variety of causal antecedents but rather the threatened loss of individuality in the obliteration of causal options as a whole. If in this, however, Twain seems to have more in common with the conservative fears of Sumner than the democratic aspirations of Howells, it should be noted that his overall concern was probably less political than moral or spiritual, as his interest in the central facts of identity throughout his work suggests.

Many critics have commented on Twain's obsession with identity from different perspectives. An esteemed tradition of criticism has recently emerged in the writings of scholars interested in the social and political ramifications of Twain's interest in identity. Susan Gillman, for example, attends to the thematic emphasis on twins or doubles in Twain's works and the questions they raise about "whether one can tell people apart, differentiate among them." "Without such differentiation," Gillman writes, "social order, predicated as it is on division—of class, race, gender—is threatened."[51] Like Gillman, Eric Sundquist writes of the social and political implications of Twain's interest in *Pudd'nhead Wilson* in the legal criteria for racial identity, juxtaposing this tale about babies of different races switched at birth with the Supreme Court decision in *Plessy v. Ferguson*. Unlike Gillman, however, Sundquist is interested in exposing the possibility of political subversion in Twain's text.[52] Still other critics in this tradition focus more on the implications of Twain's writing for the social construction of gender; in an influential article on transsexuality in Twain, for example, Myra Jehlen discusses the episode in *The Adventures of Huckleberry Finn* when Huck puts on a dress and tries unsuccessfully to pass himself off as a girl.[53] Other critics tend to turn their attentions more to identity in the context of Twain's own personal development as a writer, seeking to define or find sources for what it was about identity that seemed most to concern Twain. Thus, most recently, Randall Knoper has written of Twain's sustained interest in theatricality and the changing self as being rooted in certain dominant nineteenth-century psychologies, such as automatism.[54] At the same time, Bruce Michelson[55] argues that having recognized the irrevocable loss of his boyhood self over time, Twain struggled throughout his life to keep the self somehow above the political or cultural fray—to keep it, as if in some fantasy of cultural and political purity, unconstructed.

But if these critical opinions are as divided in their emphases as Twain's own representation of the divided self, they do tend toward one general conclusion: at one time Twain seems to have believed in an individually good or responsible self that he came to realize was, as collective forms of behavior took over, increasingly difficult to maintain. In an article on Twain and Albion Winegar Tourgee, the lawyer for Homer Plessy in *Plessy v. Ferguson* and an occasional novelist as well, Brook Thomas makes the clearest case for such a belief on Twain's part, demonstrating a gradual dwindling in the viability of a natural self from *Huck Finn* to *Pudd'nhead Wilson*. "For Twain," Thomas writes, "the demise of the natural self creates a society ruled by prejudiced custom."[56] But if Thomas's focus is on the detrimental effects of "training" in the late nineteenth century—a time when authority, for better or for worse, came increasingly to be vested in communities of trained professionals—my own is on the effects of mechanization which had a similar but perhaps more visibly disastrous effect on the notion of individuality and in particular that of individual agency.

To assert that mechanization diminished the possibility of individual agency, however, does not mean that I wish to promote a simplistic argument about the debilitating effects of technology on the human subject. Indeed, in light of Mark Seltzer's recent argument about technology in the late nineteenth century, it is no longer even possible to conceive of a simple opposition between the human body and the machine. In his enlightening book, *Bodies and Machines*, Seltzer argues that far from demonstrating an opposition between the human or natural and the technological, the late nineteenth century exemplified a profound intimacy between them.[57] Moreover, for Seltzer, it is the naturalist novel—the novel of Frank Norris, Henry James, and Jack London, for example—that most visibly reveals the double discourse he identifies. In pointing to a more intimate relationship between the natural and the mechanical, however, Seltzer is not arguing for an identity between them. Rather, his book proves again and again that the two discourses, however close, were in a constant empirical and semantic flux. For example, while locomotion was a sign of agency in liberal culture, it was, as Seltzer points out, a sign of automatism in machine culture—a paradox that provoked what he calls the "melodramas of uncertain agency" (17) that characterized the age. Thus, Seltzer's argument, the intricacies of which have been only briefly registered here, strengthens rather than weakens the claim that Twain retained a belief in an individual self whose agency had been altered profoundly and uncertainly by the forces of the modern world in general and by mechanization in particular.

TWAIN'S ANXIETY ABOUT AGENCY

We can trace Twain's anxieties about mechanization and its effects on the individual in a number of his writings. But it is most instructive to begin with the work that constitutes the locus classicus of this theme, *A Connecticut Yankee in King Arthur's Court* (1889). This novel, which represents Twain's most extended meditation on the manipulative potential of causation, concerns the exploits of Hank Morgan, a company boss in the Colt arms factory in nineteenth-century Hartford, who finds himself transported in time back to sixth-century England. Imbued with the hindsight of thirteen centuries, even the most mundane of Morgan's actions takes on a magical aura: the simple act of lighting a match causes a stir throughout the kingdom. But to his credit, Morgan brings unusual skill to his tasks, and the combination catapults him into a position of

high authority and rank, "in power . . . equal to the king."[58] Known as
The Boss, a name that recalls Morgan's reverence for nineteenth-century
business hierarchy, Morgan continues to flaunt his "master intelligence
among intellectual moles" (56), by capitalizing on his advanced knowledge of technology. With great ingenuity, he reinvents complex devices
like the telephone and telegraph, and masterminds elaborate schemes
like that involving the electric fence that kills some thirty thousand
knights at the novel's end. But despite the pleasure Morgan derives from
the display of his technological prowess, he guards its secret carefully,
letting only his trusted servant, Clarence, and a few privileged others, in
on the "magic" involved. Indeed, Morgan does nothing to dispel the popular impression that he is an even greater wizard than Merlin, his arch-
enemy and rival. In having Morgan take advantage of the ignorance of
the people, moreover, Twain puts the mystery of technology on a par
with the medieval mystery of religion, the only source of mystification in
Arthurian England arguably greater than Morgan's. Even the all-power-
ful Morgan concedes that the church is "a trifle stronger than both . . . [he
and the king] put together" (53). By concealing the true source of his
power, then, Morgan makes a religion out of technology, suggesting at
once how easy it is to turn something that is causally explicable to some
(the Morgans of nineteenth-century America), into something that is
causally obscure and seemingly accidental to others (the inhabitants of
Arthurian England).

In perhaps the best example of a technologically induced "accident" in
the book, Morgan discovers a useful anonymity in the causal confusion
his "magic" generates. Traveling incognito through the countryside, the
King and Morgan find themselves under attack by a group of errant
knights who, failing to recognize them for the important and powerful
figures they are, assume the two are marauding strangers. When the
king's protestations fail to convince the knights of his eminence, Morgan
takes matters into his own hands. When the knights are within only thirty
yards of him, their lances pitched for battle, Morgan throws a bomb at
them. The result, Morgan notes, is a thing of beauty—on a par with the
Amaranth or the *Pennsylvania* disasters. "Yes, it was a neat thing,
very neat and pretty to see. It resembled a steamboat explosion on the
Mississippi; and during the next fifteen minutes we stood under a steady
drizzle of microscopic fragments of knights and hardware and horse-
flesh" (199). More notable, however, than the morbid pleasure Morgan
takes in the human suffering that surrounds him, is the satisfaction he
feels in knowing that the mystery of the bomb and his part in it will never
be explained. "There was a hole there," he remarks, "which would afford
steady work for all the people in that region for some years to come—in
trying to explain it, I mean" (199). As usual Morgan does not attempt an

explanation himself, preferring to let people attribute it to his sorcery. But even for the King, to whom Morgan does disclose the secret, the explanation does not register. "The information did . . . [the king] no damage," Morgan observes, "because it left him as intelligent as he was before. . . . [I]t was a noble miracle, in his eyes, and was another settler for Merlin" (199).

The agency- and identity-obscuring significance for Twain of this transformation of science into superstition is anticipated in another work that reveals many of the same concerns Twain came to thematize in *A Connecticut Yankee*. In *Life on the Mississippi*, superstition is invoked to explain not just one accident but a pattern of steamboat disasters. Here the presence of a gray mare and preacher on board is said to have caused several steamboat disasters, most notably that of Twain's "first friend the 'Paul Jones'" (189). The "historian," Uncle Mumford, Twain's source for this particular piece of river lore, acknowledges that for some the mere presence of a gray mare and preacher may seem an unlikely cause for an accident, but to the "many ignorant people who would scoff at such a matter, and call it superstition," he has a ready answer:

> "But you will always notice that they are people who have never travelled with a gray mare and a preacher. I went down the river once in such company. We grounded at Bloody Island; we grounded at Hanging Dog; we grounded just below this same Commerce; we jolted Beaver Dam Rock; we hit one of the worst breaks in a fight; we burnt a boiler; broke a shaft; collapsed a flue; and went into Cairo with nine feet of water in the hold. . . . The men lost their heads with terror. They painted the mare blue, in sight of town, and threw the preacher overboard, or we should not have arrived at all" (189).

For Mumford, the facts are self-evident; the proof that the combination of gray mare, preacher, and accident are causally linked can be found in their repeated recurrence, since, in the spirit of true superstition, numbers tell all. Though such a notion of proof is strained, it clearly has its virtues. "That this combination—of preacher and gray mare—should breed calamity, seems strange," Twain writes, "and at first glance unbelievable; but the fact is fortified by so much unassailable proof that to doubt is to dishonor reason" (189). While Twain's comment here is clearly sarcastic, it points to the unimpeachable, if circuitous, logic of superstition that helps to explain its mass appeal.

Even Twain, it seems, who had served several years as a steamboat pilot, and who clearly knew steamboats better than to attribute supernatural powers to them, seems to have indulged in such fantasies on occasion. In particular, in a memorable scene from *Life*, Twain imagines that steamboats are capable of a kind of auto-locomotion which removes them from the realm of human agency altogether. In this scene, Twain recounts the story of a somnambulist pilot who, while sleepwalking one night, relieves the pilot on duty and steers the boat through a particularly treacherous part of the river. "The black phantom assumed the wheel without saying anything," Twain writes, "steadied the waltzing steamer with a turn or two, and then stood at ease, coaxing her a little to this side and then to that, as gently and as sweetly as if the time had been noonday" (107). Unaware that the pilot is steering in his sleep, the on-duty pilot goes below deck, satisfied that the boat is in good hands. But no sooner does he leave his post than he learns that the somnambulist has left it as well. "The next moment . . . [the on-duty pilot was] flying up the pilot-house companion-way, three steps at a jump. *Nobody there!* The great steamer was whistling down the middle of the river at her own sweet will!" (my emphasis, 108). The tale of the sleepwalking pilot and, more important, of his disappearance from the helm, is undoubtedly part of the river pilot's lore, but its underlying premise is significant. For in imagining an empty pilothouse with "nobody there," Twain invests the steamboat with the kind of independent agency that recalls the scene about blamelessness and the erosion of human responsibility with respect to steamboat accidents in *The Gilded Age*.

BLAMELESSNESS AND THE ECONOMY: *THE GILDED AGE*

The fantasy (that was fast approaching a reality) of an independent mechanical agency that made it possible for Twain to envision an unmanned helm—a helm with "nobody there" and nobody responsible—also made it possible, if not necessary, to reconceive the definition of legal liability. For in a world in which machines were seen to initiate actions on their own, liability lost its original purpose: namely, to identify a source of *human* compensation to make the victim whole. To be sure, attempts were made to find the parties responsible for building, designing, or operating the machines in question, but the notion that the machine itself might ultimately be behind any given accident or wrongdoing substantially diminished the legitimacy of attributing responsibility to any one individual. Indeed, the record suggests that in many cases brought in steamboat accidents, claimants vainly pursued one after another of the potentially responsible parties until the very top of the hierarchy of responsibility had been reached. After attempts, for example, to name and locate the actual operatives failed, many claims were brought against steamboat owners; but while owners' names were usually a matter of public record, even their relatively visible identities were often hidden.

"The ease with which owner-operators or their employees could escape legal process by moving into other trades," Hunter reports, "the difficulty of obtaining owner names and identifying their persons, and the frequently irresponsible character of steamboat officers greatly handicapped creditors in bringing the responsible parties into court."[59]

Fueling this evasion of responsibility was what one legal scholar has called "the nineteenth-century ethos of injury"[60]—an ethos that explicitly placed the burden for injuries on the accident victim as opposed to the perpetrator. Under the doctrine of negligence, in other words, with its emphasis on fault, the point of accident litigation (until sometime near the end of the century) was not to compensate accident victims and thus restore them to their pre-accident condition, but to identify a blameworthy agent; only in the presence of such blameworthiness—a presence that, as we have seen, was increasingly difficult to establish—would compensation be made. Oliver Wendell Holmes best captured the anti-compensatory thrust of negligence when he wrote that "the general principle of our law is that loss from accident must lie where it falls. . . ."[61] To place legal, moral, and financial blame on a non-blameworthy perpetrator, for an act that could not have been avoided was, for Holmes, both futile and ill-advised. "As action cannot be avoided," he clarified, "and tends to the public good, there is obviously no policy in throwing the hazard of what is at once desirable and inevitable upon the actor" (95).

Twain would doubtless have deplored the sentiment of Holmes's statement for it not only left many accident victims and their families without recourse, but it condoned and even perpetuated, through its hands-off policy on accidents, the indiscriminate effects on personal agency and responsibility of an economy already heavily marked by indiscriminate and speculative fluctuations. Twain's comments about the contemporary social situation reveal his great dislike and fear of an economy that was increasingly divorced from, even impervious to, human labor and the production of actual value, and more sensitive by far to the internal movements of money and the buying and selling of stocks.[62] For Twain, importantly, the decoupling of the economy from questions of real value was a betrayal of the "good heart" that he thought could flourish in a democratic system. From his many disparaging remarks about the English monarchy, for example, it is clear that what he valued about America and democracy was not its leveling of all class difference but its sensible maintenance of it. America, Twain wrote, was a land "where inequalities are infinite—not limited, as in monarchies; where inequalities are measured by degrees & shades of difference in capacity, not by accidental differences of birth; where 'superior' & 'inferior' are terms which state facts, not lies."[63] Acknowledging the necessity of economic class division, then, Twain takes issue not with the condition of poverty, or of wealth for that matter, but with an economy that imposes one or the other condition unmeritoriously. Of course, much of Twain's anxiety about the vicissitudes of the economy was inspired and borne out by events in his own life. Not only did Twain live through several financial panics, including the panic of 1873, the year in which *The Gilded Age* was written, but he teetered on the brink of personal financial ruin most of his life. Always feeling the need to earn more money to support his large family and somewhat lavish lifestyle, Twain not only wrote for money, but invested heavily and unsuccessfully in several business ventures. After the failure of the Paige typesetter,[64] a machine whose development cost Twain years of misery and over $200,000, Twain was forced to declare bankruptcy.[65]

The best known manifestations of Twain's dissatisfaction with an economy that ignored individual merit, that rewarded the frauds over the earnest laborers, is his critique of speculation in *The Gilded Age*. In his satire of get-rich-quick schemes in this novel, the writer's resentment clearly comes to the fore. Embodying the first articulation of the phrase "the gilded age" that came to characterize the era, the novel by that name depicts the illusory and ill-fated nature of an economy based on graft and corruption that affected the sensibilities and practices of street vendors, Wall Street bankers, and national legislators alike. ". . . [T]he business prosperity of the world," the narrator claims at one point, "is only a bubble of credit and speculation, one scheme helping to float another which is no better than it, and the whole liable to come to naught and confusion as soon as the busy brain that conceived them ceases its power to devise, or when some accident produces a sudden panic" (343). The best examples of such a "bubble" in the novel concern the well-intentioned but dead-end schemes of Col. Sellars, and the plight of the ill-fated Tennessee land whose questionable value keeps the Hawkins family in an insidious cycle of poverty and hope. Also targeted by the satire are the members of Congress and their minions whose wheeling and dealing lie at the very heart of the nation's economy. But less visibly, although no less insidiously, the novel also registers the effects of the volatile economy in the story of the steamboat accident and its consequences for Laura Hawkins, the little girl orphaned by it.

Like all the victims of the *Amaranth* disaster, Laura is profoundly affected by the official finding of blamelessness since such a finding precludes her ability to recover financially for her injuries. But the severity of the accident's effect on her identity is reinforced by the fact that in the accident Laura loses her family, her family's wealth, even her name. In the hours and days immediately following the disaster some abortive attempts are made to locate Laura's parents, to see if they survived, but no sign of them emerges. Inquiries reveal only her first and family name—Laura Van Brunt—and her place of embarkation. Her dainty clothes and fine manners, however, suggest that she is the daughter of a well-to-do family, and later information confirms this suspicion. But if Laura was rich before the accident, she is relatively impoverished afterwards, having been adopted by the financially troubled Hawkinses—a family whose middle-class status (they own a slave) clearly hangs by a thread (they can barely afford to feed their children) and threatens to disintegrate into poverty at any moment. Thus in losing her parents in the disaster, Laura loses the two most essential kinds of identity simultaneously—that of family and that of class.

Lest the lasting effect of the accident on Laura be overlooked, Twain takes pains[66] to describe the unsettling consequences that accompany Laura's discovery of her origins. Although Laura's place within the Hawkins family is secure, even indistinguishable from that of the Hawkins' other children—"I love [her] just the same as I love my own," Mrs. Hawkins says (51)—the secret of her birth turns her life around completely. That her sense of self is disrupted by the news of her adoption is, itself, not remarkable. But what seems more important to Laura than the knowledge that she has another family or that her father might still be alive, is the information that her family had been rich and that her father had been a "handsome featured aristocratic gentleman" (85). It is, in short, the knowledge that she once belonged to a different class, and to a higher caste, that sparks her self-reevaluation. Based on this information, Laura begins to feel like an outsider in the settlement town of Hawkeye where she is raised after the accident re-classed her. And while she is still devoted to the Hawkinses, she begins to feel that she is destined for something better than the life they have afforded her. ". . . the mystery of her birth at once chagrined her and raised in her the most extravagant expectations," Twain writes. "She was proud and she felt the sting of poverty" (140). Capitalizing on her beauty, the only palpable sign of her refinement, Laura directs all her energy and intelligence into making money and climbing the social ladder. In endearing herself to Senator Dilworthy, among others, Laura secures an invitation and a train ticket to Washington, where she realizes her fondest dream, to mingle with a more sophisticated and powerful set of people. Life in Washington completes the transformation in Laura's personality. "When Laura has been in Washington three months," Twain writes, "she was still the same person, in one respect, that she was when she first arrived there—that is to say, she still bore the name of Laura Hawkins. Otherwise she was perceptibly changed" (243). Since learning that she was born to money, Laura is transformed from a guileless girl into a conniving woman. And in this she becomes another victim not only of the steamboat accident with which the book begins, but of the gilded age economy of which the legal adjudication of accidents was both a symptom and a cause. For in seeking her fortune by influence-peddling and manipulation, Laura is, finally, like all the other corrupt participants in the "bubble of credit and speculation" for whom fortune, disarticulated from labor or true merit, is always just around the corner.

ACCIDENT INSURANCE

The fortune Laura seeks differs in one respect from that of the other fortune hunters in the novel: it functions as a substitute for legal compensation. For Laura, that is, the impulse to finagle is set in motion by the failure of the law to restore her to her pre-accident state. And in seeking some other source of compensation for her injuries, Laura's quest, importantly, becomes a figure for accident insurance—a novel and burgeoning industry in America in the second half of the nineteenth century. Indeed, although *The Gilded Age* does not directly raise the issue of accident insurance, its absence is conspicuous, lurking in the background of the literary narrative as it does in almost every accident case: it provides the impetus, among other things, for Laura's search for her father (the family, after all, was the earliest form of insurance) and for the money and connections she lost in the accident itself. Fortunately, however, we need not rely exclusively on the shadowy presence of insurance in *The Gilded Age* to learn more about how it figured in Twain's life and work, in general, and in his notions about responsibility, in particular. Although his references to insurance tend to be scattered throughout his novels, stories, letters, and speeches, Twain's life and writings circled back to the subject of insurance many times.

Like so many of the technological and business innovations of his day, the accident insurance industry both attracted and repelled Twain. At first glance, the benefits of insurance seemed to outweigh the disadvantages. In fact, Twain witnessed the flourishing of insurance in its most idealistic period, as it grew from its very limited and local beginnings as an offshoot of the steamboat and railroad inspection services in the first part of the nineteenth century,[67] to the point of mass-production in the period following the Civil War.[68] Daniel Boorstin notes that in becoming accessible to more people, insurance, for a time, seemed to embody the promise of the first truly democratically produced commodity.[69] Moreover, Twain could not have been unaware of the purpose accident insurance served for accident victims whose needs for compensation would have otherwise been left unmet by the frequently harsh and unsympathetic verdicts handed down by the courts under negligence.

In *A Connecticut Yankee,* Twain takes obvious pleasure in the fate-altering power of insurance, one of Hank Morgan's most valuable anachronisms. Indeed, in Arthurian England, Morgan's insurance business is perceived not simply as a threat to the judicial system, but to God's law. Morgan rants:

> The priests opposed both my fire and life insurance, on the ground that it was an insolent attempt to hinder the decrees of God; and if you pointed out that they did not hinder the decrees in the least, but only modified the hard consequences of them if you took out policies and had luck, they retorted that that was gambling against the decrees of God, and was just as bad (212).

Interestingly, although the priests effectively demolish Morgan's *life* and *fire* insurance businesses, the otherwise God-fearing knights who "could see the practical side of a thing once in a while" continue to support his *accident* insurance business. "[A]nd so of late," Morgan boasts, "you couldn't clean up a tournament and pile the result without finding one of my accident-tickets in every helmet" (212). On the advice of a friend who, like Morgan, saw insurance as a moneymaking venture, Twain purchased $23,000 of stock in the newly established Hartford Accident Insurance Company. Living in Hartford (then as now the insurance capital of the world),[70] Twain was surrounded by the insurance community and, not surprisingly, counted many of its leading members among his friends. In fact, until The Hartford Accident Insurance Company failed in 1874, Twain served as one of its five directors, attending every Board meeting, as he notes in his *Autobiography,* for a year and a half.[71]

After suffering a sizeable financial loss from his failing stock in the Hartford Insurance Company, Twain's enthusiasm for insurance understandably waned, but other more reprehensible aspects of the business also figured in his gradual disenchantment with it. If it solved the problem of limited liability, it seemed nevertheless to contribute to the erosion of individual responsibility that Twain so valued. Thus, like many, Twain grew uncomfortable with the financial valuations insurance placed on the loss of human life and limb, not simply because they figured loss in monetary terms, but because the valuations themselves seemed random and disproportionately measured. If a finding of blamelessness tended to deplete a victim's resources, insurance tended to inflate it.[72] While an uncompensated accident could make a rich person poor, as is the case with Laura Hawkins, accident insurance could do just the opposite. In a speech given in his capacity as a director of the Hartford Insurance Company in honor of the Englishman Cornelius Walford, one of the pioneers of the insurance industry, Twain let his displeasure with this phenomenon be known.[73]

> There is nothing more beneficent than accident insurance. I have seen an
> entire family lifted out of poverty and into affluence by the simple boon of a
> broken leg. I have had people come to me on crutches, with tears in their
> eyes, to bless this beneficent institution. In all my experience of life, I have
> seen nothing so seraphic as the look that comes into a freshly mutilated
> man's face when he feels in his vest pocket with his remaining hand and finds
> his accident ticket all right. And I have seen nothing so sad as the look that
> came into another splintered customer's face, when he found he couldn't
> collect on a wooden leg.[74]

So effective was insurance in substituting for the law's failure to compensate, according to Twain's satiric description of it here, that it denatured accidents altogether, making them desirable where they had formerly been aversive by promising their victims substantial financial rewards.

By spreading the burden formerly unique to the perpetrator across insured society as a whole, insurance accelerated the trend toward the diminution of the perpetrator's responsibility originally set in motion by a legal verdict of blamelessness. Secure in the knowledge that the cost of injuries had been assumed by someone else, perpetrators were freer than ever to act irresponsibly. (Interestingly, bankruptcy, also a novel and rapidly growing area of the law in the second half of the nineteenth century and one that Twain was ultimately driven to, had the same effect on responsibility and was clearly part of a trend in the law and the culture at large toward the acceptance of an individual's diminishing control over economic circumstances.)[75] So widespread was the diffusion of responsibility in economic affairs, in fact, that the expectation that insurance companies would offer compensation where the perpetrator himself had not was far from guaranteed. "The companies," one legal scholar notes, "acted almost as if their 'single function' was to collect premiums, and not to pay claims at all."[76] When this trend reached scandalous proportions in 1906, and the insurance companies were taken to task for their part in this public deception, Twain joined in the tirades against them. In a letter from that period, he writes:

> The gospel ["of getting rich by any means"] does seem to be universal. Its
> great apostles today are the McCurdies, McCalls, Hydes, Alexanders, and
> the rest of that robber gang who have lately been driven out of their violated
> positions of trust in the colossal insurance companies of New York. . . . It
> has been imagined that the cause of the[ir] death strokes was sorrow and
> shame for the robberies committed upon the two or three million policy
> holders and their families, and the widow and the orphan—but every now
> and then one is astonished to find that it is not the outraged conscience of
> these men that is at work; they are merely sick and sore because they have
> been exposed."[77]

Central to Twain's critique of this "robber gang," and their "universal gospel" is the heartlessness and hypocrisy that fueled their profits—their ability to take the misfortunes of some and turn them very literally into the fortunes of others. Underlying his scorn for their business practice, however, lies a more scorching indictment of what such a practice signified for the identities of the parties involved. For in literally capitalizing on accidents, the insurance industry, in Twain's view, seriously perverted the notion of individual responsibility, overturning age-old expectations about how people at risk should behave.

Specifically, in making accidents the source of a lucrative business, for both insurer and insured, insurance created an incentive for negligence, turning otherwise cautious perpetrators and victims into deliberately careless actors. Although Hank Morgan has no trouble peddling accident insurance in the sixth century, fledgling insurance companies in the nineteenth century were not as confident or as secure. Large-scale disasters, involving up to several million claims, could severely test the resources of an insurance company; but the companies that managed to survive were typically able to increase their rates and attract new policyholders. Twain witnessed the profit-making potential of the Chicago fire of 1871 on the Hartford firms that were so successful in recruiting new business in its aftermath that when fire broke out in Boston the very next year, they not only paid their claims easily but raised their premiums and reserves to new levels.[78] In his speech on accident insurance, Twain parodies the eagerness of insurance executives for accidents, mocking himself in the process:

> Ever since I have been a director in an accident insurance company, I have felt that I am a better man. Life has seemed more precious. Accidents have assumed a kindlier aspect. Distressing special providences have lost half their horror. I look upon a cripple, now, with affectionate interest—as an advertisement. I do not seem to care for poetry anymore, I do not care for politics—even agriculture does not excite me. But to me, now, there is a charm about a railway collision that is unspeakable.[79]

But more insidious even than the insensitivity of insurance directors to the suffering of those injured by accidents, was the insensitivity of the victims to their own injuries. Because of the potential financial rewards from accidents, accident victims became even more irresponsible and careless than accident perpetrators. Twain continues:

> No man can take out a policy in . . . [the Hartford Accident Insurance Company], and not get crippled before the year is out. Now there was one indigent man who had been disappointed so often with other companies that he had grown disheartened, his appetite left him, he ceased to smile—

said life was but weariness. Three weeks ago I got him to insure with us, and now he is the brightest, happiest spirit in the land—has a good steady income and a stylish suit of new bandages every day and travels around on a shutter."[80]

TWAIN'S INSURANCE PARODIES

Twain's, of course, was not the only voice to be heard excoriating the institution of insurance. Indeed, the tendency of insurance to diminish individual responsibility had been noted by many members of the legal establishment, including the noted theorist of liability, Oliver Wendell Holmes. In fact, it was because it had a tendency to deter individual initiative that Holmes actively disapproved of the idea of compulsory insurance—a compromise gesture within legal circles in his day that avoided the attribution of costs of injurious action to any one actor but promoted the distribution of them across the group of potential actors over all. "The state might conceivably make itself a mutual insurance company against accidents, and distribute the burden of its citizens' mishaps among all its members. . . ." he wrote in *The Common Law*. "[But] unless my act is of a nature to threaten others . . . it is no more justifiable to make me indemnify my neighbor against the consequences, than to make me do the same thing if I had fallen upon him in a fit, or to compel me to insure him against lightning."[81]

Holmes's choice of lightning as an example of an injury the blame for which could not be traced to any human agent finds an echo in Twain's own writing. Indeed, Twain seems to have parodied the idea of an insurance fund for lightning victims for many of the same reasons Holmes had: it epitomized the difficulty of finding a blameworthy agent and thus of structuring a legal system of liability around such an inquiry. The idea first crops up in Twain in a bizarre little story of a fraudulent accident insurance scheme, entitled, "Abner L. Jackson (About to Be) Deceased."[82] Frustrated in his attempts to gain a pension at various points in his life, Jackson finally hits upon the perfect way to insure the well-being of his family. He arranges first to take an excursion on a steamboat (a notoriously hazardous affair, as we have seen), buys $100,000 of Travelers Accident tickets, and then enumerates how he would like the money to be distributed upon his death. Indeed, the story consists mainly of Jackson's grocery list of the relatives and charitable organizations he has designated as his beneficiaries. Of the items included in this list, however, is money set aside for a pet project of his: "To print my medical pamphlet entitled 'Advice to Persons About to Be Struck by Lightning'" (312). One can only assume what Jackson's pamphlet would reveal for his interest seems to lie more clearly in advising people (provided they are properly insured) in how to seek out strikes by lightning than in how to avoid them. But one thing is certain: Jackson, who is "about to be deceased" in a steamboat disaster, has entertained the notion of insurance fraud at least once before.

The idea of turning a natural disaster (like death by lightning) to one's advantage is elaborated in a hilarious story Twain wrote just a year before he died, entitled "The International Lightning Trust" (1909).[83] Here Twain takes the idea germinating in "Abner L. Jackson" one step further, fleshing out the details of what a lightning insurance scheme would look like if it were put into effect. In this story, Jasper Hackett and Stephen Spaulding, two down-and-outers on the verge of starvation and eviction hit upon the idea of insuring people for lightning precisely because so few people are hit by lightning and yet so many are plagued by the fear of it. In creating something out of nothing, the men take their place in the tradition of true speculators. The first thing they need to do, they reason, is to issue a "few thousand numbered tickets in series A ($1); series B ($5); and series C ($10)."[84] The next thing they need "is a man laid out dead by lightning, with a one-dollar ticket in his vest pocket—after which, oh *see* us sail along" (86). At first, the two young entrepreneurs figure that they will need to fabricate their own evidence, finding a victim and then planting an insurance ticket on him in order to make the effectiveness of their premiums clear. After that, presumably, the people will be convinced and will buy tickets on their own. But something still bothers Hackett about this idea, and he refines the scheme in order to increase the potential size of his customer base.

The constraint that irritates Hackett and motivates him to refashion his insurance scheme is the requirement that there be proof—proof both that lightning caused the victim's death and that the victim was in fact insured with the company. Indeed, the genius of Hackett's idea for lightning insurance is to obviate the need for proof of any kind. In this story, Twain makes a mockery of the notion that one could trace the blame for an injury, any injury, by flouting the need for proof of its cause at all. The idea of proving that lightning was involved is given brief consideration when Spaulding protests that Hackett has forgotten to include mention of it in his advertising circular. Noticing Spaulding's hesitation, Hackett engages him in a clarifying dialogue:

"What are you looking so perplexed about?"

"Well, it's this. The circular doesn't say anything about *proof*."

"I'll fix it in two words. There—now it says the verdict of the inquest shall be sufficient proof that the owner or bearer of the ticket was killed by lightning."

"Oh, that's all very well, but suppose they don't hold an inquest?"

"Why, hang it, they've *got* to. Don't you know that much? It's a case of 'visitation of God,' as they call it. Well, when He calls on a person in that informal way you don't take the compliment on trust, the law makes you call an inquest and prove it. . . ." (87)

The first thing to notice about this apparent concession on Hackett's part to the requirement of proof is the preposterousness of the idea that one could prove a "visitation of God." It is as if Hackett concedes the point only because he knows full well that there is little that can be done to prove natural or divine disasters since these, more than any other kind of accident, can never by definition be traced back to their source. The inquest Hackett envisions, therefore, into an "act of God" serves as the very model of the kind of inquest with which this chapter began in which, seemingly, "nobody is to blame."

Even more telling of Twain's parody of blamelessness is Hackett's suggestion that proof not only of lightning but of the victim's insurance is to be taken lightly as well. In fact, Hackett proposes that in order to increase sales he and Spaulding continue to plant accident tickets on their victims—a scheme that seems counterintuitive to Spaulding (and the reader) at first. Spaulding complains: " '[T]he ticket doesn't contain the candidate's name, it only says Owner or Bearer. That is, Owner or somebody else—*anybody* else. Don't you see? Any lightning-victim that holds the ticket can collect the money. You didn't happen to notice that, did you?" Hackett explains again in a patient exchange:

"Oh, yes I did."

"Well then, why didn't you correct it?"

"I didn't want to. . . ."

"Explain it, then—explain it."

"The explanation is this: it secures to us the *entire* trade; the lightning—struck trade of the whole country."

"How? Why. . . ?"

" . . . As soon as the public find out that we don't care how the corpse got the ticket, everybody will buy one and lay for a chance to sell it to a cadaver. By and by we'll have a hundred million tickets out, and the money in the bank" (87–88).

Hackett, then, doesn't care whether he's received premiums from any given accident victim as long as that person's injury or death generates premiums from others. In short, his scheme severs the links to blame of any kind. For the beauty of insurance for Hackett is that as a business it can remain unconcerned with causal attribution and still thrive. Of course, most actual insurance companies, as Twain surely knew, did require proof of injury, barring payments to accident victims who could not document either the injuries or their own insurance coverage. And increasingly, as insurance of all kinds became widespread, proof was often required to enable the victim's company to sue for recovery of their award from the company insuring the perpetrator. Even so, especially when compared to the system of liability embodied in the legal doctrine of negligence, insurance does effectively remove the requirement of proof of individual agency, diffusing, as Holmes predicted and Twain so greatly feared, the costs of injuries and the knowledge of blame across the entire population. Thus, the characters of Spaulding and Hackett, humorous as they are, give voice to Twain's lifelong frustration in not being able to solve the problem of who was to blame—for his brother's death or for the gradual disappearance of the morally responsible individual.

CHAPTER FIVE

The Law of the Good Samaritan

CROSS-RACIAL RESCUE IN STEPHEN CRANE
AND CHARLES CHESNUTT

> A certain man went down from Jerusalem to
> Jericho, and fell among thieves. . . . And by
> chance there came down a certain priest that way;
> and when he saw him, he passed by on the other
> side. And likewise a Levite, when he was at the
> place, came and looked on him, and passed by on
> the other side. But a certain Samaritan . . . went
> to him, and bound up his wounds . . . and
> took care of him.
> (Luke 10:30–37)

> . . . [T]he priest and Levite who passed by on the
> other side were not, it is supposed, liable *at law*
> for the continued suffering of the man who fell
> among thieves, which they might and *morally*
> ought to have prevented or relieved.
> (*Buch v. Amory Manufacturing Co.*, 1897)[1]

MIDWAY through Stephen Crane's *The Monster* (1899), after the black driver, Henry Johnson, rescues the young Jimmie Trescott from his burning house and literally loses his face as a consequence, the elders of Whilomville ponder Johnson's future. When Dr. Trescott, who is Jimmie's father and Johnson's employer, decides to assume responsibility for the physically and mentally disabled man, Trescott's friend Judge Hagenthorpe gives him some advice. "Perhaps we may not talk with propriety of this kind of action," the judge remarks, "but I am induced to say that you are performing *a questionable charity* in preserving this negro's life. As near as I can understand, he will hereafter be a monster, a perfect monster, and probably with an affected brain."[2] On the surface, of course, the charity is questionable for Hagenthorpe because Johnson's life as a "monster" would, presumably, be so impoverished as not to be worth living. But the charity is questionable in other ways as well. A tale of double rescues—the one by the black man of his white employer's son, the other by the white man of his black employee—*The Monster* is also a tale of a legally engendered double standard in the exercise of charity. The act of a black man and a subordinate, Johnson's rescue is not only welcome but in some sense compelled, while Trescott's is not only optional but actively, even legally, discouraged.

Although Hagenthorpe speaks to Trescott not as a judge but as a friend, his advice bears the stamp of his professional authority. In assessing Trescott's situation, Crane notes, "[t]he judge retreated to the cold manner of the bench" (448). It is no accident, then, that in attempting to dissuade Trescott from "preserving" Johnson's life, Hagenthorpe gives voice not simply to a personal opinion but to the prevailing legal one: a bystander has no duty to rescue. More specifically, then as now, under the law of the good Samaritan, an individual who is not involved in the creation of risk has no obligation to prevent it or to aid those who have fallen victim to it. In existence in some form since Biblical times, the law was of particular interest in the late nineteenth century when unprecedented urbanization, industrialization, and poverty made the question of social welfare and altruism an urgent one. Featured prominently in hundreds of cases at the time,[3] the law of the good Samaritan had a tendency, as will be demonstrated, to tax the underclass of post–Civil War America more heavily than the well-to-do.

Crane's story is a fictional treatment of the effects of the law of the good Samaritan on relations between the classes. More important, in figuring the problem of good Samaritanism in the context of black-white relations, Crane investigates the law's less obvious effect on relations between the races. Less noted than the infamous law mandating segregation set down in *Plessy v. Ferguson* (1896),[4] the law of the good Samaritan was no less invidious in perpetuating the subordination of blacks in the post-Reconstructionist period. Unlike *Plessy*, however, the law of the good Samaritan makes no explicit mention of the races. Indeed, on the surface it appears to be neutral, requiring no one, of any color or class, to come to the aid of another. But its discriminatory effects did not go unnoticed as the work of Crane and of Charles Wadell Chesnutt, who wrote several short stories and two novels *The Marrow of Tradition* (1901) and *The Colonel's Dream* (1905) that touch on the subject, demonstrate.

AFFIRMATIVE DUTIES AND CRANE'S *THE MONSTER*

In its refusal to enforce acts of good Samaritanism, the law turned its back not only on an important Biblical precept, but on the long-standing tradition of modeling itself after and incorporating ethical teachings of all kinds. That the priest and the Levite failed to relieve the suffering of the man who fell among thieves, when they "might and *morally* ought to have," did not, as the judge in the *Buch* case reminds us, make them "liable *at law*." In distancing itself from its moral underpinnings, the law assumed a neutral cast. "Law," the legal scholar Morton Horwitz writes, "once conceived of as protective, regulative, paternalistic and, above all, a paramount expression of the moral sense of the community, had come to be thought of as facilitative of individual desires and as simply reflective of the existing organization of economic and political power."[5] Following on the heels of the Revolutionary period in which the law had been openly suffused with morality, this aversion to morality typified the direction of legal reform in the nineteenth century. Hoping to make the law more objective and thus impervious to any one of the many competing moral codes, the leading jurists of the time attempted to standardize legal rhetoric and procedures. Spearheading this movement were such luminaries as Oliver Wendell Holmes whose pathbreaking work, *The Common Law* (1881), became one of the leading texts in the effort to separate the law and morality. For Holmes, the ultimate goal was to turn the law into a science concerned only with empirical and observable phenomena. "A man may have as bad a heart as he chooses," Holmes admonished, "if his conduct is within the rules."[6]

Central to Holmes's effort to standardize and externalize the law were his notions about accident law in particular. In fact, in the second half of the nineteenth century, accident law became one of the primary venues for sorting out ideas about morality and the law. Several attributes of accident law contributed to its salience for this purpose, most prominent of which was the invocation by negligence of a notion of blameworthiness. Morality also continued to figure in the determination of accident damages. In particular, concern arose about the existence of punitive damages in accident cases—damages that went beyond the actual "cost" of the victim's injuries. The fear was that in allowing for punitive damages, accident law would exceed its compensatory function—to settle claims between two individuals—and begin to regulate and confiscate wealth according to purely moral (and social) goals. One treatise writer strongly defended morality's place in this calculus. "Compensation is the measure of redress for the *legal* wrong," he wrote. "[B]ut for the *moral* wrong, the recklessness of the act, the personal malice with which it is done, the violence and outrage attending it, reasonable exemplary [punitive] damages will be allowed."[7] Given the widespread distaste for moral intervention by the law, however, most jurists took the opposite view. Several state supreme courts even went so far as to overthrow the doctrine of punitive damages entirely.[8]

But of all the aspects of accident law that proved troublesome for the morality and law debate, none were as vexing or as visible as those that arose in the context of the good Samaritan. Addressing itself to the ac-

Fig. 2. A young cotton mill worker injured by machinery. Photo by Lewis Hines, 1912. UPI/Corbis-Bettmann.

tions not of accident perpetrators but of bystanders, the law of the good Samaritan is perhaps the clearest example of how far nineteenth-century jurists were willing to go to divorce law from morality. Taking up the explicitly anti-Christian view that bystanders had no duty to rescue, the authors of good Samaritan cases often found themselves in the awkward position of having to defend the law's flagrant disregard for the most fundamental tenets of human decency. Ultimately constrained by precedent, the cases are nevertheless full of dicta (nonbinding language) that suggest the profound ambivalence of most judges about the law.[9] Most prominent among them is the *Buch* case (1897) in which the court invoked the Biblical parable of the good Samaritan only to dismiss it as legally irrelevant. In *Buch*, the court ruled against imposing liability on a factory overseer who failed to prevent an eight-year-old German immigrant factory worker from getting his hand caught in his brother's weaving machine. "The duty to do no wrong is a legal duty," the court wrote. "The duty to protect against wrong is, generally speaking, and excepting certain intimate relations in the nature of a trust, a moral obligation only, not recognized or enforced by the law."[10] Accidents of the kind adjudicated in *Buch*, in which young children lost digits or limbs to factory machines, were widespread. Figure 2 shows one such boy who was crippled by the loss of two fingers in an industrial accident. In this case, the payment of $1.00 released the employer from responsibility for the mishap. Following the precedent set by *Buch*, but with possibly even more heinous consequences, was the case of *Union Pacific Railway Co. v. Cappier* (1903). In *Cappier*, a railroad engineer who saw a train run over a pedestrian "failed to call a surgeon, or to render [the victim] any assistance after the accident, but permitted him to remain by the side of the tracks and bleed to death."[11] Like the court in *Buch*, the court in *Cappier* held that no matter how reprehensible his inaction, the engineer was in no way responsible for mitigating or ameliorating the severity of the injury, or for acting in accord with the "laws of humanity." Acknowledging that "the failure to respond to the calls of worthy charity" would be punished by a "higher law," the judge in *Cappier* maintained, reluctantly, that "with the humane side of the question the courts are not concerned."[12]

In support of their morally untenable position, advocates of the good Samaritan law resorted to increasingly legalistic rationales. The duty to rescue, they argued, like most positive duties—to *do* certain things—would prove difficult, if not impossible, to enforce. As a member of the 1837 commission to revise the penal code of India, Thomas Babington Macaulay was among the first to call attention to the administrative problems associated with the enforcement of positive duties in general and of good Samaritanism in particular. He wrote:

> It is true that none but a very depraved man would suffer another to be drowned when he might prevent it by a word. But if we punish such a man, where are we to stop? How much exertion are we to require? Is a person to be a murderer if he does not go fifty yards through the sun of Bengal at noon in May in order to caution a traveller against a swollen river? Is he to be a murderer if he does not go a hundred yards?—if he does not go a mile?—if he does not go ten?[13]

The examples Macaulay draws on are concerned with good Samaritanism in the criminal context, but his argument had obvious relevance to the accident context as well. Nor have the problems he identified diminished with time. In addition to the line-drawing problem Macaulay articulates, legal scholars and philosophers continue to point to the special challenge posed by the enforcement of positive duties. According to the philosopher Richard Trammel, for example, the duty *not to do* something is capable of being "discharged completely" by the individual, whereas a duty *to do* something often is not.[14] To this observation the philosopher Joel Feinberg adds that positive duties, like the duty to rescue, require an often unattainable degree of social coordination. "We must . . . consult with our fellow citizens to determine a suitable rule . . . governing our positive duty to rescue," Feinberg writes, "because . . . [i]t would be unfair to those who attempt to do so on their own if others do not make similar efforts, and utterly chaotic if everyone tried. . . ."[15]

More forceful even than the administrative objections to positive duties, however, were nineteenth-century objections based on substantive, causal grounds. According to the logic of legal causation, in the violation of a negative duty (for example, littering where it is forbidden to do so), it is possible to trace an action to its consequence (someone litters and that is *why* there is litter on the ground). In the case of a violation of positive duties, however (for example, failing to save someone from drowning), the causal trajectory is less clear (the drowning could be the result of suicide, murder, a lifeguard's incompetence, or a bystander's failure to intervene). Put more simply, in the first case, a *commission* lends the causal inquiry clarity, while in the second the *omission* clouds the results. For this reason, the law has long distinguished between commissions and omissions, linking commissions with misfeasance (the act of wrongdoing) and omissions with nonfeasance (the so-called "act" of doing nothing at all). Moreover, questions about the legal distinction between misfeasance and nonfeasance have prompted increasingly elaborate justifications. When, in his 1908 article "The Moral Duty to Aid Others as a Basis of Tort Liability," for example, the legal scholar Francis Bohlen suggested that most acts could be characterized as belonging neither to misfeasance nor to nonfeasance alone but to a "borderland" between the two,[16] the law responded by divorcing the concept of "passive action" from the realm of misconduct altogether. "However revolting the conduct of the man who declined to interfere [in an emergency]," wrote the legal scholar James Barr Ames in his essay "Law and Morals," also published in 1908, the same year as Bohlen's, ". . . he did not increase the jeopardy; he simply failed to confer a benefit upon a stranger."[17] In equating the failure to "interfere" with the failure to confer a benefit, Ames explicitly transforms good Samaritanism from a duty into a gratuity—the act of going, very literally, beyond the call of duty—to which no possible judgment of wrongdoing could apply.

Crane's literary rendition of good Samaritanism makes reference to many of these same arguments. In fact, the philosophical subtleties of both distinctions—between misfeasance and nonfeasance and between duty and gratuity—figure in the rhetorical strategies adopted by many of the characters in *The Monster*. It is clear, for instance, that while Judge Hagenthorpe, the story's legal authority on good Samaritanism and one of Whilomville's most upstanding citizens, would never think of *killing* Johnson and thus of committing an obvious act of misfeasance, he is not only willing but eager to insure that no steps be taken to keep Johnson alive. Short of murder, there is much that he and others in Whilomville can do (or, more accurately, fail to do) that falls under the legally permissible category of nonfeasance. In fact, the law's indifference to nonfeasance suggests why most people in Whilomville believe that Trescott should have let the black man die. Bainbridge, a railway engineer, who is waiting for a shave in Reifsnyder's barber shop, articulates this view in a dialogue in which the phrase "let him die" is repeated so often that it begins to acquire the intentionalism and malice—the misfeasance, in short—that it otherwise tries so conspicuously to avoid.

> "Oh, he should have let him die," said Bainbridge. . . .
> "Let him die?" [Reifsnyder] demanded. "How vas that? How can you let him die?"
> "By letting him die, you chump," said the engineer. . . .
> "How vas that?" [Reifsnyder] grumbled later. "How can you let a man die when he vas done so much for you?"
> "When he vas done so much for you?" repeated Bainbridge. "You better shave some people. How vas that? Maybe this ain't a barber shop" (454–55).

By literally throwing Reifsnyder's question back at him, even to the point of mocking his German accent, Bainbridge undermines the potential basis for sympathy between Reifsnyder, an actual immigrant, and Johnson, a virtual immigrant in his own land. But he also suggests that doing "so much," even when "so much" means saving a life, is less important than being a barber and doing no more than what is asked of you, thus rhetorically turning nonfeasance into an ideal of (non)action.

Moreover, by dismissing Reifsnyder's question—"How can you let a man die when he vas done so much for you?"—Bainbridge's speech also has the effect of deflating Johnson's act of rescue: although Reifsnyder insists that it was "so much," it is clearly not enough in Bainbridge's mind to warrant reciprocal action on anyone else's part. But the arguments arrayed against the possibility of reciprocity do not stop here. Just as Johnson's act becomes, in Bainbridge's parody, not "so much," Trescott's act becomes, in Hagenthorpe's mind, much more than it actually is. In helping Johnson, Hagenthorpe explains in his version of Ames's logic, Trescott is not returning a favor, or responding in kind, but conferring an enormous, almost godlike, benefit. " 'He will be your creation, you understand,' " he warns Trescott. " 'He is purely your creation. Nature has very evidently given him up. He is dead. You are restoring him to life. You are making him, and he will be a monster, and with no mind' " (448). In order to emphasize the philanthropic and noncompulsory nature of Trescott's action, of course, Hagenthorpe not only conflates the act of restoration with creation, but falsifies Johnson's predicament altogether. Despite what Hagenthorpe says, Johnson is not dead yet, and nature has only "given him up" if the people of Whilomville "let him die."

MORAL REFORM AND THE MIDDLE CLASSES

Given force in the context of Crane's story and of Whilomville's small-town prejudices,[18] the law's position on good Samaritanism begins to reveal essential biases. For what Crane's literary text does that even the most graphic of legal cases cannot do is to linger on the human consequences of the law until its claim to neutrality is seriously undercut, if not invalidated altogether. In their colloquial invocations of nonfeasance, for example, both Hagenthorpe and Bainbridge expose the underlying callousness of the law. But if the scene in Reifsnyder's barber shop displays the law's fundamental indifference to human suffering, the scene with Hagenthorpe belies an even more insidious aspect of the law. For in attempting to dissuade Trescott from helping Johnson, Hagenthorpe is not simply indifferent to Johnson's role as a victim; he is actively concerned with Trescott's role as a good Samaritan. In short, for Hagenthorpe, the law's amorality, although a step in the right direction, is not a sufficient safeguard against any given individual's optional act of charity—an act that in this case threatens to establish a relationship of reciprocity in which the white middle-class Trescott would be as liable to come to the aid of the black working-class Johnson as the other way around. In fact, good Samaritanism was predominantly figured as a class threat in this period that had less to do with keeping the law amoral than with keeping the law and its unavoidable morality under the exclusive control of the middle classes.

In the nineteenth century members of the middle classes were the self-appointed arbiters and custodians of morality. Their efforts to promote mores that continue to be associated with Victorianism, including sexual prudishness, temperance, and a general social conservatism, scarcely need mentioning. But they were also at the forefront of moral reform efforts that catered especially to the underclasses in the form not only of Bible societies and Sunday schools, but of fundraising for widows, orphans, and others in need. As many historians have pointed out, however, the zealousness of the middle classes' work in this regard belied a deeper anxiety about their own class status. Sacvan Bercovitch has written of the ambivalence of the middle classes' efforts at forming a cultural consensus in the nineteenth century—a consensus that, in Bercovitch's terms, reinforced their own distinctive and dominant identity and yet held out the promise for the absorption of other, more marginalized groups over time.[19] According to Joseph Gusfield, who is perhaps the most explicit proponent of this view, middle-class reform movements were "one way in which a declining social elite tried to retain some of its social power and leadership."[20] By championing moral reform among the masses, Gusfield and others argue, the middle and upper classes were able to standardize and naturalize their own behavior and beliefs. Perhaps even more important, they were also able to insure the ongoing dependence and subordination of the working classes and to keep them from seeking redress for their problems through the formation of unions, strikes, or other forms of protest that were unquestionably violent and socially threatening. In the hands of the middle classes, then, morality was sometimes less the expression of altruistic tendencies[21] than an instrument of class consolidation.

To this ideological use of morality, the middle classes' position on the law of accidents was no exception. From the start, spokesmen for the middle classes within the legal establishment favored the introduction of negligence and its inherently moral standard of liability. Attributing liability only to those who were morally at fault, they argued, was a welcome change from the harsh and ostensibly unfair consequences of the doctrine of strict liability which attributed liability without regard to a concept of fault altogether. But like their efforts to bring moral reform to the lower classes, the middle classes' penchant for morality in the law had a hidden agenda: the negligence standard catered to their political, class-specific needs. In predicating liability on moral fault, in short, negligence introduced a liability-limiting principle whose effect, not surprisingly, was of greater benefit to the middle classes—primarily the factory owners and managers most commonly cited as accident perpetrators—than to any others. If strict liability held to a notion of liability based on causation alone, Morton Horwitz writes, "negligence, by contrast, was the doctrine of an emerging entrepreneurial class that argued that there should be no liability for socially desirable activity that caused injury without carelessness."[22] Holmes, a fervent advocate of capitalist risk, was adamant on this point. To his mind, strict liability was a dangerous deterrent to risk-taking activity which he recognized as essential for commercial growth. ". . . [T]he public generally profits by individual activity," he wrote, and "as action cannot be avoided and tends to the public good, there is obviously no policy in throwing the hazard of what is at once desirable and inevitable upon the actor."[23]

With respect to negligence, then, Holmes undergoes an apparent reversal of his own intellectual aversion to morality in the law. But the reversal was, it is important to note, only "apparent." To be sure, in upholding the validity of the fault-finding aspect of the negligence doctrine, Holmes gave his assent to a standard loosely identified with personal and moral intentionality, but in his mind the notion of intent had itself been stripped of the kind of subjectivity typically associated with morality.[24] By the late nineteenth century, in fact, negligence had already proved to be a lasting exception to the general trend toward amorality in the law, and efforts were made to turn fault itself into an objective standard. Holmes was instrumental in this process, linking fault to customary and typical behavior—considered to be legitimate bases for objective standards at the time—rather than to a subjective state of mind. Thus, to determine fault required only that one compare the defendant's conduct to that of a "reasonable" or "prudent" person in similar circumstances, a standard, importantly, that any reasonable or prudent judge or reasonable or prudent jury would, according to Holmes, be able to recognize instantaneously.

The important element in this redefinition of blameworthiness for an understanding of Holmes's logic as a legal theorist and later as a justice of the Supreme Court lay in his invocation of and profound faith in a notion of majority opinion. For implicit in the notion of reasonableness was for Holmes a sense of what most people would do at any given time. Of course, *most* people, especially in the context of Holmes's theories of tort law, referred to an explicitly middle-class and not working-class majority. But to his credit, Holmes's valorization of majority opinion did not always position him as a social or political elitist. For example, in the landmark case of *Lochner v. New York* (1905), Holmes's dissent upholding the power of public sentiment aligned him with the distinctly liberal voices of labor reform. Indeed, what seemed to matter to Holmes in this case was that the ostensibly constitutional theory of freedom of contract (a freedom between bakeries and their employees to work long hours which the majority opinion upheld) not interfere with a more important political interest of the people in shorter working hours and in the health of bakery workers. But if Holmes was affiliated more with liberal interests in the *Lochner* opinion and more with conservative ones in his tort decisions, the cases nevertheless share a prototypically Holmesian cast of mind for both manage to advocate and advance the political and economic interests of one or another class in the name of the majority.

GOOD SAMARITANISM AND THE ISSUE OF CLASS IN CRANE, HOWELLS, PHELPS, AND CATHER

Reinforcing the majoritarian basis of the law of the good Samaritan and helping to veil its many objectionable elements was the language of neutrality in which it was written. For the law's ostensible neutrality—its mandate that no one of any class was required to rescue any other—worked in favor of the middle classes by limiting the liability of society's most resourceful rescuers. Nor was the middle classes' aversion to morality in the law necessarily at odds with their role as the standard-bearers of morality in society at large, since by wresting the observance of morality from the law, the middle classes emphasized the voluntariness of their charity. As with negligence, the preponderance of legal cases on good Samaritanism, for example, speaks to the unnecessary nature of the middle classes' responsibilities to those beneath them, not the other way around.

Although not exactly on all fours with the typical good Samaritan case, an incident in Crane's personal life raises issues about the law's hidden class prejudice and further motivates his long-standing obsession with the subject. In September of 1896, in his capacity as a muckraking journalist, Crane was commissioned to write a series of exposes of the New York City police courts for William Randolph Hearst's New York *Journal*. To this end, on the night of September 15, Crane interviewed three "chorus girls," one of whom was a streetwalker known to the police as Dora Clark.[25] As the interview came to a close, at about 2 A.M., Crane left two of the women at a corner to help the third catch an uptown cable car. He returned moments later to find that Clark and her friend were being arrested for soliciting. Just as Crane had parted from them, it seems, the police spotted two men in their vicinity and despite the fact that no communication had been made—the men were walking swiftly and the women deep in conversation—they were sure they had witnessed a solicitation. In quickly securing the release of one of the women by posing as her husband, Crane left the other, Clark, without an alibi. Clark, not surprisingly, spent the rest of the night in jail while Crane spent the night contemplating his obligation to her. He was, he wrote in the newspaper account of the incident, a "reluctant witness," torn between his "duty as a man . . . [not to] stand tamely by," and his fear that in the performance of this "duty," he would ruin his reputation.

> Suppose I were a clerk and I interfered in this sort of a case. When it became known to my employers they would say to me: "We are sorry, but we cannot have men in our employ who stay out until 2:30 in the morning in the company of chorus girls." Suppose, for instance, I had a wife and seven children in Harlem. As soon as my wife read the papers she would say: "Ha! You told me you had a business engagement! Half-past two in the morning with questionable company!" Suppose, for instance, I were engaged to the beautiful Countess of Kalamazoo. If she were to hear it, she would write: "All is over between us. My future husband cannot rescue prostitutes at 2:30 in the morning." [26]

Of course, the rescue at issue in this incident is not from an accident but from an unjust prosecution, but the law's subtle pressure against it is indicative of the legal attitude toward cross-class good Samaritanism as a whole. Thus, just as Trescott was advised by Judge Hagenthorpe not to intervene in the affairs of his black servant, Crane was advised by a "friendly" police sergeant not to rescue Dora Clark. " 'If you monkey with this case,' " the sergeant said, " 'you are pretty sure to come out with mud all over you.' "[27] Indeed, in the weeks and months following Crane's court appearance, in which he testified on Clark's behalf, the police interrogated him about questionable aspects of his past, searched his rooms for evidence of illicit activities and, in the end, created a scandal that injured his personal reputation and career more than any other incident in his life. Memorialized in both his newspaper account and his short story "Adventures of a Novelist," the incident became for Crane an object lesson in the inherent inequality of the law's position on good Samaritanism, for here was proof that while the law discouraged *all* acts of bystander intervention equally on its face, it seemed to work more aggressively to discourage the intervention of an otherwise upstanding, middle-class citizen on behalf of a lowly prostitute.[28]

In rescuing Dora Clark, Crane threatens the reputation of the middle classes through a process of contamination—by sympathizing too closely with and intervening too directly in the injuries of the underclasses. His real offense, then, is not the offer of charity per se (for the middle classes, as we have seen, prided themselves on their philanthropy), but the proximate and unmediated nature of that charity. For the most part, the middle classes' contribution to the rise of moral reform and charity, in particular, was an institutional one: members of the middle classes were more frequently found on the boards or organizing committees of voluntary associations than in the reform schools, orphanages, or poor houses themselves. Partly a function of realpolitik which taught them that altering politics, lobbying for new legislation, and raising funds were ultimately more effective than providing hands-on individual relief,[29] their removal from the poverty and alleged depravity of the lower classes had a purifying effect as well. It kept the masses and their ignorant, and possibly evil, ways at a safe, noninfectious, distance. In addition, institutionalization allowed the middle classes to reassert their class hegemony over the distribution of charity through group or class participation. As individuals, acting singly, members of the middle classes could never achieve class cohesion, but through the medium of membership in large organizations, admission into which, as Stuart Blumin confirms,[30] was an important aspect of their class identity and affinity, they could control the class character of their efforts.

The growing trend toward the institutionalization of charity was of signal importance in Crane's writings. Many of his stories depict the displacement of individual actions and the eventual disempowerment of individual agents by professional benefactors. In "When a Man Falls, a Crowd Gathers," and "When Everyone is Panic-Stricken," to name just two stories, he concerns himself with the strangely disaffected nature of urban bystanders who would rather wait for professional help than offer aid themselves. In fact, in the late nineteenth century the institutionalization of charity went hand in hand with the trend in legal reform that relieved the law of its jurisdiction over acts of good Samaritanism and replaced bystanders with designated rescuers—police and fire officials, and other trained emergency professionals. In *The Monster*, institutionalization surfaces as a means of keeping the underclasses, in this case exemplified by Johnson, at a distance. When their arguments for "letting him die" fail to dissuade Trescott from helping him, the people of Whilomville propose another form of mediation, the option of letting others care for him. At first a private form of institutionalization is suggested. John Twelve, the local grocer and one of the richest men in town, suggests that Trescott allow Johnson to live by himself, out of sight, with an occasional attendant, " '. . . I have a little no-good farm up beyond Clarence Mountain that I was going to give to Henry,' cried Twelve, aggrieved. 'And if you—and if you—if you—through your house burning down, or anything—why all the boys were prepared to take him right off your hands, and—and—' " (474). When this appeal fails, however, a stronger measure is proposed. "Suddenly a man stirred on his chair. 'Well, then, a public institution—' he began" (474), but before he can finish his sentence, Trescott dismisses the suggestion out of hand. Acknowledging the need for institutionalization generally, Trescott refuses to support it personally. " 'No,' said Trescott; 'public institutions are all very good, but [Johnson] is not going to one' " (474). In refusing to send Johnson away, Trescott not only refuses to shift the burden of his responsibility to a distant agency, but insists on keeping Johnson around—in a shed in his own backyard, as it turns out—as a constant reminder to the people in Whilomville of the underclasses' threat to their own social superiority.

Given its potential for threatening the ostensible integrity of the middle classes, it will come as no surprise that the subject of cross-class good Samaritanism also surfaces in the work of the writer most completely identified in the nineteenth century (by himself and by others) as middle class, namely, William Dean Howells. While the subject is not emphasized in any one novel, it does make an important appearance toward the end of *A Hazard of New Fortunes* (1890) which is, like so much of Howells's work, concerned with questions of blame, responsibility, and risk in general.[31] This novel which takes as its subject the creation of a new literary magazine revolves around the fortunes of several different middle-class characters, one of whom, Conrad Dryfoos, struggles more than any other with his status as a member of a middle-class literary elite. Conrad, whose father is the financial backer of the magazine and who represents some of the best and worst of the newly monied middle class (he made his fortune as a farmer who found natural gas on his land), is an ethereal, idealistic type who is very obviously bothered by his father's acquisitive mores. Rather than follow in his father's footsteps, then, Conrad hopes to become a minister to those less fortunate than he. Although he has consented for the time being to serve as an editor at the magazine in order to placate his father's ambitions for him, he spends most of his spare time in New York's soup kitchens and streets ministering to the needy. In the novel's climactic scene, in fact, Conrad wanders unthinkingly toward the working-class district and finds himself in the thick of a violent struggle between a group of striking streetcar workers and an increasingly brutal police force.

Motivated in part by his growing love for a like-minded woman who has recently enjoined him to take action in the strike and in part by his long-term sympathy for the underdog, Conrad decides to stop the violence—to act, in short, as a good Samaritan. But before he can do anything, he notices Lindau, an old German socialist who has done occasional translations for the magazine and who at that very moment is in the process of being pummeled by a policeman's club. Howells writes: "He [Conrad] was going to say something to the policeman, 'Don't strike him! He's an old soldier! Don't you see that he had no hand!' but he could not speak, he could not move his tongue."[32] Shots are heard in the crowd and just at that moment, the novel's protagonist and the magazine's editor-in-chief, Basil March, alights from a carriage to see Conrad fall forward, "pierced through the heart by that shot fired from the car" (384). Indeed, it is through March's assessment of Conrad's death—"'I fancy life was an awful thing to Conrad Dryfoos,'" he remarks (391)—that we come to see the futility of Conrad's direct efforts to bridge the classes. For even though Conrad's death ultimately makes his father more sympathetic to the needs of the working classes, it does nothing to ameliorate the plight of the workers; and his self-sacrifice strongly suggests that unmediated, noninstitutional attempts by the middle classes to offer aid to the working classes will, like Trescott's offer to aid Henry Johnson, continue to be censured by designated protectors of the middle classes, like judges or, in this case, the police.

But the aversion to direct intervention by the middle classes in the lives of the working classes was most visible not in street riots such as that depicted in Howells's novel but in the workplace itself where such aid was less dramatically but more regularly required. In fact, it was in the workplace where most cases of good Samaritanism arose, and where they went from being problems between strangers to being problems between employees and employers. Already heavily contested in the battleground between negligence and strict liability, the responsibilities of employers continued to be limited by the law of the good Samaritan, as the *Buch* case reveals. Indeed, the law's ostensibly neutral stance with respect to rescues was adopted in conscious recognition of the fact that while the middle classes were not in need of frequent rescue, the working classes were.

The lack of obligation on the part of the typical employer is graphically and tragically dramatized in two works by Elizabeth Stuart Phelps, one of several women novelists who were concerned with the question of industrial conditions and industrial accidents.[33] In her novel, *The Silent Partner* (1871),[34] Phelps depicts the courageous efforts of a woman who inherits part of a cotton mill from her father to be more than simply a silent partner who collects dividends, that is, to help the poorly paid and educated workers gain some degree of independence so that they are no longer at the mercy of unhealthy working environments and of the all too frequent industrial accidents that maim and kill them. The novel is studded with such accidents and takes care to depict the disastrous consequences the loss of a family member and his or her wages could have on a working-class family. But it focuses primarily on one such story, a story of two girls orphaned by the factory system: the young and stalwart mill worker, Sip Garth, and her sister Catty, who is blinded from an early age as a result of rubbing her fingers, which were diseased from picking wool, into her eyes. With the exception of Perley Kelso, the silent partner of the title, there is no one to care for or militate on behalf of these girls.

But the Phelps story that more perfectly captures the neglect suffered by factory workers in the context of an accident is the little known but powerfully elegiac "The Tenth of January" (1868), a short story about a young mill worker in Lawrence, Massachusetts, who dies in a factory fire. Asenath Martyn is a good-hearted and contemplative girl who lives with her elderly father and a boarder named Dick with whom she has fallen in love. But while Dick is kind to her and has even promised to marry her, Asenath, whose mouth is scarred and whose face is sickly, knows he is really drawn to another, a young, healthy mill worker named Del. Thus, the stage is set for Asenath's sacrifice in the factory fire as she offers to let Del escape before her, falling victim herself to the flames. But if the love plot compels Asenath's martyrdom, the narrative as a whole tells another story, a story of a life wasted as a result of grossly negligent error. For the building in which Asenath dies has, as Phelps emphasizes, been poorly designed, and it was just a matter of time before it was fated to collapse and kill dozens if not hundreds of workers. "Years before," she writes, "an unknown workman in South Boston, casting an iron pillar upon its core, had suffered it to 'float' a little, a very little more, till the thin, unequal side cooled to the measure of an eighth of an inch."[35] But where another author might have been content to attribute responsibility for this error to the "unknown workman," Phelps makes it clear that others in positions of more authority were in the know and that the error was the fault of a careless and invisible management. "Who shall say," she writes, "what it [the building collapse] was to the seven hundred and fifty souls who were buried in the ruins? . . . What to that architect and engineer who, when the fatal pillars were first delivered to them for inspection, had found one broken under their eyes, yet accepted the contract, and built with them a mill whose thin walls and wide, unsupported stretches might have tottered over massive columns and on flawless ore" (342). Nor does Phelps let the negligence of the management escape notice during the torturous operation to rescue the injured workers which is conceived and executed entirely by good Samaritans. A management that would have been both equipped and trained to handle such an emergency is nowhere in sight and the rescue effort, as a result, comes to an end when a volunteer carelessly drops a lantern and ignites the ruins in which Asenath ultimately dies.

But if the managers and employers who were responsible for the accident were conveniently absent during the rescue operation Phelps depicts, they were in many other cases present but officially relieved of any obligation to come to their employees' aid through the operation of two legal doctrines that worked in conjunction with negligence; products of the antebellum period,[36] as we saw in the Introduction, and contemporaneous with the earliest expressions of the modern concept of negligence, the "fellow-servant rule" and the doctrine of "the assumption of risk" continued throughout the postbellum period to eliminate any residual notion that middle-class employers had a special obligation to rescue employees, and yet to reinforce the existing, if unstated, assumption that working-class employees were nonreciprocally and inequitably bound to rescue them. By redesignating as voluntary the risks that accompanied even the riskiest of jobs and in opening up countless new possibilities for expanding the liability of employees and limiting that of employers,[37] the doctrine of the assumption of risk had particular relevance for injuries incurred in the context of work-related rescues. The accidents occasioned by machine malfunctions, which were increasingly common as machines became more complex and safety measures failed to keep up with them, led to countless on-the-job rescues. Regardless of the fact that they were often forbidden to do so, moreover, workers were increasingly impelled, for reasons of efficiency, to make their own mechanical repairs, or to help their fellow workers make them, rather than operate faulty equipment or wait for the breakdown to be acknowledged and fixed by management. Indeed, the incidence of accidents that followed in the wake of this practical imperative receives special attention in Marx's critique of factory labor in *Capital*. Quoting a factory inspection report, Marx writes, "It is . . . the constant practice . . . that the workpeople do, unreproved, pick out waste, wipe rollers and wheels, &c., while their frames are in motion. Thus from this cause only, 906 accidents have occurred during the six months."[38] But the courts held that employees who came to the aid of their fellow workers, employers, or employers' machines, even at some risk to themselves, did so voluntarily and thus abrogated the duty that might otherwise inhere in their relationship.

It was just such a practice that came to interest Willa Cather, an author noted for her concern with farm employment but concerned with urban industry as well. In particular, in her story "Behind the Singer Tower" (1912), Cather gives voice to the tragic loss of lives in the construction industry and to the negligence of an increasingly corrupt and arrogant management. In an almost eery echo of Phelps's story about the burning of the mill in Massachusetts, Cather's story revolves around the collapse and burning of the Hotel Mont Blanc in New York. Told from the perspective of a famous engineer who chose to begin his apprenticeship by helping to dig this building's foundation, it details the pitiful journey of a young Italian immigrant, Caesarino, who moves to New York to support his mother and brother who remain on the small Italian island of Ischia. Despite protestations from the young engineer, the builder, Stanley Merryweather, refuses to pay for new cabling for the building, and the structure eventually collapses, crushing Caesarino and countless others. " 'One of his maxims was that men are cheaper than machinery,' " the narrator says of Merryweather. " 'He smashed up a lot of hands, but he always got out under the fellow-servant act. 'Never been caught yet, huh?' he used to say with his pleasant, confiding wink.' "[39] The callousness of Merryweather's response and of his financial calculus only begins to tell how profitable the fellow-servant act was for employers even if, like Merryweather, they finally had to replace the old, faulty machinery with new equipment. " 'Well, I guess you've got your new cabling out of me now, huh Freddy?' " Merryweather says to the narrator on witnessing the accident and toting up his financial losses. " 'That wasn't so worse,' " he concludes (289).

Case after case revealed the unequal burden placed on the employee by the legal concept of voluntariness. In *Sann v. H.W. Johns Mfg. Co.* (1897), for instance, a workman who was rescuing a fellow employee from the shaft of a felt-washing machine was caught by the belt of the machine and fatally injured. Despite the fact that the belt itself was defective (it was not in compliance with the Factory Law of 1890), the court held that the master was not liable for the act because it was "voluntary."[40] Similarly, in the case of *Allen v. Hixson* (1900), a laundry worker who was helping her supervisor search for a hidden defect in her folding machine, got her hand stuck between two of the machine's rollers for half an hour. The court absolved the laundry of any responsibility for both the injury and the failure to assist on the grounds that the employee was a "volunteer" who was "acting entirely outside the scope of her employment."[41] In *Saylor v. Parsons* (1904), moreover, a case whose facts most closely resemble those of Crane's *The Monster*, an apprentice mason was injured while attempting to save his employer from the danger of a falling wall. Here the court held that the employer owed no duty to the employee who saved him no matter how dangerous or heroic his actions, for in endangering himself the employer could not have "anticipated that some one would, upon discovering his danger, undertake to shield him from harm."[42] By stressing the voluntary nature of the "servant's" act, moreover, the law maintained the fiction of its even-handedness toward both employer and employee, even as it acknowledged that the employee might be motivated to rescue his employer (or employer's property), in Holmes's words, by "fear of losing his place."[43]

The language of the voluntary assumption cases as a whole, and of *Saylor* in particular, reveals how far the law was willing to go to limit entrepreneurial liability, for in failing to compensate workers for injuries incurred in the course of a rescue, the courts failed to protect the best employees—employees whose devotion and vigilance not only made them exemplary workers, but drove them to acts of good Samaritanism as well. But the courts were just as unforgiving of workers whose performance fell below par, or whose special needs, had they been acknowledged, would have reinforced the employer's responsibility for them. It is in this light that race becomes an especially important factor in the analysis of the law on good Samaritanism, for workers distinguished by race or ethnicity from the predominantly white workforce were also more likely to belong to one or the other of these extremes: workers who because of their legacy of subordination were more likely to feel the obligation to rescue, or workers who because of their inherent or imagined limitations were more often in need of being rescued.

At times even during slavery, the courts were able to acknowledge and articulate the difference race made in the employment context, and this had an impact on the application of the fellow-servant rule to slaves. Although they acknowledged the logic of Justice Shaw's *Farwell* decision, many southern courts (e.g., in Georgia and Florida) failed to enforce the fellow-servant rule in slave cases because they could not justify in the case of the slave the concept of voluntariness that determined the average worker's fate. In *Scudder v. Woodbridge* (1846), for example, the judge was quite explicit about why the fellow-servant rule was inapplicable to slaves. In this case, a slave, hired by Scudder as a carpenter on a riverboat, was killed by a waterwheel. The jury found Scudder's employee negligent and awarded Woodbridge $500. The judge wrote:

> But interest to the owner, and humanity to the slave, forbid its [the fellow-servant rule's] application to any other than free white agents. Indeed, it cannot be extended to slaves, *ex necessitate rei*. The argument upon which the decisions referred to mainly rest [*sic*] is, that public policy requires that each person engaged on steamboats and railroads should see that every other person employed in the same service does his duty with the utmost care

and vigilance. . . . Can any of these considerations apply to slaves? They
dare not interfere with the business of others. They would be instantly chas-
tised for their impertinence. . . .

. . . [N]either can they exercise the salutary discretion, left to free white
agents, of quitting the employment when matters are mismanaged, or por-
tend evil. Whether engaged as carpenters, bricklayers or blacksmiths . . .
they have nothing to do but silently serve out their appointed time, and take
their lot in the meanwhile in submitting to whatever risks and dangers are
incident to the employment.[44]

For the slave, then, according to the judge in *Scudder*, both the contractual and tort basis of the fellow-servant rule are inapplicable because the
slave is neither free to contract for and assume the risks of his labor nor
in a position to compensate as a fellow servant for the risks he might
inflict on another. Of course, the restrictions the judge in *Scudder* recognizes as relevant to the slave or hired slave pertain specifically to the antebellum period, but his remarks anticipate the problems of the racialized
servant after slavery as well who was, as Crane's Johnson reveals, the
perennial victim and rescuer.

RACIAL IMPLICATIONS OF THE LAW

The law's indifference to workers who were less rather than more competent at their jobs is best documented in the countless cases involving
children in the workplace. Typically, the judges in these cases denied
even the most obvious of differences between children and adults, including the fact that children were often too uncoordinated, too imprudent,
or simply too short to perform the tasks assigned to them safely. Figure
3 shows two spindle boys in a Georgia cotton mill who are too short
to operate their machines without standing on part of the apparatus. In
the cases in which children were injured and employers called to task
for failing to rescue them or warn them of dangers, the courts insisted
that the sensibilities of children were no different from those of adults.
In *Buckley v. The Gutta Percha and Rubber Manufacturing Co.*,[45] for
example,[46] the court reasoned that a twelve-year-old was no less capable
of assessing the danger of getting his hand caught in a machine he
had never used than were older, more experienced workers. "It is idle,"
the court wrote, "to say that this plaintiff did not know as well as a
grown man that if he placed his fingers between the revolving cogs he
would be injured" (848). "It might as well be required," the court added,
"to warn a boy twelve years old, who was working about boiling water

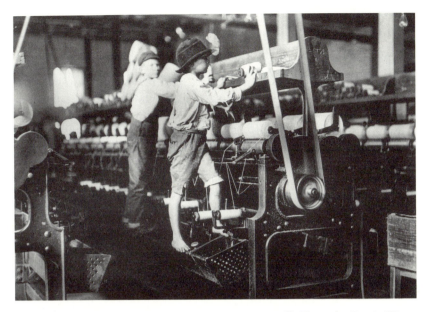

Fig. 3. Spindle boys working in a Georgia cotton mill. Photo by Lewis Hines, undated. UPI/Corbis-Bettmann.

or a hot fire, not to put his hand into the water or the fire" (849). But if, for the purposes of relieving employers of responsibility, the courts were careful to attribute to children more developed sensibilities than they actually had, they were no less careful to avoid giving the impression that children were as skilled as their older counterparts. In this way, the law legitimated the common and insidious practice of paying children less (and often working them harder) than adult employees. This two-pronged strategy, which simultaneously denied and reinforced the incompetence of children in the workplace, is reiterated in the law of the good Samaritan, which reinforced the characterization of the workplace as a potential site of rescue, while allowing employers to divorce themselves from the paternalistic ideology—the association of employer with benevolent father and good Samaritan—that characterization had once served.

Of course, the legal strategy in cases involving children would have had only limited relevance to the good Samaritan situation in general had it been confined to children alone. But the strategy was commonly invoked in cases involving other workers whose competence was called into question—workers, that is, from other marginalized groups. Of these groups, immigrants figured most frequently since by the end of the nineteenth century foreign-born workers had flooded the northern industrial workplace. Like the cases involving children, the cases dealing with immigrant workers and their injuries suggest how reluctant the courts were, on the one hand, to acknowledge their special limitations—their inability to speak English and their lack of familiarity with American customs—and yet how quick they were, on the other hand, to undervalue them precisely because of these same limitations.[47] The *Buch* case, where the victim was both a child and a non-English-speaking immigrant, reveals just how insensitive the courts could be in this regard. "The only negligence charged," the *Buch* court wrote, "is that inasmuch as they [the employers] could not make the plaintiff understand a command to leave the premises, and ought to have known that they could not, they did not forcibly remove him" (810). Needless to say, for the court the "negligence charged" was unconvincing, for an employer who had no obligation to warn a child of danger in the first place could hardly be compelled to warn that child in a language he could understand.

But if immigrants were subject to a legal indifference that heightened their status as victims in the workplace, black Americans were even more seriously disadvantaged in this regard. Of course, the plight of blacks in the industrial workplace is not as visible in the legal cases on accidents as that of immigrants since blacks themselves did not enter the northern workforce in significant numbers until the beginning of the twentieth century. Moreover, unlike some immigrants and children, their limitations as workers was more imagined than real. But their absence as accident victims in the legal cases is in no way indicative of their absence from that role in the culture at large. In fact, in the nineteenth century African-Americans were cast in the role of accident victims par excellence. They were repeatedly characterized as accident-prone if not in the legal cases, then in countless other cultural documents. Most conspicuous were the images of blacks in literature[48] where they were stereotyped as lazy and incompetent, giving play to the popular image of the "low-comic Negro." More revealing, however, were the widespread images of blacks in the blackface minstrel shows, where they were vividly portrayed in the context not of industrial but of urban accidents.

Most typically, the urban black of the minstrel show was either a dandy, a trickster, or a criminal. But the culture's discomfort with the postbellum influx of blacks into the city was also played out in terms of the black man's physical incompetence and accident-proneness. Most commonly, blacks were seen as befuddled by technology, taxed by the logic of machines, and confused by urban congestion in general. Many of the most frequently staged farces and burlesques—with names like "The Black Chemist," "Our Colored Conductors," and "Rival Barber Shops"—included images of blacks as bewildered users, consumers, and purveyors of urban technologies and commodities. Others specifically highlighted the consequences of blacks' physical incompetence, like "Black Blunders" by George Coes.[49] According to Robert Toll, a minstrel historian, blacks were often seen as accident victims, "getting run down by trolleys, [and] shocked by electric batteries. . . ." (69). Many scholars have argued that blackface minstrelsy served to ease tensions both within the working classes and between the races.[50] But Toll takes this argument one step farther by explaining that the minstrel shows, especially those having to do with accidents, served to teach whites, many of whom were confronting city life for the first time themselves, about the perils of urban technology. Toll writes: "Using the incompetence and stupidity of these laughable imbeciles, who had to learn everything the hard way, as models of how *not* to do things, minstrels explained new inventions, current events, scientific principles, and city life."[51] Echoing Toll' s assessment is George Lipsitz who argues that the minstrel show Negro presented white society with a representation of "the natural self at odds with the normative self of industrial culture."[52]

Toll's argument about the function of black accidents in the minstrel shows is also pertinent to the good Samaritan law. For even though it made no explicit mention of African-Americans, the law of the good Samaritan helped significantly to designate them as a class of expendable accident victims—a class defined by its existing marginality and by its actual or imagined incompetence, whose purpose was to have the accidents and bear the injuries the middle classes would then be more fit to avoid. This phenomenon helps to explain the peculiar nature of the discrimination aimed at Henry Johnson in *The Monster*. For while Johnson is the subject of some derision from the white community in Whilomville before the accident, he is heroized immediately afterward, elevated in public opinion to the level of a saint. In the local paper, which prematurely announces the death of Henry Johnson in the days immediately following the accident, "[t]here was also an editorial built from all the best words in the vocabulary of the staff. The town halted in its accustomed road of thought, and turned a reverent attention to the memory of this hostler" (446). Although it is admittedly more dramatic and more laudatory of Johnson's action than any legal case would be, this scene shows how welcome Johnson's rescue is. When the news that Johnson has survived and that Trescott has pledged to keep him alive emerges, however, Johnson goes from being a martyr to an outcast overnight. Of course, in insisting on his rescue, Trescott does nothing to change the nature of Johnson's heroism. But he interferes with the *utility* of Johnson's accident—the significance to the community of having a black man, not a white man, experience the degree of risk and injury required by the rescue at hand.

BLACK AND WHITE RESCUE IN *THE MONSTER*

The adversity suffered by black victims was compounded by their legacy of subservience, for not only were they designated as society's all-purpose accident victims, they were also society's *de facto* rescuers. Like so many white workers, the black worker was typically motivated to fix machines or otherwise aid employers not for altruistic reasons but, to reiterate Holmes's observation, "for fear of losing his place." Making their situation even worse than that of whites was the fact that blacks had been conditioned by more than a century of slavery to see whites as their masters—their financial, moral, and emotional superiors. Indeed, although there were exceptions to the rule, the image of the self-sacrificing slave predominates in the antebellum literature about slavery. There is, of course, no more widely discussed example than Harriet Beecher Stowe's portrait of the infamously obsequious Uncle Tom in *Uncle Tom's Cabin*.[53] A work from the postwar period, *The Monster* revisits the effects of this subservience in terms of its legacy to more modern blacks like Henry Johnson. In the critical scene of the rescue, as Johnson fights his way through Dr. Trescott's laboratory where he is ultimately overcome by smoke and burning chemicals, the specter of slavery looms before him. "He was submitting," Crane writes, "submitting because of his fathers, bending his mind in a most perfect slavery to this conflagration" (441).

For Johnson, however, the issue of subordination is even more complicated than it was for his "fathers," for Johnson, as his actions suggest, is both free and enslaved at the same time. Thus, we might think of the antebellum literary representation of slavery, and of the Uncle Toms with which it abounds, as establishing a kind of literary prehistory for *The Monster* which takes up the issue of black subservience at the point where slavery leaves off. In focusing specifically on the phenomenon of postwar subservience, Crane re-creates the tension—the pull toward freedom and then back toward slavery—that so many blacks experienced in this period. We get one glimpse of this tension in an exchange between another of the story's black characters, Alek Williams, and Judge Hagenthorpe. Williams, who has agreed to become Johnson's caretaker for a time, finds the job more taxing than he had originally expected. In asking Hagenthorpe for a raise from five to six dollars a week, Williams is, on the one hand, represented as an equal bargaining partner whose labor is measured and repaid in wages. Yet the more Hagenthorpe resists his request—reminding him that compared with what he used to earn, his current salary allows him and his family to "live like millionaires" (451)—the more a race-based sense of incumbency prevails. "'Yes I know,

Jedge,' said the negro wagging his head in a puzzled manner. 'Tain't like as if I didn't 'preciate what the docteh done, but—but—well, yeh see, jedge,' he added, gaining a new impetus, 'it's hard wuk. This ol' man nev' did wuk so hard. Lode, no' " (451). Thus, while Williams manages to persuade the judge that he deserves an extra dollar a week, he has been reduced to begging and expressing his gratitude for "what the docteh done" as if he were a slave.

If Williams's efforts to negotiate a contract with Judge Hagenthorpe reveal some of the hypocrisy of the post-Reconstructionist implementation of equality between the races, Johnson's action as a good Samaritan brings it further to the fore. In releasing *everyone* from the obligation to rescue, the law of the good Samaritan appeared, in theory, to benefit blacks as well as whites: technically, the law was colorblind. But in practice, as we have seen, the law only more starkly highlighted the racially inflected nonreciprocity of the obligation it aimed to obliterate: blacks remained unofficially bound by the obligations they incurred under slavery, while whites remained officially unencumbered. The ambiguity of Johnson's position as both free and bound is perfectly rendered in the description of the moments leading up to the rescue itself and in Crane's representation of his divided motivations for it. On the one hand, Crane portrays Johnson as having come to the decision to rescue Jimmie freely, without any external prodding or constraint. He responds to the news that the house is on fire and the boy still trapped inside without a moment's hesitation. Moreover, even if a sense of responsibility for the boy impels his actions, it is, some have argued, a responsibility that he has shouldered voluntarily. In support of this interpretation, the Crane critic, David Halliburton, reads Johnson as a father surrogate, noting that Trescott himself is tending to business rather than to his family when the fire breaks out. "In the absence of the father," Halliburton writes, "[Johnson] does what the father would do. Rescue here constitutes . . . an image for authority."[54]

The first hint that Johnson's act is not completely self-motivated, however, and that his assumption of "authority" has all of the drawbacks of fatherhood and none of its rewards, is in the sharp demands made on him by Mrs. Trescott to save her son. In fact, in beseeching Johnson to act in her husband's place during the emergency, Mrs. Trescott essentially demands that Johnson risk his life for Jimmie as, presumably, only a parent would. "At the head of the stairs Mrs. Trescott was waving her arms as if they were two reeds. 'Jimmie! Save Jimmie!' she screamed in Henry's face." (440). Having just learned that her house is on fire and her son trapped inside, Mrs. Trescott's appeal is clearly uttered in panic; but her panic, conspicuously, does not compel her to make a rescue attempt herself, and her words have the ring more of an order than of a plea.

In addition to Mrs. Trescott's assumptions about the extent of Johnson's obligation to her, Johnson must cope with the burden of obligation imposed on him by Dr. Trescott. Throughout *The Monster*, Crane suggests that life in the Trescott household is authoritarian, and that Trescott himself is a harsh taskmaster who demands order and obedience in every aspect of his life. Even in his professional capacity, it seems, Trescott demands and to a large extent achieves a measure of control over a subject as unruly and untameable as the human body. After assessing the effect of his cure on one patient—a particularly difficult case—Trescott feels a sense of relief that is indistinguishable from a sense of mastery. Trescott leaves the patient's home, Crane writes, "glad that his last case was now in complete obedience to him, like a wild animal that he had subdued" (443). But the doctor is no less insistent on order in the domestic sphere. In the opening scene of the novella, Trescott is described as not mowing the lawn but as "shaving . . . [it] as if it were a priest's chin" (430). When Jimmie who is pretending to drive a train on the lawn accidentally destroys one of the doctor's peonies with the wheel of his cart, Trescott issues a stern rebuke. As his servant and chauffeur, of course, Johnson is no less subject to the doctor's discipline, making him an especially sympathetic partner for the boy. "Whenever Jimmie became the victim of [his father's wrath] . . . he went to the stable to solace himself with Henry's crimes," Crane writes. "Henry, with the elasticity of his race, could usually provide a sin to place himself on a footing with the disgraced one" (431). In fact, Johnson, we learn, is like Jimmie in many ways, even to the point of bearing a twin-like resemblance to him: "In regard to almost everything in life they seemed to have minds precisely alike," Crane writes. Even as he takes on "an image for authority," then, Johnson is infantilized, reduced through his position and his race to the status of a young and helpless boy.

It is relevant to the nature of Johnson's infantilization that the claims on him are made by a young boy, that is, someone of relatively infantile stature. But *The Monster* suggests that the claimant's youth alone is not the central factor in the older man's debasement. On the contrary, the same kind of infantilization threatens Dr. Trescott as soon as he expresses an interest in returning the favor Johnson performs. Indeed, for the Whilomville community, the infantilization seems linked to the act of rescue itself as if the expression of sympathy or concern for another that it implies is by definition degrading. Any indication of active or lasting sympathy on Trescott's part is thus quickly and strongly countered. For daring to express a sense of obligation to Johnson and for daring to act on it, Trescott is punished severely. For harboring and preserving the unsightly Johnson and for setting a precedent that might infantilize himself and other whites and expand their limited liability, Trescott risks not his life, like Johnson, but his livelihood. After Johnson is moved into Trescott's home, the people of Whilomville refuse the doctor's medical care, and ostracize him professionally. John Twelve, the wholesale grocer, emphasizes the financial cost of the doctor's good Samaritanism. " 'You have changed from being the leading doctor in town to about the last one,' " he explains. " 'We want you to get out of this trouble and strike your old gait again. You are simply killing your practice through your infernal pigheadedness' " (473). Although Twelve admires Trescott for his effort, he admits his admiration is not enough to " 'change the minds of all those ninnies' " in town who disagree. Prominent among these "ninnies" is Martha Goodwin, a woman who devotes her days to gossip and voyeurism. " 'Serves him right if he was to lose all his patients,' she said suddenly, in blood thirsty tones" (464). For Twelve, then, as his name implies,[55] Trescott's problem is one of simple arithmetic. The sheer number of people who oppose him makes Trescott's action insupportable.

The calculus that is central to Twelve's argument—of the many against the one—finally convinces Trescott that he should do as Twelve suggests. In a moment that is characteristic of Crane's interest in failures, inactions, and absences, Trescott recognizes the pain he himself is inflicting in the scene in which his wife receives only one guest at a tea party to which she had invited fifteen. "As he sat holding [his wife's] head on his shoulder," Crane writes, "Trescott found himself occasionally trying to count the cups. There were fifteen of them" (475). Although the mechanical and repetitive nature of the counting may be comforting to Trescott, the counting also demonstrates the operation of a legally binding calculus. The fifteen teacups represent not only the many missing guests, but the many people who have made Trescott's life unbearable. At this point Trescott's options are limited: he can either persevere in his devotion to Johnson and continue to lose his footing in the community or abandon his efforts to care for Johnson and be welcomed back into the middle-class fold.

It is, as much Crane criticism has shown, a subject on which reasonable people can disagree. David Halliburton, for example, believes that ". . . there is no reason to think the doctor will give up the arrangement,"[56] and thus sees Trescott as something of a martyr to the cause of charity. My reading of this scene, however, and of *The Monster* as a whole suggests otherwise: that the missing guests are a final and conclusive reminder that Trescott's act of good Samaritanism is not viable;[57] it has repercussions for his family—in the absence of friends, Trescott's wife cannot be happy and in the absence of business, Trescott cannot live—and for the entire community. The more important point, however, is that Trescott's act, or rather failure to act, is mandated by the law for while the decision to care for Johnson remains a moral one in the eyes of the law—a "matter of conscience," as Hagenthorpe refers to it derisively (449)—the decision to discontinue caring is a legal one, compelled not by edict as much as by the law's silence and aversion to morality. In failing to attend Mrs. Trescott's tea party, the citizens of Whilomville not only censure the Trescotts silently but validate a law whose silence and apparent neutrality continued to induce the black good Samaritan to rescue whites, while inducing the (potential) white good Samaritan, like the priest and Levite before him, to "pass by on the other side."

CHARLES CHESNUTT AND THE RACIALIZED GOOD SAMARITAN

If the final tension in *The Monster* suggests that the story is ultimately more concerned with the white man's decision to act as a good Samaritan than with that of the black, it was, importantly, not the only view of cross-racial rescue available. Indeed, the work of the African-American author and lawyer Charles Waddell Chesnutt, who fashioned many of his narratives around the literary trope of cross-racial rescue, reveals the effects of the culture's double standard on good Samaritanism from a more explicitly black perspective. In his novel, *The Marrow of Tradition* (1901), for example, the rendering of the racial inequality inherent in the law of the good Samaritan is, in many ways, even starker than Crane's because of the socioeconomic, educational, and professional equality between many of his black and white characters.

Although it does not involve an accident, *The Marrow of Tradition* registers the inequality and nonreciprocity of black-white relations in a narrative that involves the rescue of a white boy by a black man and that has striking similarities to Crane's account. In this case, however, the black man in question is not a chauffeur but a doctor and the rescue, a medical intervention, is one he is not eager but reluctant to perform. Based on the Wilmington, North Carolina, race riot of 1898, the novel tells the story of Major Carteret, an upstanding white newspaper editor in the fictional town of Wellington who although ordinarily law-abiding harbors a racial prejudice that eventually gets out of hand. A creature of the old South and its peculiar institutions, Carteret is not hostile to the residual class of blacks who occupy many of the same subservient positions that they did under slavery but only to the "new Negro" or middle-class black whose accomplishments, he fears, will put an end to the social and political hierarchy as he knows it. In the novel, the preeminent example of this class is Dr. William Miller, whose wife, it turns out, is the octoroon half-sister of Major Carteret's wife, and who is himself an extremely successful doctor with a medical training equal to if not surpassing that of the other white doctors in town. Unlike Henry Johnson, in other words, Dr. Miller is a black whose middle-class status gives him the appearance of being able to choose when, where, and whom to rescue, all of which complicates his role as a good Samaritan.

Perhaps even more important is the complication provided by the charged history between Miller and Carteret: Miller is the direct and recent recipient of race-based injuries inflicted by the very man whose son he is asked to save. Thus, in the novel's moving final chapter, as Carteret's son lies dying from the croup, with no way to survive but through the medical aid provided by Miller (the white doctors have either died in the riot or are out of town), Miller contemplates the injuries he has suffered at Carteret's hand. To begin with, when months earlier Miller had been asked by an esteemed white physician to help in a delicate operation on Carteret's boy, Carteret refused to let him enter his house by the front door, much less attend to his son's injury. More significant is the fact that Carteret himself, in masterminding the race riot, incited the violence that led to the death of Miller's young son.

Not surprisingly, the question of reciprocity evoked by the good Samaritan paradigm is at its clearest in this chapter, for while Carteret has in effect killed Miller's son, Miller is asked to save Carteret's. Of course, as a doctor, it could be argued that Miller is under a professional obligation to help Carteret's son. Indeed, it is Miller's sense of professional ethics on which Carteret relies when he appeals to Miller to help him. "Nevertheless, he could hardly refuse a professional call," Carteret thinks, "—professional ethics would require him to respond."[58] But if Miller contemplates his professional duty, he does so only to dismiss it as irrelevant. Nor were the courts inclined to enforce it since they had in similar situations ruled that doctors, like everyone else, were under no special obligation to be good Samaritans, even if that meant failing to tend to the illnesses of patients they had long served. For example, despite the fact that "no other doctor was procurable in time, and that decedent relied on him for attention," the court in *Hurley v. Eddingfield* (1901) wrote, the doctor had no obligation to render medical assistance. The practice of medicine "is a preventive, not a compulsive, measure," the court reasoned, and "the analogies drawn from the obligations to the public on the part of innkeepers, common carriers, and the like, are beside the mark."[59]

But if professional ethics do not compel Miller to help Carteret, his sense of human kindness and, more important, of a race-inspired resignation, finally does. Having reluctantly accepted the logic of Miller's refusal (Carteret's own impending personal tragedy seems to have opened his eyes to the suffering of blacks as a group), Carteret goes home empty-handed. His wife, however, returns to Miller's house to beg for her son's

life, willing to sacrifice her name and reputation in the bargain. When she
arrives, Miller turns the decision over to his own wife whose injuries at
the hands of Carteret's wife, her half-sister, are now foregrounded. For
some time, Miller's wife had tried to elicit from Mrs. Carteret an ac-
knowledgment of their relationship only to find herself openly scorned
and ignored. But even she seems to see the pointlessness of avenging her
son's death by sacrificing the life of another, and after refusing her sister's
apologies and rejecting her share of the family fortune—a fortune to
which she was legally entitled—she encourages her husband to save the
Carterets' boy. In severing ties to this distinguished white family, Miller's
wife seems to gain the moral high ground, but it is in reality a poor substitute for freedom. For as with Johnson, there is for Miller and his wife no
real option but to acquiesce—to rescue the sons not simply of white men
but of white supremacists who will almost certainly perpetuate a racist
society in the future.

In the end, then, although Chesnutt focuses more than Crane on the
intricacies of the black man's decision to rescue, Miller appears to make
no decision at all, but rather like Johnson, his social inferior, submits to
the demands of a dominant white society. Indeed, Miller often functions
as a spokesman for Chesnutt's melioristic approach to the race problem—an approach that urged reconciliation over conflict. Having been
forced to part company with Dr. Burns, for example, his white friend and
traveling companion (and the very doctor who asked him to assist in the
first of the operations on Carteret's son), by a law that required him to
ride in a separate, "colored" railway car, Miller strives to see the virtue in
his humiliation.

> His philosophy had become somewhat jaded on this journey, but he pulled
> it together for a final effort. Was it not, after all, a wise provision of nature
> that had given to a race, destined to a long servitude and a slow emergence
> therefrom, a cheerfulness of spirit which enabled them to catch pleasure on
> the wing, and endure with equanimity the ills that seemed inevitable? . . .
>
> "Blessed are the meek," quoted Miller at the end of these consoling reflec-
> tions, "for they shall inherit the earth." If this be true, the negro may yet
> come into his estate, for meekness seems to be set apart as his portion
> (61–62).

Of course, for Chesnutt, this posture of meekness is acceptable only insofar as it is distinguishable from the abject servitude of the slave. In fact, it
is of the utmost importance that Miller's acts and attitudes be seen as a
compromise between the other two models of black behavior that find
expression in the novel, that of the old blacks and that of the "new Ne-
groes." But despite Chesnutt's efforts to cast Miller's action as a dignified

compromise in this regard, it bespeaks an attitude of submission that prevailed even among that class of blacks that had achieved a degree of socioeconomic parity with the elite of white society.

A slightly different manifestation of socioeconomic parity between the races is undercut in another of Chesnutt's stories that deals with the legacy of slavery and its repercussions for the act of good Samaritanism. In the short story, "The Averted Strike," the black man who acts the part of the good Samaritan is a black mill hand whose value, ironically, is acknowledged by his white superior, the mill's owner and manager, but challenged by his white peers, the mill's predominantly white workforce. The story begins as the owner of the mill, a Mr. Strong, is told that his trusted white foreman of many years is resigning. Not long after, he receives a deputation from the mill hands asking that the man next in line to be foreman, a black man named Walker, be passed over in favor of a less qualified white man. Strong, a generally fair man who prefers Walker to any other for the job because of his experience and proven expertise, bridles at the workers' obvious racial prejudice.

> "Humph!" said Mr. Strong, "and what objection have you to Walker?"
> "Well sir" [began the leader of the workers' committee], "we're not used to working under niggers—perhaps I should say colored men—and we don't like it, and don't want to keep it up."
> "You've worked with Walker for several years," said Mr. Strong, "and no one has objected to him. He's the same color now that he has been all along."
> "Yes, sir," rejoined the spokesman, "and we haven't objected to working *with* him; what we don't want is to work under him."[60]

Although the language of the workers' spokesman is unambiguous—he doesn't mind being on a par with the black man but will not tolerate any sign of his own inferiority—it is in actuality a much more complicated matter. In stating their opposition to his promotion, in other words, the white workers deprive Walker of his status as their equal for it is a generally accepted rule among mill hands, at least the mill hands in this factory, that the foreman will be chosen from their midst based on seniority and a demonstration of the requisite skills without respect to color. In short, the question of Walker's potential superiority as a worker—a superiority that would be assumed in his promotion to foreman—is less important than and actively subordinated to the question of his equality with respect to race.

Walker, for whom race is immutable, is thus forced to prove an *equality* with his white peers through an act of non–race-based *superiority* and supererogation. The pattern is a familiar one for black good Samaritans and Chesnutt's story is no exception. Thus, soon after the delegation of white workers lodges its protest against Walker's promotion, a fire breaks out in the mill that allows for just such an opportunity. As it turns out, not only is the mill's main building at risk in the conflagration, but so too are Strong's daughter and daughter's friend who have coincidentally chosen this time to visit and tour the factory. The narrative emphasizes Strong's desperation and the apparent futility of rescue. "'Can nobody get them down?' cried Mr. Strong. 'I will give a thousand dollars, ten thousand dollars—anything—everything—to anyone who will save them.'" But every avenue of approach from within the burning building seems blocked and any attempt to reach the girls who are visible on the topmost floor of the building's tower seems impossible. Impossible that is until Walker appears with a ladder and a small coil of rope. Even as Walker enlists the aid of other bystanders to help him place the ladder against the building, however, they try to dissuade him, reiterating the implausibility of his success. "'You'll never get up, Walker,' they cried, wondering what he meant to do. 'The ladder doesn't reach within twenty feet of the roof'" (388). But Walker reassures them with a recital of his wall-climbing skills—skills, interestingly enough, that he says he acquired as a sailor where he, like the many common seamen pictured in the narratives of chapter 2, was ostensibly put in the position of effecting similar rescues.

Indeed, the parallels between the nautical stories cited in chapter 3 and "The Averted Strike" resonate even more loudly when we note that Walker himself equates his ultimate success in rescuing the girls not to any superior ability of his own but to his training and to his duty. "'I was in the Navy, sir,'" Walker says to Strong, "'any able seaman could do as well'" (389). This form of self-deprecation, moreover, grows more pronounced when Walker is faced with Strong's expression of gratitude and his efforts to reward him. "'I haven't done anything to deserve all this, sir. I only did my duty, and it was easy for me to do. You don't need to give me anything, sir'" (390). But Strong persists, and Walker eventually accepts his praise and gratitude at a dinner that he and his daughter give in his honor.

The full extent of Walker's "reward," however, makes a mockery of the term, for in recognition of his extraordinary heroism and self-sacrifice, he is the beneficiary of little more than the promotion he had earned in the course of his regular, nonheroic endeavors. As a token of his personal gratitude, of course, Strong does not forget to throw in an added bonus—five thousand dollars of the newly reorganized company's stock. Even in the face of this generosity, however, the reader is nevertheless struck by the relative paucity of the reward compared to Strong's initial promise of a "'thousand dollars, ten thousand dollars—anything—every-thing. . . .'" to the person who saved his daughter. But the irony of Strong's failure to make good on his promise to give "anything—every-thing," much less the full "ten thousand dollars" he had initially offered, to the black man who managed against all odds to rescue his daughter pales in comparison to the hypocritical recognition and reward bestowed on Walker by his white coworkers. For even if the white workers have changed their minds about Walker, their belated and opportunistic ap-preciation of him has a decidedly hollow ring. "'We realize that he saved your daughter's life,'" the spokesman of the workers' committee remarks to Strong, adding in an apparent after-thought the real reason the men now endorse Walker's promotion, "'and [he] probably saved our jobs'" (390). Indeed, Walker, the formerly snubbed African-American, is pro-moted because he has proven himself not just useful but indispensable to the mill's existence and to the workers' prosperity, achieving through the demonstration of his obvious superiority a much more coveted, although for that reason, supremely tenuous, equality.

But if "The Averted Strike" and *The Marrow of Tradition* reveal the way in which good Samaritanism came to haunt the lives of otherwise competent and highly skilled post-Reconstructionist blacks, at least one Chesnutt story addresses its effects on the lives of blacks truly left behind by the abolition of slavery—blacks, that is, who because of their age or inability to adapt to changing economic conditions could only legitimate their existence through an act of slave-like loyalty for which good Samar-itanism was the most widespread and acceptable substitute. Thus, in his novel, *The Colonel's Dream* (1905), Chesnutt demonstrates how an act of good Samaritanism provides an opportunity for a former slave to re-deem himself in the eyes of a white community that saw him as superflu-ous. The man in question is the old and feeble Peter who though he had once served a thriving French family in the southern town of Clarendon has since their deaths and the departure of the one remaining French heir, the eponymous colonel, fallen on hard times. Indeed, the novel begins in earnest as the colonel who decides to revisit his hometown (he takes a potentially prolonged vacation from his duties as a financier in New York) discovers that his old and trusted servant Peter is about to be ar-rested for vagrancy. The colonel, in the style of the more responsible slaveowners, not only takes Peter under his wing but puts his young son in his care. The purpose of this arrangement is ostensibly to provide a relatively comfortable retirement for the old man, but in reality it puts him in the position of the house slaves whose roles as guardians of their masters' children revealed not only the trust and high regard in which their white owners held them but also the absolute enormity of their responsibility. For in return for their role as confidant and caretaker of their young wards' well-being, the slave in this position was regularly required to sacrifice his or her own.

Indeed, it is a commonplace of many plantation and slave novels from the antebellum period to show house slaves not only adopting the goals and concerns of the slaveowner's family but functioning as surrogate parents for the white children in their care who were often wholly dependent on them for expressions of emotional or physical affection. This kind of surrogacy perfectly describes the relationship old Peter and the young French boy develop. For "Uncle Peter" not only becomes the boy's boon companion but is clearly on hand more often than his father to comfort him in his boyish sorrows and to give him sage advice. The intimacy breeds both knowledge and responsibility. So close in fact do the young French boy and Uncle Peter become that when the boy fails to respond to his call one day, Peter alone can divine his whereabouts. " 'I hyus the train comin,' " Peter tells the colonel. " 'I 'spec's he's gone up ter de railroad track.' "[61] And no sooner does he come into view of those tracks than he sees the boy huddled under the end of a flat car calling to a cat who had scurried beneath it. Perceiving at once that the engine with several other cars in tow is about to couple with the flat car which is at the other end of the track, Peter does what he can to alert the brakeman and engineer of the boy's existence. But the engine has already started steaming down the track and it is too late to make them stop it. Moving more quickly than any other bystander, with the quickness, in fact, of an animal protecting its young, Peter hurls himself between the cars to protect the boy who because of Peter's interference manages to live for several days but dies finally of irreparable internal injuries. Peter, on the other hand, dies instantaneously, in a blaze of glory that is as Chesnutt makes clear the result simultaneously of his extraordinary efforts as a good Samaritan and of his obligation to the boy. A verdict delivered by bystanders that renders the tragedy "an accident, pure and simple, which ordinary and reasonable prudence could not have foreseen" (259), emphasizes the uniqueness of Peter's prescience and intervention. And yet from the perspective of his vestigial place as Colonel French's manservant, and his son's personal slave, self-sacrifice begins to seem like the only opportunity Peter might have to lend meaning to an otherwise meaningless life. It is, after all, only because of such an act that the colonel can legitimately command that "every honour, every token of respect . . . be paid to his [Peter's] remains" (259).

That Peter's attempted rescue legitimates his existence only in death makes his good Samaritanism seem fatalistic. But the fatalism of Peter's good Samaritanism stems not only from the futility of his life as an exslave but also from the inexorability of the railroad as an agent of his demise. Indeed, Chesnutt seems to view the railroad accident, even more than other accidents, fatalistically—as unpreventable for both blacks and whites alike. In yet another of his stories about accidents, in fact, "Stryker's Waterloo," the fatalism of railroad accidents comes to the fore. In this story, a young entrepreneur by the name of Napoleon Stryker, who is given to concocting elaborate financial schemes on the off chance that he will strike it rich, is badly injured in a train wreck. Chesnutt documents his medical condition as the story begins: "[Stryker], he writes "was taken from the wreck to a hospital, where an examination showed that his skull was fractured. In addition to this he had sustained a compound comminuted fracture of the left humerus, a simple fracture of the right femur, numerous painful contusions, and a severe concussion of the spine."[62] Though Stryker is a schemer, in short, the accuracy and graphic detail of this description leaves no doubt in the reader's mind that he has not fabricated these particular injuries. Yet the imaginary nature of Stryker's illness is precisely what is at stake in the story, for Stryker's natural healing process not only lessens his pain but weakens his claim for compensation from the railroad company. Determined to milk the company for all it is worth, Stryker, in cahoots with his lawyers, is forced to simulate his injuries after they have vanished, even going so far as to hide his health and general well-being from his own family. He continues to limp when he otherwise could walk upright and to grimace with pain he does not feel. In fact, as his case is appealed through a succession of courts, Stryker, despite his health, manages to convince even the railroad's lawyers of the chronic nature of his debilitating condition. But just as a final verdict is about to be rendered in his favor his masquerade is revealed: responding to shouts of "Mad dog! Mad dog! Run for your lives!" Stryker who has been limping alongside his lawyer on his way to court and who has harbored an unnatural fear of rabid dogs from his infancy drops his crutches unceremoniously and runs past a crowd of witnesses and doctors who have come to testify on his behalf. "The second trial of Stryker vs. The Railroad Company," Chesnutt writes, "was never finished," and Stryker, newly impoverished, dutifully resumes "the quest of fortune" (373).

The part of "Stryker's Waterloo" that parodies the accident victim's attempt to prolong his injuries artificially reinforces the fatalism with which Chesnutt viewed the railroad accident. But an unresolved sympathy for Stryker himself evokes what is the more interesting narrative for even as the story parodies the accident victim's desperation, it also parodies a legal system that requires as a condition of compensation that the injuries the victim incurs be sustained over the course of the many years it takes to bring a case through the court system. Indeed, while Chesnutt voices his protest against gold diggers like Stryker, he also protests the absurdity of a legal system that effectively retries a case until the original reasons for the litigation are moot. Indeed, while Stryker's injuries are still palpable, a jury composed of "twelve presumably intelligent men," renders a verdict in Stryker's favor of $45,000, and it is only to collect this money, fairly awarded to him, that Stryker begins to sham. Moreover, Chesnutt seems aware that the settlement that the railroad offers Stryker at the beginning of the story to induce him not to go forward with his suit, while sufficient for Stryker's immediate needs, falls far below the punitive sum necessary to serve as an incentive to the company to prevent future railroad accidents. Taken together, then, *The Colonel's Dream* and "Stryker's Waterloo" invite us to ask specific questions about accident prevention (by good Samaritans and by others) in the context of the railroad, a new and imposing instigator of accidents whose effects on the future of legal liability are the subject of the next chapter.

CHAPTER SIX

Stop, Look, and Listen

THE SIGNS AND SIGNALS OF THE RAILROAD ACCIDENT

The ordinary dub thinks what he should have
done to avoid disaster after it is all over;
Bartholomew thought before.
(Frank H. Spearman, "The Million Dollar
Freight Train")[1]

ON August 24, 1924, a hot and sticky summer day in New York City, a railroad-related accident occurred that helped to redefine the question of causation and to alter the understanding of individual responsibility in accident law and accident narratives as a whole. The facts of this accident, which resulted in what is arguably the most famous accident case in the annals of American law, are at once simple and perplexing as the fact statement, written by Judge Benjamin Cardozo of the New York Appellate Court, reveals:

> Plaintiff was standing on a platform of defendant's railroad after buying a ticket to go to Rockaway Beach. A train stopped at the station bound for another place. Two men ran forward to catch it. One of the men reached the platform of the car without mishap, though the train was already moving. The other man, carrying a package, jumped aboard the car, but seemed unsteady as if about to fall. A guard on the car, who had held the door open, reached forward to help him in, and another guard on the platform pushed from behind. In the act, the package was dislodged, and fell upon the rails. It was a package of small size, about fifteen inches long, and was covered by newspaper. In fact it contained fireworks, but there was nothing in its appearance to give notice of its contents. The fireworks when they fell exploded. The shock of the explosion threw down some scales at the other end of the platform many feet away. The scales struck the plaintiff, causing injuries for which she sues.[2]

Noted here for its striking succinctness, Cardozo's description of the events that led to Mrs. Palsgraf's injuries makes an unusually attenuated series of events seem remarkably clear. Indeed, Cardozo takes what has to be one of the strangest series of events—events more reminiscent of a

Rube Goldberg contraption[3] than an everyday occurrence—and makes it sound almost logical.

Despite his certainty about the causal trajectory of these events, however, Cardozo decided the case against the plaintiff, and in 1928, Mrs. Palsgraf, who had waited four long years while her case was tried and appealed, saw the damages she had been awarded in the lower court vanish. That the decision was not made in Mrs. Palsgraf's favor despite the obvious role played by the railroad in causing her injuries generally points to a bias in negligence law in favor of industry and enterprise. But more particularly it points to the devaluation of causation in determining the liability of agents involved in accidents. For unlike the many causally obscure legal and literary narratives analyzed in chapter 4, the causal role of the various agents in this case, including the two men on the platform who were railroad employees, is far from murky. On the contrary, what is noteworthy in the *Palsgraf* case is not that the causal trajectory of the accident is confusing but rather that it is explicitly ignored. Indeed, for Cardozo the decision in the *Palsgraf* case had more to do with duty than with causation. "The law of causation," he wrote, "is thus foreign to the case before us" (101). Rather, for Cardozo the central question concerned the "orbit" of danger contemplated by the law, making the negligence or wrongdoing of those who caused the accident an issue only for the immediate parties: the railroad and the passenger whose package was dislodged. Given this limited scope, Mrs. Palsgraf was seen as an interloper who, while undeniably injured, was not legally protected. "The risk reasonably to be perceived," Cardozo wrote, "defines the duty to be obeyed, and risk imports relation; it is risk to another or to others within the range of apprehension" (100).

The unusual, some would say twisted,[4] logic of Cardozo's focus in the *Palsgraf* case marks an important moment in the history of accident law and of accident narratives, for in turning away from causation, this case turned away from the one feature that had linked most accident narratives throughout the nineteenth century. Specifically, the case points to a time when causation lost its salience in determining the nature of human responsibility within the accident context. Indeed, the story of individual responsibility and blame at the turn of the century and throughout the first quarter of the twentieth century is shaped by this paradox: as technology improved, especially the technology of signaling which was designed to protect passengers and personnel on the railroad, the causal trajectory of accidents became in many ways more certain, and yet the nature of the human role or what was often called the human equation was lost. In 1927, just as Mrs. Palsgraf was fighting to preserve the sanctity of causation in determining liability, Werner Heisenberg published scientific findings about causation that shook the world. Known as the uncertainty principle, Heisenberg's theory demonstrated that the position and velocity of subatomic particles could only be known in relation to each other. It followed that all things in nature were relative and interdependent.

The intellectual historian Thomas Haskell explains the far-reaching consequences of this causal crisis for social thought.

> Things near at hand that had once seemed autonomous and therefore suitable for causal attribution were now seen as reflexes of more remote causes. Those factors in one's immediate environment that had always been regarded as self-exacting, spontaneous entities—causes: things in which explanations can be rooted—now began to be seen as merely the final links in long chains of causality that stretched off into murky distance.[5]

In other words, the uncertainty principle established that no one thing could necessarily be disassociated causatively from any other. This kind of uncertainty came at an obvious cost since if no one thing could be divorced from any other in a hypothetically endless chain of causality, then causation in general, and human agency in particular, lost much of its earlier meaning. Cases like Mrs. Palsgraf's clearly model this paradox, but the literary representations of accidents from this period give voice to it as well. In fact, in the years in which signaling technology was developing most rapidly—from about 1890 to 1930—there was an explosion of pulp fiction[6] about the railroads that was preoccupied with the mediation of human responsibility by signaling. An heir to the dime novel and the penny dreadful, this fiction adopted many of the formulas peculiar to the popular genres. But it distinguished itself from much of the sentimentalism and melodrama of most popular fiction by introducing characters who were not simply victimized by technology but struggled heroically to take responsibility for it.

SIGNALING SYSTEMS

The use of causation in determining liability—a use that had faltered in the face of evidence pointing to the multiple and intervening causes that had plagued cases like that involving Twain's brother described in chapter 4—gained in validity when the railroads joined the public to campaign for greater safety. Of course, the late nineteenth century was characterized by a proliferation of safety movements and devices, including the safety razor, safety revolver, and safety bicycle,[7] but the greatest efforts in this period to reduce risk were focused on the routine and increasingly frequent railroad accident. Taking shape under the auspices of the Safety First movement, a joint venture by both the public and the railroads to increase safety in railroad travel, the most significant contribution to railroad safety was the introduction of radically new mechanical and automated signaling systems that facilitated inquiries into causal links and responsible agents.

In addition to providing cautionary guidelines about accidents, in other words, signs and signals transformed the accident from an apparently unique and frequently incomprehensible event to a commonly understood and reiterable one.[8] In marking the accident with a system of visible and audible milestones, signals clarified the trajectory of the accident's often inscrutable action and invested that action with a previously unknown materiality. The consequences of this materiality for determining responsibility were enormous, for now when accident perpetrators and victims reported on their actions and injuries, they could document by means of signals the time, place, and often the person or mechanism that had played a part in them.[9] Moreover, by incorporating this information about signs, the accident narrative was able to trace the accident back in time to the moment at which its existence was first foreshadowed (by signs), and thus to sustain a story about the accident's action that went beyond the moment of impact. That signs were already discursive in nature—conveying information from one person and place to another— made their role in determining the causal trajectories of an accident even more indispensable. Thus, signals further enhanced the ability to determine liability for the accident by providing a discourse—more accurately, a meta-discourse—with which to represent what had always been a relatively inarticulate and nondiscursive event.

Standing in for the mental analogues available to other forms of narrative with access to the internal states of characters before, during, and after a given event, signs and signals increased the chances of identifying a responsible party by augmenting the set of attributes of a given accident, rescuing it from the indistinctness and generality with which it was typically surrounded and endowing it with a particularity in which certain warnings and certain modes of conduct were prescribed. Specifically, signs made the accident more concrete by investing the accident site with a technologically complex apparatus. Of course, as a means of conveying intelligence between carriers on land and water some form of signaling had long been in use. But with the rapid increase in railroad travel came a new and unprecedented congestion which made the need for faster, safer, and more complex signaling systems more pressing than ever. Gone were the days in which lanterns were used instead of lights and in which signalmen, dressed in top hats and waistcoats, signaled to the occasional train by means of a primitive set of hand gestures. With advances in engineering science came more elaborate devices and a host of mechanical, pneumatic, hydraulic, and electrical mechanisms, involving new technologies of wires, electricity, relays, motors, and lights. In fact, so considerable were the advances in railroad signaling technology that it became the standard for controlling the greater congestion brought about by the arrival of the first mass-produced automobile.[10] Indeed, between about 1910 and 1930, when the automobile decisively edged out the railroad as the preferred mode of transportation, the conjunction of railroad and automobile traffic at grade crossings remained one of the greatest challenges for signaling technology.[11]

Many of the new safety signals increased the clarity of the accident's causation by increasing the number of people to whom information about an impending accident could be communicated. In some cases, safety signs were aimed at travelers approaching points of danger, while in others they were aimed at signalers whose job it was to space trains at safe distances. The first category included signs designed for the better protection of grade crossings and junctions where the greatest number of accidents among pedestrians and, later, motorists, occurred. The second category included more automated signaling systems like the block system in which signals placed at the entrance to a designated section of track, or block, would indicate whether the track was clear of other traffic.[12] Initially tied to the movements of signalmen in elevated signal towers, the block system soon became automated, allowing the train itself, upon entering the block, to trip a warning circuit. In addition there were systems that made the movements of trains mutually dependent. Of these the most famous was the interlocking system which mechanically and later automatically joined the signals of two or more tracks so that the signalman in the tower would not simultaneously throw open the track to trains with conflicting routes.[13] Indeed, had no other safety device ever been invented, the interlocking system alone would have revolutionized railroad travel.

Keeping pace with the advent of increased train and car traffic, many signs soon came to embody nuanced forms of communication designed to indicate more complex and varied information than ever before. Lights and semaphores, for example, were now capable of displaying not just the three traditional indications—stop, proceed, and proceed with caution—but the four or five necessary to direct information about specific blocks, divergent tracks, or multiple trains. Although a vast improvement on the older model, even this ability to render multiple aspects was no match for the most sophisticated of all carrier communications systems, the telegraph. With the introduction of the telegraph and the gradual spread of the Morse Code in the middle of the nineteenth century, train dispatchers were able to convey extraordinarily detailed information about trains over distances once thought unbridgeable.

Indeed, the vastness of the American railroad system which covered hundreds of thousands of miles of track and stretched across a wide and diverse continent inspired a welter of rules and codes about signaling that further sharpened and singularized the narrative of causation and responsibility. Almost every railroad had a code that was conducive to its own purposes, its own sense of professional conduct, and to the peculiarities of its own terrain. For example, there was little or no uniformity among railroads as to the colors used to indicate caution or as to the numbers used for an emergency wire dispatch to indicate that the track needed to be cleared. (Often this diversity was unintentional, but just as frequently it was the result of an intense competition among railroad lines vying for distinction.) Moreover, signal aspects changed not only from line to line but from day to night and among signaling systems—a yellow light meaning one thing under a manual block system and quite another under an automatic block regime.

The great diversity of signals across signaling systems was furthered by the need for bigger, better, more specific signs by a public that exhibited a resistance to forming safe habits and a general heedlessness that ultimately gave rise to an even more rigorous emphasis on safety in the literature on railroads and signaling. At grade crossings, especially, a curious tendency to ignore the rules established by railroad signage added to the already staggering number of injuries and fatalities from train collisions. (There were about three thousand fatalities from train collisions but twice as many fatalities from grade-crossing accidents per year from 1900 to 1905, according to one tally.)[14] Despite these statistics, however, this strange crossing behavior persisted to the consternation of many a professional observer. In article after article, critics speculated as to what led pedestrians or motorists to exhibit such a high, even suicidal, degree of impatience and carelessness while crossing railroad tracks. "He may be absorbed in watching another train. He may be absent-minded, thinking of a debt he owes, of his home or wife or child. . . ,"[15] one author speculated. Others hazarded the guess that people crossing tracks were in too much of a hurry to wait for trains or signals. But anecdotal observations of those running the trains soon put an end to this hypothesis. "'The funny thing about people dodging under the gates and running across ahead of a fast train,'" one engineer is reported as saying in an article bluntly titled "People Act as If They Wanted to Be Killed," "'is that in almost every case they stop afterward, turn around, and watch the train go by! That shows how much of a hurry they really were in.'"[16]

Fig. 4. A staged collision of train and automobile in Florence, California, in 1924. Such stunts graphically showed the outcome when drivers fail to "Go Slowly" when approaching railroad crossings. UPI/Corbis-Bettmann.

As the author of this article suggests, crossing accidents seemed in part the result of a strange compulsion among a certain segment of the population to defy the train, to come as close as possible to a near-death experience. To deter these so-called "crossing maniacs,"[17] the railroads began a vigorous safety campaign intended specifically to prevent grade-crossing accidents and characterized most prominently by the colorful, often frightening, warning posters that began to dot the roads and highways. "Jail Might Stop Them—We Can't" read one particularly threatening poster issued by the Long Island Railroad Company in 1916.[18] Even more widespread was the series of posters issued by the American Railway Association in the 1920s and 1930s, each with a different drawing of a head-on collision between train and automobile and a caption that read in boldface: **"Cross Crossings Cautiously."**[19] Some railroads went so far as to stage grade-crossing accidents to get their message across. Figure 4 shows one such publicity stunt staged by the Southern Pacific in 1924. Photographs of these "crashes" were published widely, as a warning to careless motorists. But of all the warnings that characterized this safety campaign, the one most frequently invoked was that embodied by one of the oldest and yet most vexing of all railroad signs—the sign that read "Stop, Look, and Listen."[20] In these words lay the seeds of a controversy that ultimately found its way into the courts and that epitomized the role of signs in clarifying and at the same time confusing human agency and liability.

THE CROSSING CASE

Like its literary counterpart, the legal accident narrative gained in focus and clarity from the signs posted along the path of the accident and from the safety debate they generated. Indeed, in considering questions about the general adequacy of signs—their visibility, audibility, efficacy, and legibility—the causal focus of the law on accidents became more detailed and more predictable than ever. The predictability provided by signs, moreover, was especially conducive to the generalizing impulse behind negligence law which describes a failure to abide by a standard of conduct and care exercised by a person of *ordinary* prudence *under the same or similar circumstances.*

Of all the jurists to capitalize on the generalizing impact of signs for negligence law, Oliver Wendell Holmes was perhaps the most articulate. A leading proponent of the movement to remake the law in the image of a science, Holmes preferred the law to speak in general rather than specific terms whenever possible. The greatest virtue of the law, he wrote, was its ability to fashion rules and regulations "of general application."[21] Of course, Holmes was not unmindful of the particularities of a given case; he was simply driven to combine and generalize from them, turning the lessons of experience into laws. To this end, Holmes searched for what the law has come to call *familiar* cases—cases that reenact virtually the same fact pattern over time—an example of which he believed he found in the crossing case scenario. In the crossing case, Holmes identified several shared features—an approaching train, the pedestrian or motorist who was inevitably run down by it, and most significant of all, the ubiquitous "Stop, Look, and Listen" sign which not only warned those crossing of a potential danger but prescribed a set of specific and presumably preventative acts. While the typical "Stop, Look, and Listen" sign was a bland affair, some railroads embellished it with eye-catching paraphernalia. One railroad in Texas went so far as to perch a wrecked automobile above such a sign (fig. 5).

All of these features were present in the case of *Baltimore & Ohio Railroad Company v. Goodman* (1927).[22] Here Goodman, a motorist, was hit by a passing train at a railroad crossing in which the "Stop, Look,

Fig. 5. A variation on the "Stop, Look, and Listen" sign that warned drivers to be alert and use caution at railroad crossings. Texas, 1922. UPI/Corbis-Bettmann.

and Listen" sign was present. Holmes had no trouble ruling that Goodman was at fault. The possibility that there might have been unusual or extenuating circumstances having to do with the apparent risk or with Goodman's opportunity to deal with it did not enter into Holmes's calculus, for from the presence of the sign alone Holmes deduced that Goodman, not the railroad, had failed to take the necessary precautions and that this failure had caused the accident. Indeed, given the repetitive nature of the crossing case and the standardization made possible by the "Stop, Look, and Listen" sign, Holmes believed that the *Goodman* case was ripe for generalization—specifically for the formulation of a rule that would remove the determination of causation from the fact specific inquiry of the jury and place it firmly within the hands of established, judge-made law. Thus, it was in direct disregard of the causal factors of Goodman's actual situation that Holmes established a standard of conduct for crossing motorists that required them not only to stop, as suggested by the sign, but when otherwise unsure of the approaching danger, to *get out of their vehicles* and to survey the area.

The opinion, a mere four paragraphs long, is a masterpiece of vagueness and circumlocution. It speaks more of men in general than of Goodman in particular. "When a man goes upon a railroad track," Holmes writes, "he knows that he goes to a place where he will be killed if a train comes upon him before he is clear of the track. He knows that he must stop for the train, not the train stop for him" (69–70). In fact, so steadfast was Holmes in his desire to read into the sign a standard that could "be laid down once for all by the Courts" (70) that he dismissed all suggestions in the court record to the contrary. Specifically, he paid no attention to the testimony provided by Goodman's spouse (who had been in the car) that while her husband had not stopped at the sign, he had slowed to an appropriate speed near the track in order to scan the area but found that his view remained obscured by an obstacle on the railroad siding. "We do not go into further details as to Goodman's precise situation," Holmes writes, "beyond mentioning that it was daylight and that he was familiar with the crossing, for it appears to us plain that nothing is suggested by the evidence to relieve Goodman from responsibility for his own death" (69).

The mere existence of the same signs at more than one similar grade crossing, however, could no longer guarantee the kind of congruence required by the law since the sign itself, it was soon recognized, was characterized by an almost infinite number of variables including placement, wording, and visibility. Indeed, articles about the pitfalls of various signaling systems appeared regularly in journals with sizeable circulations. A frequent complaint, for example, concerned the time it took for signaling aspects to change from one indication to the next in the semaphore systems that relied on blades or signaling arms. During a typical delay the semaphore would either display no signal at all, or render itself in a configuration that was somewhere in between signals, leaving the train conductor to guess which way the signal was to turn. More troublesome still was the use of white lights in certain lighted semaphores as the indication for "proceed" since white was a notoriously impure color which might look reddish or greenish in different situations. Indeed, it was not until 1908, as a result of intensive railroad sponsored research at Corning Glass Works, that a standard-color lens was developed and the red-yellow-green color scheme so familiar to us today was put into use.[23] But mechanical signals were not the only ones subject to this kind of confusion or ambiguity. For example, a simple "Stop, Look, and Listen" sign located twenty feet from the railroad track was, for the purposes of a law determining reasonable or normal conduct, not the same as or even similar to a "Stop, Look, and Listen" sign that was forty feet away and thus harder to see from certain angles. More important, the variability of the sign raised the possibility, and at times even the necessity, of a variable plan of human response or agency which Holmes's decision in the *Goodman* case refused to acknowledge. Indeed, the popular wisdom on the subject was that written signs were often too small to read, poorly worded, or obscured by obstacles on the railroad siding. "With an apparently cynical disregard for the peril involved," the author of a magazine article entitled "Speed" notes, "this [the sign] is often placed where it cannot be seen until one is upon the tracks. . . . As he [the motorist] drives or motors along the country road he knows not what moment he may see too late the maddening little sign 'Railroad Crossing,' and a flying express be upon him."[24]

The popular wisdom reflected a legal impatience with a standard approach to signs, and it wasn't long before Holmes's ruling was seriously challenged in the courts. In particular, the decision that cast the greatest direct doubt on the holding in *Goodman* was that of *Pokora v. Wabash Railroad Company* (1934).[25] In this case, Justice Cardozo, the same Cardozo who had written *Palsgraf* a mere six years earlier, argued that Holmes had gone too far in trying to establish a rule of "general application" that put the burden of responsibility on the pedestrian or motorist in cases involving railroad crossing accidents. Moreover, the decision in the *Pokora* case was much more threatening to the standard Holmes established in *Goodman* since it was, as Cardozo himself would have acknowledged, an unquestionably familiar one: like Goodman, Pokora was a motorist who was struck and killed by a train at a grade crossing and who claimed, through his survivors, that his view of the main track was obscured. Unlike Holmes, however, Cardozo insisted on the significance of Pokora's attempt to cross safely and in accordance with the warning of the "Stop, Look, and Listen" sign, placing the blame in the end on the railroad for failing to maintain its right of way in the proper manner.

As Cardozo's detailed fact statement reports, Pokora did all he could short of getting out of his car to ascertain whether a train was approaching: he stopped and listened before he crossed. His failure to "Look," the only one of the three requirements specified by the sign that he did not meet, Cardozo found understandable. "The record does not show in any conclusive way that the train was visible to Pokora while there was still time to stop" (100), he wrote. Indeed, for Cardozo, the obstruction—a line of boxcars on the switch track left there by the railroad—defamiliarized the case sufficiently to warrant a new analysis. "Illustrations such as these bear witness to the need for caution in framing standards of behavior that amount to rules of law," he wrote. "Extraordinary situations may not wisely or fairly be subjected to tests or regulations that are fitting for the common-place or normal" (106). Specifically, Cardozo held that in Pokora's case, trying to comply with Holmes's standard would probably have constituted an act of negligence itself. "To get out of a vehicle and reconnoitre is an uncommon precaution, as everyday experience informs us. Besides being uncommon, it is very likely to be futile, and sometimes even dangerous. If the driver leaves his vehicle when he nears a cut or curve, he will learn nothing by getting out about the perils that lurk beyond. By the time he regains his seat and sets his car in motion, the hidden train may be upon him" (104). Of course, Cardozo's ruling in this case did not suggest that stopping and leaving one's vehicle was never in order; he simply reinstated the need for a case by case determination of the motorist's agency with respect to the sign or signal in question in order to gain an accurate, legally justified, and narratively precise idea of the causative factors involved in the accident at hand.

Indeed, just as Holmes's rhetoric reduced Goodman's accident to a brief, overly general, virtually nonnarrative form, Cardozo's reinforced the narratability of Pokora's by stressing the causal specificity of signaling details. Thus, Cardozo's opinion is substantially longer than Holmes's in part because he seeks to corroborate his intuitions with facts about causation, including calculations about the zone of human visibility that took account of such frequently overlooked items as the distance from the front of the truck to the driver's seat where Pokora was seated. Where Holmes dismisses the relevance of the details of Goodman's case, Cardozo pauses to linger over Pokora's, insisting on getting them perfectly straight before he renders the story in legal terms. That Cardozo's decision in *Pokora* indicates a way for the human agent to alter or exert some control over the accident does put his decision in *Palsgraf* in a somewhat ironic light. For while the two cases present very different fact situations and were decided on very different theories of law, the *Pokora* decision nevertheless indicates an acceptance of causal variability and a sympathy for the human causal agent (as opposed to the corporate or technological agent) that *Palsgraf* does not. Often cited by legal theorists as an indication of Cardozo's independence of mind, the contradictoriness of Cardozo's decisions could just as easily be cited by students of railroad fiction as an indication of the accident narrative's interest in the struggle between the human agent and railroad technology.

SIGNALING AND SENSORY FACULTIES

The literature about railroad signals reveals the extent to which the technology of signaling was simultaneously dehumanizing and uplifting. Of course, most technological innovations have been received with mixed emotions since their inception, with each new achievement representing an improved quality of life for a certain segment of the population while typically lowering it for another. That machines, since their inception, have had a debilitating effect on the human body and mind, reducing the idiosyncrasies of the human mind to rote and repetitive gestures, has also been well documented. An especially acute witness of the gradual disappearance of arts and crafts and the rise of mechanization at the turn of the century, Henry Adams bemoaned the decline of human agency in his famous contrast between the heavenly Virgin, represented by beauty and religion, and the hellish Dynamo, represented by machine-age technology.[26] But as if the advent of mechanization itself was not sufficiently dehumanizing, theories popularized by people like Frederick Winslow Taylor contributed greatly to the sense that humans would have to conform in order to compete with mechanical devices.[27] Taylor's notorious notion of efficient time-motion labor took hold after his book, *The Principles of Scientific Management*, published in 1911, revolutionized many industries including that of the railroad. One of the most enduring legacies of Taylor's principles was that rote work as well as the worker's obedience to the machine and to the orders of management increased efficiency.

But there was a special quality to the technology of safety which allowed it to be celebrated as an unadulterated improvement for society as a whole. In fact, safety measures taken on the railroad were almost universally endorsed by a public that wanted to feel safe when traveling. Indeed, one of the most popular forms of entertainment in this period was the safe staging of train wrecks by the safety-conscious showman and promoter Joe Connolly—the Evel Knievel of his day. For his first staged wreck, for example, Connolly instructed engineers in their every move and hired firemen and mounted police to keep the crowds at a safe distance. When not one of the eighty-nine thousand people who paid to see Connolly's collision was injured, Connolly knew he had a success on his hands. Indeed, in the next thirty-six years, "Head-On" Joe Connolly, as he came to be known, staged seventy-five more collisions, one bigger, more explosive, and more lucrative than the next. But in all this time, he never lost a single person to death or injury. In fact, as Connolly knew, it was the guarantee of safety that drew people in and that allowed him to capitalize on their morbid interest in accidents. For what the public wanted was to see a *simulation* of disaster, free of risk. As he told reporters at the end of his life, he had had a "lifelong desire to see such a disaster without danger to himself, and thought many other people harbored the same secret desire. . . ."[28]

Of all the safety mechanisms developed in this period of rapid invention, however, none was so welcome as signaling technology for it promised effective protection of life and limb at relatively low cost to workers. Indeed, there lingered about the operation of signals an aura of self-sufficiency and human inventiveness, for signaling technology, more than any other kind of technological achievement in this period, mimicked the peculiarly human attribute of language. Many descriptions reveal an uncertainty about whether signaling was a human or a mechanical operation.

One Lionel toy train catalogue boasts of its "Semaphore-Train-Control" signal which automatically stopped and started trains. "You will be absolutely thrilled as you watch the unique action of this almost-human railroad device," the catalogue exclaims.[29] Consider too the strange mix of religiosity and mechanization in the following description:

> If there are two classes of men on a railway who must implicitly trust and understand one another, they are the signalmen and the engine-drivers. The driver lets his engine fly round a blind corner or into the darkness of the night with full faith in the message just given him by the lowered arm or green light of the semaphore. The signalman, jumping from lever to lever in *obedience* to mysterious signals rapped out by the telegraph, takes it for granted that if he says a thing through the medium of his rods and wires the driver will act accordingly.[30]

Here the signalman acts in "obedience" to something higher and yet is clearly called upon to interpret the "mystery" of what he hears. Similarly, the same author hesitates between depicting the signalman as an artist or a robot when he invites us to imagine the signalman as a musician: "Imagine yourself standing in Waterloo signal-box," he writes, "where over 200 bright levers ranged side by side, resemble a gigantic keyboard. . . . [E]very action is business-like as they [the signalmen] improvise, *or seem to improvise*, strange combinations on their keyboard, bending out a lever here, another there, and a couple more maybe far down the line."[31] In describing the signalmen as *seeming* to improvise, of course, the author gives his attitude about the signalman's work away, for there is little or no improvisation required. "On the shoulders of these men," he continues, "rests an enormous responsibility, too heavy indeed to be borne, did not mechanical invention come to the aid of human fallibility. How easy it would be for a tired signalman to pull over the wrong lever, were it as independent of its fellows as one note of a piano is of the rest!"[32]

The truth about signaling, therefore, was that it was as dehumanizing as almost any other kind of technology, and more prone than most to the Tayloristic demands of obedience, for nowhere else did so much hinge on the correct, quick, and strict application of rules. In order to convey his ideas about a legal order calibrated according to the actual harm done and not to what he perceived as a shifting and often baseless moral reckoning, the sociologist E. A. Ross invoked the example of railroad signaling. "A scientific penology," he wrote, "will graduate punishments primarily *according to the harmfulness of the offence to society*. . . . It will be hard on the careless train despatcher, because mistakes *must not* occur in despatching trains."[33] Indeed, it was on the subject of human fallibility that many of the mechanical metaphors came into play. The mechanical systems left room for human error in which overtired telegraph dispatchers or signal operatives either failed to send messages in time to avoid collisions or misconstrued the often intricately coded signals they received. One observer even likened the human brain to a mechanical device in a prescient moment when he invoked a signaling metaphor to describe the neural apparatus of the human brain. "The tired brain refuses to connote intelligence," he wrote; "the signals slip by, shining into eyes held open with sheer strength, but no strength can control the brain to which the weary *nerves fail to convey* the news of the signal."[34] As we saw in the legal battle over the "Stop, Look, and Listen" sign, so critical was the ability to perceive signs and signals that it often devolved on scientifically informed assessments not only about the audibility or visibility of the sign or signal in question, but about the capacity of the human being to take it in. Thus, many of these stories include details gleaned from a growing literature that was either authored by or drew on insights from behavioral or cognitive scientists. An example of the widespread dissemination of such information is the article "Stop, Look, Listen," in *The Outlook* of August 23, 1913, in which the author brings behavioral and psychological insights to bear on his argument for installing more noticeable signal markers. In particular, the author raises questions about the peculiarities of the human ear and audiology and attests to the strange habit, epidemic among accident victims, of claiming that train whistles—whistles that other witnesses clearly heard—had never been sounded. "Many persons fail to sense the sound of the bell or whistle," he writes, "and then say, 'If they had been sounded, I would have heard them.' How many of you readers, heard your clock strike the most recent hour?" (930), he comments skeptically. Moreover, just as frequently, the author claims, the ear can deceive in the opposite direction, leading people to think that they have actually heard bells that were never rung. "Some years ago at W——, a team, with a wagon occupied by two men, was struck by a limited train. Two reputable farmers, 'who set their clocks by that train,' gave statements to the effect that they were about to enter their barn when their attention was attracted to the train by the 'crossing whistle.' And yet—and yet—the whistle was not sounded for the crossing, nor others in the vicinity. The whistle valve had broken. . . ." (930), he explains.

Of all the sensory faculties subject to scientific investigation the one most widely reported on and investigated by scientists and fiction writers alike was the sense of sight, for sight was the primary target of most signals and also the greatest source of signal misperception. In particular, the concern of most studies in this period involved the newly significant affliction known as color blindness. Diagnosed in the late eighteenth century, color blindness did not become a source of obsessive concern until the advent and widespread use of color signals. It was then that railroad companies and signal historians began to issue treatises[35] about it and scientists began to explore its etiology and symptoms. In his 1907 article "Railway Disasters at Night: The Psychological Need of Revising the Signals," George Stratton, a psychology professor at The Johns Hopkins University, suggests that the affliction is sufficiently serious and common to induce the railroads to replace the trinity of red, yellow, and green signal lights with a different set of colors altogether. "And as if by a kind of diabolic perversity," he writes, "the colors which are so vital to the signal system, red and green, are the very ones with regard to which the abnormal eye more often goes astray."[36]

In addition to being overtired, signalmen were often thought of as being incapable of understanding the complex mechanisms that had to be manipulated. Indeed, signalmen were the object of patronizing attitudes on the part of the engineers of the signal operations. Noting that signalmen were not the inventors of the signal apparatus, one treatise explains that "the signals must be simple in their operation because worked by men not skilled in scientific ideas or appliances."[37]

Although as members of a group they resisted this characterization, at least one signalman himself recognized the need for the routinized quality of the signalman's work, for creativity or individuality rarely played a part in the prevention of an accident. In one exceptionally revealing book, entitled *Confessions of a Railroad Signalman*, the author, a retired telegrapher and towerman of twenty-seven years, emphasizes repeatedly the need for the signalman to obey the rules handed down to him.

> Every rule in the time-table has its history written in suffering and dollars; and while, of course it is advisable for employees to be conversant with their meaning and significance, it is evident that the principle of dogged obedience is the only safe method for employees to pursue in regard to them. An inflexible enforcement of this principle would be looked upon as little short of tyranny; and yet, seriously and fairly considered, it is nothing but the subordination which every railroad man owes to the community in the interest of safety and general efficiency.[38]

But as he kowtows to the official rhetoric about the need for the subordination of human agency to technology, even this signalman identifies the importance of the human as opposed to the mechanical agent, for the human agent alone has emotions. Indeed, in a chapter entitled "The Human Equation," the author of this book holds up the signalman as a model of the kind of human compassion that could and should govern railroad management and could also lead to the prevention of accidents. Castigating the management's habit of translating accidents into statistics and tolerating as many as efficiency and cost-effectiveness would warrant, the author points to the signalman's ability to feel for the injured as a way of turning the indifference of a railroad around. "The railroad employee," he writes, "as a unit, is whole-souled and sympathetic; not a suspicion of indifference can be imputed to him, either as a man or as a brother. Individually speaking, when a passenger or an employee is injured, there is no sorrow like his sorrow, but unfortunately, the organizations or machines through which alone his desires and sympathies can be expressed, have never shown any disposition to interest themselves in any practical way in matters relating to the safety of the public, or of the employees, *whenever such interest is liable to develop into a probe of the conduct and efficiency of the railroad man*" (132–33). But the story of the railroad man's and in particular the signalman's "desires and sympathies," was in fact told many times in the railroad fiction that thrived just as this signalman was confessing.

AGENCY AND THE PULP FICTION

The fiction about railroads that flourished from the turn of the century to about the 1930s displays the same kind of concern with human agency in the face of a monolithic technology that can be seen in Cardozo's *Pokora* decision and in the writing about railroad accidents in the contemporary nonfiction. Unlike *Pokora*, however, the fiction is less concerned with the agency of accident victims than with that of the railroad men and signalers themselves who were caught up in a language and gestural vocabulary that threw the causal trajectory of the railroad accident into relief and yet tended to subordinate their own role as independent causal agents. As if to counteract this trend, the railroad stories turn the focus on causation made possible by signs and signaling away from the *events* of the accident and toward the human *experience* of the signaler. Indeed, because signals expanded the scope of the accident narrative to include the steps leading up to the accident, many railroad stories could now account for a period of time that had previously been too indistinct or too precipitous to undergo accurate representation. Into this period the railroad authors often interjected descriptions of the subjectivities of signalers whose motions were rote but whose emotions were volatile. The result is the literary transformation of accident causation into a source of human, not mechanical, drama.

Not surprisingly, a disproportionate amount of space is devoted in these stories to the acts and sensations of those who know the accident is coming, and yet for whom time seems, literally, to drag. Thus, in Harold Titus's classic railroad story, "A Little Action,"[39] Titus shifts repeatedly between descriptions of the frenzied motion generated by a train that has come uncoupled from its locomotive and is hurtling toward certain disaster, and the odd and highly idiosyncratic thoughts and images running through the mind of George, the telegrapher, who is among the first to learn about the runaway and who contemplates its impending collision with other trains from afar. "I'm giving it to you as it came to George," Titus writes. "It takes time for me to give it as he saw it. It takes time, too, for me to tell how he remembered the Scouts at noon and thought their shrilling like that of happy crickets" (67). For Titus, in fact, slowing the narrative down becomes a protest not only against the subordination of the signalers' agency but of his own subordination as the author of these events. "It takes more time *for me to write*," Titus asserts, "that his moustache bristled as he thought what those voices would sound like if that runaway met their engine" (67–68, my emphasis).

The record that Titus so carefully provides of the signaler's mental and emotional state in the moments before an accident, during the time of potential accident prevention, is intensified in a series of stories that center on emergency situations and the need for human agents to take extraordinary measures not offered by routine signaling procedures. Common to these stories are the last-minute rescues effected by the wire dispatchers, semaphore operators, flagmen, and the like who, by virtue of their status as signalmen, are newly empowered to act as rescuers. Not surprisingly, the scenes in which this kind of signaling is described exude an emotional desperation. For example, in Frank Packard's "The Night Operator"[40] a sense of panic pervades the signaling operation and is made all the more emphatic by the calm that precedes it. The story begins with a long section devoted to the routine business and domestic lives of the people who work in a telegraph office. But in the midst of this routine, an accident threatens. "Late summer turned to early fall, and early fall to still sharper weather," Packard writes, "until there came the night that the operator at Blind River muddled his orders and gave No. 73, the westbound fast freight, her clearance against the second section of the eastbound Limited that doomed them to meet somewhere head-on in the Glacier Canyon" (152). From this point on, nothing is routine; the friendly and somewhat aimless dialogue between telegraphers turns into a pointed call for help and a silent expression of anguish as the need to signal a stop to the misrouted trains takes center stage.

> Again [the operator] called, and again, and again. The minutes slipped away. Still he called—with life and death, the Seventeen—called and called. And there was no answer save that echo in the room that brought the perspiration streaming now from Regan's face, a harder light into Carleton's eyes, and a chill like death into Donkin's heart (154).

In this passage, Packard conveys the shared exasperation and dread of those who fear that an accident is imminent. But what is more significant is the way in which he turns a moment of potential causation—of impending collision—into one that reinforces the importance of the signalers' agency and human reactions.

Nowhere is the description of a character's internal, emotional state more clearly substituted for one of external causation than in those stories that devolve more precisely than Packard's on the signal as a means of decision-making and on the moment in which the decision—to act in the most appropriate and safety-conscious way—comes to pass. Like Bartholomew, the character cited in this chapter's epigraph, it is often incumbent upon the signalmen in these stories not only to signal instantaneously to "avoid disaster," but to have "thought before" they signaled—that is, to demonstrate the ability to use the *right* signals under pressure. The pressure of making the right signaling decision, moreover, reminds the reader that though the technology of signals may be mechanical, the signaler is the one who must put it into effect. Indeed, in a distinct grouping of railroad stories, the necessity to signal is represented as being in conflict with the necessity to do something else—often something unrelated to railroading. Typically, the struggle takes the form of a conflict between one's professional and domestic duties. And signaling,[41] which had a tendency to provoke the greatest professional devotion on the part of railroaders, also produced the most affecting of domestic dramas.

"The Semaphore,"[42] a story by the railroad author Herbert Ward, literalizes the struggle between the professional and domestic lives of railroaders in rendering all communication between the signalman, Joe Stringer, and his home impossible for the duration of the story. In this story, Ward cuts between scenes of Joe at home, tending to his sickly son and anxious wife, and scenes of the signaling operation which, in this case, involve the moving of heavy levers (such as those pictured in fig. 6) that control the blades of a distant semaphore. The general effect of this cinematic strategy does not favor one or the other storyline, but renders both more poignant. Thus, when we see Joe pulling on the levers in the signal tower, we are reminded of the emotional stress he labors under, and of the sleeplessness that clouds his vision. "Now for the first time in nine years," Ward writes of one of Joe's signaling iterations, "that straight row of levers, the red, the blue, the green, and the black, became blurred to his eyes and meaningless to his mind. . . . [But] Joe Stringer brushed his hand over his forehead, with a trembling, irresolute motion, and then began his duties. . . ." (762). At another point, we learn that "Joe set the signals back at danger with automatic listlessness" (763), and

Fig. 6. The interior of a metropolitan elevated signal tower. *Railway Age*, January 13, 1905, p. 40. Courtesy of Archives, University of Colorado at Boulder Libraries.

at still another that "he unlocked a switch, and flung it back with a resonant thud, and then, in the phrase of the tower, 'gave 'em the signal'" (763). The inability to see his bedroom window, where his wife said she would place a light to alert him to his son's condition, only serves to increase the signalman's anxiety and to tempt him repeatedly to leave his post. "He went toward the window," Ward writes. "The silent snow now came down like a dead wall between him and his wife's message. In the darkness and the density of the storm he could hardly see the other side of the four tracks. Was the child alive or dead?" (768). But a crisis on the tracks consumes his attention, infusing the very signaling motions that might otherwise appear rote with human intensity and effectively eliding the emotions of home and work.

An even more striking example of the human drama provoked by signaling itself—the thrill and urgency of throwing the large, cumbersome levers to open or close a switch, of controlling two-way traffic on a single track, of troubleshooting accidents and near-accidents at the last minute—is evident in Wadsworth Camp's story, "The Signal Tower."[43] Here two signalmen—Tolliver, the dutiful husband and father, and Joe, the sinister and far less dedicated signalman—relieve each other after twelve-hour shifts in a distant signal tower. When the story opens, Tolliver arrives to spell Joe and begin his shift only to learn that the "thirty-three," a regularly scheduled train, is running late and is at risk of colliding with the "special." The only hope for preventing the accident lies in a signaling maneuver that will have to be made during Tolliver's shift. To make matters worse, Joe, a drifter who boards at Tolliver's house and is jealous of his domestic security, threatens to seduce Tolliver's wife as soon as he gets off duty. Tolliver is thus forced to choose between staying at his post, helping to avert what is sure to be a deadly collision, and protecting his wife from unwanted advances and almost certain brutality. At first, while the accident is still only a distant possibility, he is preoccupied with his domestic situation. "It was difficult, moreover, for him to fix his mind tonight on his professional responsibility," Camp writes. "His duty toward his family was so much more compelling" (71). But as the collision nears, and the urgent signals from other towers filter through his sounder, he becomes aware of the greater significance of his signaling operation. Indeed, it is in the realization that he alone is responsible for hundreds of lives on the train that finally convinces Tolliver that he must stay in the signal tower. "It only needs you to keep all those people from getting killed" (77), Joe tells him once, and the phrase repeats in his head until he rails against it. "It was vicious to crush all that responsibility on the shoulders of one ignorant man, such a man as himself" (80), he thinks as he nevertheless settles in to monitor the thirty-three's progress, and wonder helplessly what was happening to his wife. As it turns out, of course, Tolliver's decision was the right one since his wife is able to help herself (she kills Joe in self-defense), and he alone is able to prevent the train disaster.

Of course, not all stories in this genre emphasize the heroism or devotion of the signaler. Just as often, the importance of human agency and human reactions is reinforced through an emphasis on the fallibility of the human signaler. For example, in the story, "When the Light Turned," the accident in question is rendered through the dubious ability of a color-blind engineer to perceive the traffic lights at a crossroads. "Faulkner [the engineer] had looked at a green signal-light one night," the author writes, "and seen it turn to red. He had closed his fingers over the throttle involuntarily, whereupon the lamp changed to green once more, and drops of perspiration came upon Faulkner's forehead. In five minutes the signal had changed color five times, and before it had finished its evolutions the big engineer was trembling like a man in a very bad chill."[44] So pervasive was the problem of color blindness that it figured in the thoughts of many train and signal operators who were not suffering from color blindness, as far as they knew, but were faced with unexpected signals.[45] Indeed, at least one story in this genre revolves around a mystery light that confounds all railroaders who see it but whose source remains unknown. " 'They saw the red light in the middle of the track, down on the ground, but no one was near it. The thing is getting on the men's nerves. There must be an end to it,' " one character reports. " 'You look as though you thought it might be a ghost,' " says another.[46]

Had the engineer in this story not been induced to doubt himself, however, he might very well have turned his doubt on others, for the unexpected appearance of contradictory or misleading signals could often be traced not to color blindness or misperception but to an error on the part of the signaler himself. As the author of "The Semaphore," puts it, "[the signalman] had to be alert, masterful and imaginative. Enormous interests were subject to his fidelity and control. Therefore he is a picked man. For him to render a false signal became a capital crime" (764). Indeed, the criminal nature of false signals is the subject of many railroad stories devoted to rogue signal operations.

In these stories, human ingenuity asserts itself, interestingly, not in the evil doings of the rogues themselves, but in the superior expertise and intuitions of the professionals. Indeed, in a volume of short stories by Francis Lynde collected under the title, *Scientific Sprague* (1912),[47] professionalism itself is presented as a panacea. A government official who works as a consultant for the railroads, Sprague is, as his epithet suggests, a fund of scientific information. That his particular expertise is in chemistry—he is referred to throughout as the "chemistry sharp"—is in no way an impediment to his understanding of railroads or of the people who run them. On the contrary, there is an assumption throughout Lynde's stories that an expertise in one science—any science, it seems—makes one an expert over all. Sprague thus is valuable not for his knowledge of chemistry, as such, but for his ability to "apply good, careful laboratory practice." "I wish you could stay and put this railroad of ours into a test tube. . . ." (24), one character says to Sprague, in the first story in the volume. And that is precisely what Sprague seems to do. Thus, in the story "The Wire-Devil," in which rogue wire messages are mysteriously being sent from the railroad's wire office, Sprague effortlessly masters all the technicalities of wire signaling, from the placement of the wires to the operation of the keys—everything short of the Morse Code itself. To aid Sprague in the precise language of signaling is the trusty dispatcher, Connolly, whose experience as a signaler is rendered in some detail. Indeed, the story begins with a description of Connolly "snapp[ing] his key-switch at the close of a rapid fire of orders sent to straighten out a freight-train tangle on the Magdalene district" (3). Connolly, of course, whose signaling know-how has been established in this and a host of other similar scenes, turns out to be critical in sending an important wire message as per Sprague's instructions as the mystery comes to a climax:

The message is in Morse, but Sprague, and the reader, conveniently receive a translation: "Hurry—down—to—mainline—and—throw—your—switch—to—red. Then—run—west—and—flag—your—passenger" (50), it reads. When Connolly gets his reply, which Lynde renders in Morse as "dot—pause—dot," "dash—dot—dash" (50) (which means "OK"), it all comes together for Sprague who, like a detective before a gathering of all the suspects, lingers over the technical details of the rogue operation as he unravels the mystery that has paralyzed the railroad and threatened it with a myriad of accidents.

The power of professional devotion in Lynde's story takes on a feminist cast in Cy Warman's "Mysterious Message" (1897).[48] This story opens, like so many others, with a view of the dispatcher's office where preparations are being made for the arrival of the President's special—a train carrying the newly appointed President of the railroad and its Chairman of the Board. Having sent the regular "trick" man away from his post, Goodlough, the train-master, assumes the position of dispatcher to insure that no signaling errors are made with the special. But no sooner does he send his first wire dispatch than Goodlough, who is out of practice on the keys, confuses the designation "Eastcreek" with "Westcreek," and puts the President's train on a certain collision course. Without his knowledge, however, his signaling is observed by the young Minnie Morgan, a "pale girl" whose father was killed in a train accident and who has come to the office to apply for a job. Believing that a "woman operator was bad enough, but a woman despatcher was sure . . . to make trouble" (198), Goodlough has nothing but contempt for Minnie. Thus, when she notifies him of his mistake, he responds defensively, and tells her to leave the office. Seconds later, however, when he looks back at his time sheet, he realizes the truth of what she has said, and faints in horror. Noting this, Minnie "slips" back into the office and sends a message to hold one of the two affected trains, adding the words "lap order" to indicate that compliance is necessary to prevent a collision. Since she signs it with the train-master's initials, however, Minnie's identity as the sender of the message remains a mystery until the President himself, determined to discover and reward the person who saved his life, forces Minnie to confess. Promotion in hand, Minnie now not only gains the recognition she deserves, but calls attention to the ability of women to handle critical signaling jobs. That she turns the promotion down in order to marry Goodlough who has come to see her potential not only as a signaler but as a wife only reinforces the tendency of this fiction to emphasize the human and emotional consequences of signaling in the face of a concept of mechanical causation that was both dehumanizing and increasingly arbitrary.

THE DECLINE OF CAUSATION

The subordination of the causal inquiry that emerges in many of the sab-
otage stories involving railroad signaling recapitulates the subordination
of the causal inquiry in the law. The coincidence of this points to an
important development in the history of the accident narrative for with
the disappearance of the causal link, the accident narrative tends to lose
its distinctiveness and merges with other kinds of stories—stories of criminal intent and criminal responsibility.[49] Indeed, the causal inquiry had
been a mainstay or pillar of the nineteenth-century conception of tort
liability. So central had the notion of objective causation become that
jurists like Holmes had staked their reputations on them. Of course, the
transformation of these concepts was gradual and due not only to a shift
in legal thinking about these matters but also, as we have seen, to a revolution in the sciences that had overturned notions of objectivity. In place
of a standard inquiry into causation in late nineteenth- and early twentieth-century tort cases came a notion of proximate cause which qualified
the possibility of finding an absolute cause by distinguishing between the
first and subsequent causes. But finally with the advent of *Palsgraf* and
the railroad fiction contemporary with it came a relativism that altered
the treatment of causation in fiction and in accident cases forever.

Of course, as many legal scholars[50] have noted, the *Palsgraf* case did
not put an end to the idea of causation or to the idea of doctrinal solutions
for the problem of liability in tort. Rather, Cardozo replaced the idea of
causation with another doctrine that had to do with the relation of risk
and the limitations such relations imposed on one's duty. Taking issue
with Cardozo's formulation of duty was the dissenting justice in the *Palsgraf* case, Justice Andrews, whose opinion is cited almost as frequently as
Cardozo's. Andrews argues, first of all, that Cardozo's notion of duty is
misguided. "Not only is he wronged to whom harm might reasonably be
expected to result," he writes, "but he also who is in fact injured, even if
he be outside what would generally be thought the danger zone. . . . Unreasonable risk being taken, its consequences are not confined to those
who might probably be hurt" (437). Rather, Andrews argues, the nature
of the decision determining liability and denying compensation to the
plaintiff in the *Palsgraf* case should have turned not on this new and odd
definition of risk, but on the law's reliance on proximate cause. For Andrews, the notion of proximate cause was sufficient to handle the seeming
randomness of denying Mrs. Palsgraf compensation for while causal trajectories could be followed indefinitely, he argues, it is not always right to
do so. "A murder at Sarajevo may be the necessary antecedent to an as-
sassination in London twenty years hence," yet it is only "a cause, but not

the proximate cause" (438). This, according to Andrews, would have been a more straightforward way of deciding the issue of the railroad's liability. "What we do mean by the word 'proximate,'" he explains, "is, that because of convenience, of public policy, of a rough sense of justice, the law arbitrarily declines to trace a series of events beyond a certain point." Andrews, needless to say, found Mrs. Palsgraf's injuries to be the proximate result of the railroad employees' negligence and would have affirmed the lower court ruling to that effect.

But even Andrews's notion of proximate cause tends to mask the real importance of the *Palsgraf* decision and of the railroad fiction in moving away from causation as a whole since it clings, albeit weakly, to the idea of causation. Rather, it was the extremely influential work of Leon Green (no relation to Nicholas St. John Green), a contemporary of Cardozo and of Andrews who articulated the need for the law to look away from causation as a whole. Indeed, it was Green's monograph, *The Rationale of Proximate Cause* (1927), that best captured the way in which causation had assumed only the guise of a scientific principle without a scientific aim. Causation, Green insists, is a factual inquiry and one that a jury can handle with relative ease. It need not, in his opinion, be cloaked with or hedged with all kind of other rules and regulations. "'Cause,' although irreducible in its concept, could not escape the ruffles and decorations so generously bestowed: remote, proximate, direct, immediate, adequate, efficient, operative, inducing, moving, active, real, effective, decisive, supervening, primary, original, contributory, ultimate, concurrent, *causa causans*, legal, responsible, dominating, natural, probable, and others" (135–36).

Rather, Green argues, the causal inquiry should bear only the weight it deserves, as a threshold requirement of an accident case. Then the law should turn to more nuanced forms of decision-making, away from causation altogether and toward a public policy mode. Indeed, in an article Green wrote in the *Harvard Law Review* expressly about the *Palsgraf* decision, he complains about the inadequacy of legal formulas in general and those used in the *Palsgraf* decision in particular. Of Cardozo's invocation of the relative nature of one's duty to prevent harm or what has often been called the question of foreseeability, Green writes: "The attempt to sustain the foreseeability of harm or the probable consequence formula as adequate for the determination of negligence, is futile. Howsoever far these elastic terms may be stretched, there are too many cases which go beyond their bounds." Of Andrews's innovation of proximate cause he adds that "its usefulness as an analytical term has been destroyed by resolving it into a universal formula for the very phase of responsibility. . . ." (800–801). In place of these formulas Green offers the consideration of "factors more likely to control judgment," namely, policy factors. Thus, his own consideration of the *Palsgraf* case inquires not into who or what caused the accident, but into who or what should bear the cost of it. On the one hand, he argues, "railways can always absorb or spread the loss more easily than can the hurt passenger. . . . This argues for recovery for Mrs. Palsgraf." On the other hand, in support of the decision to deny recovery to Mrs. Palsgraf, Green acknowledges: "As rich as railways may be, as easy as it is for them to spread the loss, as necessary as it is to subject them to the strictest precautions, government does not yet impose all risks upon them." On the contrary, Green enunciates the policy nature of the decision involved: "It was a matter of adjustment by government of risks which, while normal in that they occur in constant variety, can not be eliminated from the hurly-burly of modern traffic and transportation" (800).

Coincident with the introduction of a calculus geared to policy in the law came the gradual decline of accident narratives in fiction, for both began to reflect a major reconceptualization of the accident that was less conducive to narratization. Indeed, the explosion of railroad signaling fiction in which accidents appeared represents something of a swan song for the accident narrative as it came to be known in the nineteenth century for without the inquiry into all those things that had comprised the notion of limited liability—namely, fault, carelessness, and complex causation—the story began to change, moving away from linearity and in-depth characterization and toward a more modern and more politicized notion of cause.

CHAPTER SEVEN

Epilogue

> It was on the face of it, a personal injury case, and
> most such cases tended to be simple matters com-
> pared with the commercial litigation that Facher
> was used to. Yet he saw right away that there was
> nothing simple about this complaint. There was a
> long list of plaintiffs, each purportedly suffering
> "an increased risk of leukemia and other cancers,
> liver disease, central nervous system disorders,
> and other unknown illnesses and disease."
> (Jonathan Harr, *A Civil Action*)[1]

THE STORY of the accident narrative in the twentieth century begins with
the problems posed to the orthodox narrative of causality by *Palsgraf* and
by the influential monograph on causation by Leon Green. In challenging
the viability of the old notion of causation which underwrote the orthodox doctrine of negligence and fault, and in preferring a policy-based
resolution to inquiries formerly based on fault, Green foretold the development of a different kind of accident narrative—one that was thematically preoccupied with replacing causation with policy and formally or
stylistically preoccupied with the breakdown of coherent causal narratives. These narratives differ from their nineteenth- and early twentieth-
century counterparts in revealing how the choice among multiple causes
or within protracted causal sequences is not logically but socially and
politically informed.

Indeed, the political nature of causation figures prominently in several
twentieth-century narratives of the modernist period—a period preoccupied with causal discontinuities—that revolve around accidents. In narratives as diverse as Thornton Wilder's *The Bridge Over San Luis Rey*
(1928), and John Dos Passos's *U.S.A.* trilogy (1930–36), for example, the
accidents that befall certain characters give rise to reflections about
chance, with implications that are religious and humanistic for Wilder,
more explicitly political and socioeconomic for Dos Passos. And although it was written much later, Charles Reznikoff's two-volume poem,
Testimony 1885–1915 (1965–75), based directly on the law reports of

several states, echoes many of the same concerns with the political and social implications of industrial accidents. In a passage oddly reminiscent of both Wilder's novel and of the landmark case of *Palsgraf v. Long Island Railroad*, Reznikoff writes:

> The track was slippery and the train moved slowly—
> people riding even on top of the box car and on the locomotive—
> and had gone only about three miles an hour
> when a bridge beneath it gave way.
> The platform on which the young woman was standing
> slipped down
> and stopped at a steep angle among the wreckage of the bridge
> and she found herself up to her waist in wreckage,
> both of her legs caught under the platform behind her
> and one of her feet crushed against the piling.[2]

Indeed, Reznikoff's poem is both an epic catalogue of industrial accidents and a protest against the safety hazards they impose disproportionately not only on the passenger and bystander, but on the working, not entrepreneurial, classes.

The significance of the rise of a politically informed notion of causality, however, is only part of the story of negligence's decline in the twentieth-century accident narrative. For the seeds of the causal uncertainty that gave rise to such a notion and that were, importantly, already sown in the inconclusive resolution of the steamboat disaster that killed Mark Twain's brother, also put an end to the model of individualism at the heart of the negligence paradigm. For in the twentieth century, the problem is not only that the causes of accidents have multiplied and been mechanized (which was already true in the nineteenth century, as we have seen), but that they are often lodged in the products of mechanized processes themselves. In short, as the accident narrative leaves the confines of the industrial era where human negligence, though mediated by a mechanical device, is still discernible, it enters those of the post-industrial era where, in Siegfried Giedion's ominous phrase, "mechanization takes command."[3] It takes root, in other words, in a world in which mechanical products are often made by other products in an endless and virtually untraceable regression, a world in which some products are no longer even mechanical objects but processes, chemical transformations, or recombinant technologies. Even if still manufactured by human hands, these are products that are so far removed from the site of their original manufacture that they appear to have taken on a life of their own. Hence the category of accident cases known as *products*-liability.

An outgrowth of products-liability, the toxic tort represents yet another form of important accident case in the twentieth century, and yet another way in which the paradigm of accident narratives in this century diverges from the individualism that characterized the previous one. In the toxic tort, prevalent in the legal cases and fictional narratives of the late twentieth century in particular, accidents typically revolve around products that have become deadly, that are not so much products as experiments or inventions whose potential effects are often unknown. They stretch the definition of products to include dangerous chemicals and nuclear power, and of accidents to include the unintended consequences of these products, like acid rain and the contamination at Love Canal. In the fiction that concerns this kind of accident, the animism of objects is taken as a given and the focus shifts from the threat posed by individual objects to individual humans to the threat of invisible, and possibly even unknown agents that could destroy human life as a whole. For example, toxic waste, chemical spills, and ozone depletion force a massive redefinition of the accident that includes human epidemics and wide-scale injuries to the environment.

Thus, in both products-liability and the toxic tort, the nineteenth-century notion of agency and blame—a notion that was intimately related to assumptions about the individual as the basis of all agency—has been altered. By contrast, in the twentieth-century narrative, the assumption is that agency is very often collectivized, and that the determination of liability must avoid useless inquiries into individual fault. In short, in these more modern narratives, the prevalent paradigm is one of strict liability, not negligence. But if the presence of the strict liability test in some sense brings the story I tell back to its beginnings, to the standard that prevailed before James Fenimore Cooper's time, it does not come full circle. For while individualism recedes in this late twentieth-century version of strict liability, fault does not. Thus, we can observe a shift in the trajectory of liability: from the paternalism and *noblesse oblige* that informed the first appearance of strict liability to the theories of atomism and capitalism that informed the emergence of negligence to the current reappearance of strict liability which, in the context of products-liability and toxic torts, is less a return to a pre-nineteenth-century protectionism than it is the strange and futuristic admission of the irrelevance of the individualistic terms of negligence in the apparent absence of human agency.

MECHANICAL AGENCY AND HUMAN AGENCY: STEPHEN KING

Commonly acknowledged as the first products-liability case, *Escola v. Coca Cola Bottling Co. of Fresno* (1944), provides a classic example of the encroachment on human agency by product agency.[4] Decided a year before the end of the Second World War, the *Escola* case involves the explosion not of a bomb, but of a Coke bottle. Although the case is most often cited in the law for Justice Traynor's concurring opinion, which first proposed the application of strict liability to product accidents, it is cited here for the language of the original judgment in which the threshold issue of product agency was first announced. The facts are simple: a waitress in a restaurant was injured when a bottle of Coca Cola "exploded" in her hand. In the absence of evidence directly implicating the bottle as an agent, the court was forced to rely on testimonials exculpating those who came into contact with it, chief among which was an eyewitness report that the waitress "did not knock the bottle against any other object" when transferring it from its case to the refrigerator. Thus, assured that "the bottle here involved was not damaged by any extraneous force after delivery to the restaurant," the court concluded that it had to be "in some manner defective" because of "an excessive charge or a defect in the glass."

In this description the product's agency is equated with a defect, giving an otherwise inexplicable kind of agency (a bottle exploding) an identifiable source. Yet in eliding the difference between agency and defect, the court acknowledges the mystery inherent in product defects and thus acknowledges its own limitations in articulating the kind of agency products can possess. Injuries from defective products are troublesome, Justice Traynor observes in *Escola*, whether they arise because of the manufacturing process or because of a submanufacturing error or a flaw in a component part. "Manufacturing processes, frequently valuable secrets, are ordinarily either inaccessible to or beyond the ken of the general public," Traynor writes. "The consumer no longer has means or skill enough to investigate for himself the soundness of a product, even when it is not contained in a sealed package" (440).

There is a particularly disturbing moment in J. D. Salinger's story "Uncle Wiggily in Connecticut" (1948), written only four years after *Escola*, that dramatizes the inscrutability of product injuries. In the story, an alienated suburban housewife, Eloise Wengler, reminisces with a friend about her old lover, Walt, a "wisecracking G.I." who died in the war when a Japanese stove he was sending home exploded in his face. "The last thing I'd do would be to tell him he was killed," Eloise says when asked why she won't tell her husband about Walt. "And if I did— which I wouldn't—but if I *did*, I'd tell him he was killed in action."[5] The unspeakability of Walt's death is revealing, for it seems to stem not only from the recognition of the senselessness of all premature deaths, but from Eloise's sense of it compared to a death "in action." Convention dictates that any death not directly related to the contest of war—Walt's accident occurred "between battles or something"—cannot be classified as military; yet we suspect that the uncertainty surrounding Walt's death is more than simply taxonomic. Indeed, it is only when Walt's death is contrasted with wartime casualties, which it nevertheless closely resembles (the stove *explodes,* after all), that it begins to seem not just senseless but virtually indescribable.

Of course, the basic recognition that a product may be mysterious is not new to *Escola* or to the postwar period, for it was long the ruling assumption in the adjudication not of *accidents* involving products but of *contract* disputes and of breach of warranty cases. Indeed, under that law known colloquially as the law of *caveat emptor* or "let the buyer beware," which prevailed in America until the end of the nineteenth century, buyers were left to rely on their own assessment of the product in question. "Such a rule," wrote the Supreme Court in a case from 1870, "requiring the purchaser to take care of his own interests, has been found best adapted to the wants of trade in the business transactions of life."[6] Indeed, the law of *caveat emptor* worked hand in hand with negligence to serve the interests of the manufacturing and commercial industries. The difference between the doctrine of *caveat emptor* and that articulated in *Escola* is precisely the difference made by the twentieth-century recognition that the injurious nature of a product could be so inscrutable, so "inaccessible," to use Traynor's word, that no buyer could reasonably be held liable for it.

Much of Stephen King's fiction is built upon this recognition. Indeed, the horror that informs so many of his stories turns on the inscrutable animus or agency with which so many mechanical inventions have been invested. In "The Mangler," for example, an industrial ironing and folding machine proves able not only to consume its operators but, after freeing itself from the concrete moorings that held it in place, stalks its prey beyond the laundry room's doors. Similarly, in "The Lawnmower Man," in which the man who operates a lawnmower for a commercial service does not run the lawnmower itself but simply snakes, naked, on his belly after it, eating the freshly cut grass, the lawnmower goes berserk, crashing through the living room wall of a self-satisfied member of the lawn-owning middle class who does not appreciate this unconventional, albeit highly efficient, method of lawn mowing. In King's story "The Sun Dog," moreover, a Polaroid camera displays an even more highly directed sense of its own purpose when a fifteen-year-old boy prematurely assumes his mastery over it. When presented with the camera on his birthday, the boy's first thought is " 'It's mine.' "[7] To prove him wrong, the camera begins to take only the pictures it wants to take; indeed, no matter who takes the picture or what is framed in the viewfinder the camera spits out a picture of a nonexistent, mangy dog. King draws out the implications of this strange reversal of human over object agency: " 'It's mine'—that was what he [the boy] had thought when his finger had pushed the shutter-button for the first time. Now he found himself wondering if maybe he hadn't gotten that backward?" (605).

In King's vision, as in that of the anthropologist Igor Kopytoff, commodities are not simply or always commodities; they can serve other functions, even have "biographies."[8] In particular, King seems interested in the inscrutable longevity and self-direction of certain mechanical inventions. Indeed, when seen in the context of objects that are explicitly invested with a self-propelling agency, like cars, for instance, King's vision of the stalking iron or the picture-making camera no longer seems confined to the realm of horror fiction. In Ralph Nader's classic work, *Unsafe at Any Speed* (1965), the consumer advocate gives voice to the strange phenomenon of the "one-car accidents" that finally forced a manufacturer's recall of all 1960–63 General Motors Corvairs. Rather than put the car on trial, Nader notes, General Motors settled out of court with the first accident victim who lost her arm when her Corvair flipped over unexpectedly. The company feared that a trial would not only tarnish its reputation and diminish sales, but lead to strict public regulation of its product. Nader writes:

> What would legislators think—men long nourished on the diet that "it's all because of the nut behind the wheel"—when court-sanctioned investigations of evidence brought out into the open the facts about an American car that abruptly decides to do the driving *for* the driver in a wholly untoward manner?[9]

King capitalizes on Nader's nonfictional but still, for some, unimaginable conceit of the self-propelled automobile in a host of stories that focus on autonomous vehicles. In "Trucks," for example, he once again scrutinizes the potential within self-governing commodities for a reversal of master-servant relations. In this story, a group of masculinized, heavy trucks, Mack semis and interstate haulers, enact a carnivalesque reversal of power and hold their drivers captive in a truck stop. Realizing that the trucks not only have the humans surrounded, but have forced them into refueling them, one of the captives bemoans the replacement of his own agency by object-agency. " 'You want to be their slaves?' the counterman had said. 'That's what it'll come to. You want to spend the rest of your life changin' oil filters every time one of those things blasts its horn?' "[10] Another of the characters inside the truck stop, a young girl whose naive astonishment has more raw force than any sophisticated analysis, reiterates more honestly the counterman's fear. " 'We made them!' the girl cried out with sudden wretchedness. 'They can't!' " (131).[11]

In his novel *Christine* (1983), King combines all the fears about self-governing commodities—the same fears that are voiced repeatedly in products-liability cases—as he traces the vengeful career of a car that is not only self-propelled but that has the ability to regenerate. After a particularly vicious attack on the car, its owner, Arnie, finds that the car has virtually repaired itself without him. ". . . [H]e had popped some of the dents, he could remember that. But he hadn't ordered any glass (although it was all replaced), he hadn't ordered any new seat covers (but they were all replaced, too)."[12] Indeed, Christine's ability to repair herself extends to an ability to regenerate from a heap of scrap metal, and the novel ends as the soft strains of her radio emerge from the maw of the giant bulldozer that has tried, in vain, to crush her. And in ending with the promise of Christine's reincarnation, not Arnie's, the human agent who successfully redeemed himself as he redeemed the car, the novel perfectly models the displacement of human with product agency.

THE TOXIC TORT: DON DELILLO

The masterful quality of machines like Christine and the Polaroid camera of King's fiction—machines that allow the product accident to reverse assumptions made about agency in narratives dominated by nineteenth-century notions of negligence—is also a prominent feature of the toxic tort. In the toxic tort, however, the longevity of the injurious agent is complicated by factors like latency, ubiquity, and a pandemic potential that make not just the human but the individualized focus of the causal inquiry within the negligence paradigm obsolete.

Not surprisingly, the accident narrative that emerges from such a context differs dramatically from its nineteenth-century counterpart. Indeed, if we take Don DeLillo's *White Noise* (1984) as a model, we can see how the inquiry into the accident's cause that was the centerpiece of the accident story in the nineteenth century is replaced by an inquiry into the accident's effects since these have become the greater unknowns. Of course, agency is still a complex issue. Typically a matter of exposure to a chemical, vapor, or gas, toxic accidents are often invisible or, if visible, generally inexplicable. In *White Noise*, for instance, the chemical spill that permeates Blacksmith, the college town where the main character, Jack Gladney, lives and teaches, is alternately described as a "black, nebulous cloud," and an "airborne toxic event," descriptions that suggest how visually and conceptually elusive the idea of accident has become. But even more elusive than the agency of the accident are its potential consequences which haunt its victims in a way that no previous kind of accident ever could.

In other words, unlike the analyses and narratives of other accidents, which take their definition from the accidental event—a lamp falls on someone's head, a chain saw severs someone's toe—the analysis of toxic accidents proceeds inductively from the signs of their having lodged in the body. We can only know the effects of a toxic accident when someone coughs or when a liver fails. Identifying the accident, then, is tantamount to identifying an illness. But the diagnosis is complicated by the fact that the signs rarely, if ever, appear on the spot. Thus, when Gladney accidentally exposes himself to the vapors enveloping the town (he is one of the last to be evacuated), he experiences no immediate symptoms. Rather, DeLillo's novel charts the progress not of his visible injury but of his overwhelming fear and anxiety about it which emerge as the most tangible and narratable effect of his accident—an effect, importantly, that forms the basis of a new legal accident suit. Indeed, a *fear* of death has been legitimated by the law as a basis for claiming injury for toxic accidents. In many cases, courts have dropped the requirement that there be a present illness and allowed damages for injuries not yet suffered but for which there is an increased risk of disease.

Indeed, at least one court has explicitly allowed recovery for toxic effects even when it was highly unlikely that the claimant would contract the disease.[13] In the case of *Jackson v. Johns-Manville Sales Corporation* (1986), the first and most expansive of the many cases to expose the history of corporations suppressing the truth about the hazards of asbestos, the court addressed in depth the "cancerphobia" of the former shipyard worker, Jackson, who had been exposed without warning to asbestos insulation. A lower court dismissed Jackson's claim because his medical tests showed only that he had "a mild case of asbestosis," and a "15 percent disability." Furthermore, it reasoned that while asbestosis was bad, it was not as bad as cancer,[14] thus discounting evidence that in the vast majority of cases asbestosis led to cancer. On appeal, a higher court took account of the latency period of asbestosis which, as the court confirmed, takes between ten and twenty-five years to manifest itself as either full-blown asbestosis or another form of cancer. Given the latency period, the court ruled, Jackson could recover damages for his fear of cancer and death. "Jackson's fear," the court wrote, "is plainly a present injury. It is a fear which he experiences every day and every night. It is fear which is exacerbated each time he learns that another victim of asbestos has died of lung cancer. It is fear which, *regardless of whether Jackson actually gets cancer*, will haunt him for the rest of his life."[15]

In his quest to learn more about his exposure to substantiate *his* fear, however, Jack Gladney encounters a void. Indeed, once they arrive at the designated shelter for evacuees in Iron City, Jack's son, Heinrich, who has a morbid fascination with disasters of all kinds, establishes himself as a local expert on the subject, his explanations drawing crowds. As Jack listens in, Heinrich explains how the toxic cloud lingering over Blacksmith, Nyodene D, is essentially garbage, "a whole bunch of things thrown together that are byproducts of the manufacture of insecticide."

> The original stuff kills roaches, the byproducts kill everything left over. . . . Once it seeps into the soil, it has a life span of forty years. . . . After five years you'll notice various kinds of fungi appearing between your regular windows and storm windows as well as in your clothes and food. After ten years your screens will turn rusty and begin to pit and rot. Siding will warp. . . . After twenty years you'll probably have to seal yourself in the attic and just wait and see.[16]

Heinrich's advice—to "wait and see"—epitomizes the problem with Nyodene D and toxic accidents in general: they take time to understand, often time that exceeds a given individual's lifetime. Indeed, the information available about Nyodene D and its effects on humans is all very general. Thus, Jack is frustrated when, on his visits to the doctor, he learns that the information available to him is only statistical and has little meaning for him personally. A medical technician who feeds Jack's name, the substance, and his exposure time into a computer, calls up his "computer history." The computer, he tells Jack, has "your genetics, your personals, your medicals, your psychologicals, your police-and-hospitals," all of which, apparently, say very little. " 'This doesn't mean anything is going to happen to you as such," the technician advises, " 'at least not today or tomorrow.' " The only reassurance Jack receives is in the hope that if he lives fifteen more years—half the lifespan of Nyodene D in the human body—scientists may then know a lot more about the disease in humans. Until then, science must content itself with knowledge of the toxin's effects on laboratory rats, and pretend that there is no relation between rats and humans. " 'If I was a rat,' " the technician remarks, " 'I wouldn't want to be anywhere within a two hundred mile radius of the airborne event.' " But in the same breath he tells Jack, " 'I wouldn't worry about what I can't see or feel. . . . I'd go ahead and live my life. Get married, settle down, have kids. There's no reason you can't do these things, knowing what we know' " (141).

The advice the doctor offers Jack is not medical precisely, but epidemiological. Epidemiology has been defined as "the science dealing with the environmental causes of diseases in humans as inferred from observations of human beings."[17] For the most part, epidemiology is a tentative "science." It proceeds from "observations of humans" because virtually nothing is known about the diseases with which it is concerned. The uncertainty of epidemiological evidence informs the adjudication of the accident in the legal context as well. This is evident in an early toxic tort case about the exposure to the toxin benzene. In this 1960 case, after a piano and cabinet finisher died of leukemia, a complaint was filed by his widow claiming that his death resulted from an occupational disease.[18] The legal determination in this case of whether liability could be assigned to the employer's company was based exclusively on medical testimony concerning the *effects* of exposure to benzene, an ingredient that as it turned out was found in varnish removers used by most, if not all, cabinet companies.

The case of the piano finisher was among the first to translate issues of causation into questions of epidemiology dealing largely with effects. At the time of the litigation, doubts remained about the nature of the disease in question. "[A] serious defect in claimant's case," the court wrote, "is that the causes of leukemia or its aggravation are unknown." Similarly, in 1960, relatively little was known about benzene. The fact that seventeen years later, in 1977, the Occupational Safety and Health Administration (OSHA) issued a report identifying benzene as a human leukemogen, only reinforces the inadequacy of both legal and medical vocabularies for understanding and describing toxic accidents.

Even when the medical knowledge of a particular disease or substance is, within the relative terms of epidemiology, considered complete, it is generally a function of statistical incidence and variable estimates. Epidemiology is rooted in a notion of correlation—a notion that is central to the medical analysis of disease and epidemics. Epidemiologists examine the relationship between disease and the environment in the context of populations, and their findings are phrased in terms of probable effects. But complications in epidemiological probabilities arise when epidemiological evidence cannot distinguish between the incidence of a disease in people exposed to the toxic substance in question and those in the population at large. Moreover, the question of incidence is one of degree. There are cases, like that of asbestosis, in which the incidence among an exposed group is so high that it constitutes causal certainty. Similarly, there are cases like that involving adenosis, a disease found almost exclusively in women whose mothers took the drug diethylstilbestrol ("DES"), for which the incidence in the population at large is so low that the connection between the drug and disease can be considered definitive. Problems inherent in the method of correlation account accurately, however, for the legal difficulties that surfaced in claims filed by American army personnel stemming from their exposure to the defoliant dioxin, commonly known as "Agent Orange," in Vietnam, or by soldiers claiming to have been exposed to toxic chemicals in the Persian Gulf War.[19] Because there was evidence that the Vietnam veterans demonstrated no higher incidence of cancers than people who were not in Vietnam, for example, and that in the relevant ten-year time period very little dioxin was sprayed over the jungles of southeast Asia, the court felt it necessary to distinguish between the question of whether "dioxin *can cause* certain diseases and whether it *did cause* a particular disease or defect in a particular person."[20]

The uncertainty of the epidemiological evidence is complicated by the latency of many toxic effects. The technician to whom Jack appeals tries to comfort him with the knowledge that illness from toxic injuries is latent and delayed, but Jack responds to this by turning his anxieties toward the future. He quickly recognizes that the effects of toxicity are intergenerational. Not only can toxic accidents end life for the living, but they can resurface in the altered bodies of future generations. "Fire and explosion were not the inherent dangers here," he thought. "This death would penetrate, seep into the genes, show itself in bodies not yet born" (116).

The mutagenic capacity of certain chemical compounds and other toxic substances has been an issue in the courts. In a recent case in Minnesota, the court directly addressed the problem of intergenerational harm.[21] The case was brought by the grandson of a woman who had taken DES to control miscarriages more than twenty-five years before he was born. The boy's mother, who was second-generation, was largely unaffected by the drug, although she did have difficulty during her own pregnancies. Her child, the third-generation victim, was born two months premature, a quadriplegic with cerebral palsy. While the court in this case dismissed the grandson's claim as unforeseeable, presumably because it did not accept the medical evidence of the damaging effects of DES as grounds for reasonable knowledge or fear of injury, it did admit the possibility of recognizing such a claim in the near future.

White Noise takes place in this near-future in that it raises a general concern about the chromosomal alterations that Nyodene D may engender. Jack, for instance, is concerned about the possibility that his children were exposed to the chemical when he opened his car door and let the vapor in. The combination of the chemical's latency period and severe toxicity make it even more likely that while the effects may not manifest themselves within Jack's normal lifetime, they will make themselves known in the course of his childrens'. "Show[ing] itself in bodies not yet born," as Jack predicts, wiping out not just generations within a family but an entire population's ability to generate, toxic accidents are not simply latently dangerous but injurious on an order of magnitude never seen before.[22]

In DeLillo's vision, as in that of the toxic tort paradigm itself, the accident narrative tells the story of vague and potentially unsubstantiated fears. Far from being another example of postmodern paranoia, however, this version of the accident narrative legitimates even the most unverifiable fears and injuries, going so far, as we have seen, as to equate the possibility of future injuries with present ones. Thus, the elements featured in the accident story of the nineteenth century—the elements of individual agency and causation that gave rise to a notion of fault-based responsibility—have now become almost obsolete. Viewing Jack Gladney's predicament through the lens of strict liability, the paradigm that now determines the adjudication of products-liability cases and toxic torts, allows us to see accidents and the responsibility assigned for them as intergenerational and transhistorical, as *possibilities*, in fact, that exist at times only in the imaginary narratives, both legal and literary, that contain them.

Notes

Chapter One
Introduction

1. For a valuable portrait of Shaw's tremendously influential career as a jurist, see Leonard W. Levy, *The Law of the Commonwealth and Chief Justice Shaw* (Cambridge: Harvard University Press, 1957), especially chaps. 8 and 10.

2. Shaw served as Chief Justice for thirty years, from 1830 to 1860.

3. *Brown v. Kendall*, 60 Mass. 292 (1850).

4. Ibid., 292–93.

5. 2 *History of English Law*, 42, cited in Charles Gregory, Harry Kalven, Richard Epstein, eds., *Cases and Materials on Torts* (Boston: Little, Brown and Company, 1977), 76.

6. For an incisive overview of the changes in the American concept of individualism in the nineteenth century, see Sacvan Bercovitch, *The Rites of Assent: Transformations in the Symbolic Construction of America* (New York: Routledge, 1993), 308–18.

7. James Barr Ames, "Law and Morals," 22 *Harv. L. Rev.* 97, 99 (1908).

8. See, for example, *Stephens v. White*, 2 Wash 203 (Va. 1796); *Cross v. Guthery*, 2 Root 90 (Conn. 1794); *Coker v. Wickes* (R.I. 1742).

9. *Patten v. Halsted*, 1 Coxe 277, 279 (N.J. 1795). See also *Jones v. Abbee*, 1 Root 106 (Conn. 1787); *Staphorse v. New Haven*, 1 Root 126 (Conn. 1789).

10. *Patten v. Halsted*, 1 Coxe 277, 279 (N.J. 1795).

11. Indeed, some have argued that this defense appeared in England as early as the fourteenth or fifteenth century.

12. The pleading rules in accident cases were very complex. Briefly, injuries that had been inflicted directly by the injurer on the injured were typically pleaded in "trespass," while those that were inflicted indirectly, often by means of an intervening act or agent, were pleaded in "case." The accidents to which I refer here were those pleaded in case.

13. See, for example, *Ogle v. Barnes*, 8 T.R. 188, 101 Eng. Reg. 1338 (1799).

14. There has been a good deal of controversy about the significance attributed to Shaw's decision. Oliver Wendell Holmes Jr. was the first to single out Shaw's decision as a turning point for the doctrine of negligence, and many scholars since then have followed suit. See, for example, Charles Gregory, "Trespass to Nuisance to Absolute Liability," 37 *Va. L. Rev.* 359 (1951). Others, however, have taken the opposite view, claiming that Shaw's decision had absolutely no significance whatsoever. See, for example, E. F. Roberts, "Negligence: Blackstone to Shaw To?" 50 *Cornell L. Rev.* 191 (1965). Still others recognize its significance as a leading, although not unique, case, and it is this position that I urge here. See, for example, Morton Horwitz, *The Transformation of American Law: 1780–1860* (Cambridge: Harvard University Press, 1977), 90.

15. See, for example, *Percival v. Hickey*, 18 Johns. 257 (N.Y. 1820); *Fales v. Dearborn*, 1 Pick. 344 (Mass. 1823); *Sproul v. Hemingway*, 14 Pick. 1 (Mass. 1833); *Lehigh Bridge v. Lehigh Coal & Navig. Co.*, 4 Rawle 8 (Pa. 1833).

16. Oliver Wendell Holmes Jr., "The Theory of Torts," 7 *Am. L. Rev.* 660 (1873).

17. This rule was first articulated in the landmark case of *Farwell v. Boston & Worcester R.R.*, 45 Mass. 49 (1842). For a brief history and explanation of the fellow-servant rule, see Lawrence M. Friedman, *A History of American Law*, 2d ed. (New York: Simon & Schuster, 1985), 301, 470.

18. *Lamson v. American Axe & Tool Co.*, 177 Mass. 144 (1900).

19. For more on the doctrine of the assumption of risk, see G. Edward White, *Tort Law in America: An Intellectual History* (New York: Oxford University Press, 1985), 41.

20. Morton Horwitz, *The Transformation of American Law: 1870–1969* (New York: Oxford University Press, 1992), 52.

21. James Boyd White, *Heracles' Bow: Essays on the Rhetoric and Poetics of the Law* (Madison: University of Wisconsin Press, 1985), 107.

22. Owen Fiss, "Objectivity and Interpretation," in Sanford Levinson and Steven Mailloux, eds., *Interpreting Law and Literature: A Hermeneutic Reader* (Evanston: Northwestern University Press, 1988), 229.

23. Ronald Dworkin, "Law as Interpretation," in W.J.T. Mitchell, ed., *The Politics of Interpretation* (Chicago: University of Chicago Press, 1983), 263.

24. Robert Cover, "Nomos and Narrative," in Martha Minow, Michael Ryan, and Austin Sarat, eds., *Narrative, Violence, and the Law: The Essays of Robert Cover* (Ann Arbor: University of Michigan Press, 1992), 95–96.

25. Ibid., 101.

26. Brook Thomas, *Cross-Examinations in Law and Literature: Cooper, Hawthorne, Stowe, and Melville* (Cambridge: Cambridge University Press, 1987), 1–18.

27. Wai Chee Dimock, *Residues of Justice: Literature, Law, Philosophy* (Berkeley: University of California Press, 1996), 26.

28. See, for example, Alan Trachtenberg, *The Incorporation of America* (New York: Hill and Wang, 1982); Walter Benn Michaels, *The Gold Standard and the Logic of Naturalism* (Berkeley: University of California Press, 1987); Howard Horwitz, *By the Law of Nature* (New York: Oxford University Press, 1991).

29. See Horwitz, *The Transformation of American Law: 1780–1860*; Robert Rabin, "The Historical Development of the Fault Principle: A Reinterpretation," in *Perspectives on Tort Law*, ed. Robert Rabin (Boston: Little, Brown and Company, 1983); G. Edward White, *Tort Law in America: An Intellectual History* (New York: Oxford University Press, 1985).

30. See C. B. MacPherson, *The Political Theory of Possessive Individualism* (New York: Oxford University Press, 1962).

31. See J.G.A. Pocock, *The Machiavellian Moment: Florentine Political Thought and the Atlantic Republican Tradition* (Princeton: Princeton University Press, 1975).

Chapter Two
A Clear Showing

1. Oliver Wendell Holmes Jr., *The Common Law* (New York: Dover Publications, Inc., 1991), 3.

2. James Fenimore Cooper, *The Pioneers* (New York: Penguin Books, 1988). Subsequent cites are in the text.

3. Thomas, *Cross-Examinations of Law and Literature: Cooper, Hawthorne, Stowe, and Melville*, 21–44.

4. Charles Swann, "Guns Mean Democracy: The Pioneers and the Game Laws," in *New Essays on Cooper*, ed. Robert Clark (New York: Barnes and Noble, 1985), 96–120.

5. Tort has also traditionally protected against the invasion of selected non-physical interests, such as emotional harm and defamation.

6. Cooper, *The Letters and Journals of James Fenimore Cooper*, ed. James F. Beard (Cambridge: Harvard University Press, 1960–68).

7. In *The American Democrat* Cooper argues that it is the duty of the gentry to protect the rights of the individual and of democracy. "Liberality is peculiarly the quality of a gentleman," he writes. James Fenimore Cooper, *The American Democrat* (Indianapolis: Liberty Classics [reprint], 1931), 114.

8. Oliver Wendell Holmes Jr., "The Theory of Torts," 7 *Am. L. Rev.* 653 (1873). My emphasis.

9. C. B. MacPherson, *Democratic Theory: Essays in Retrieval* (London: Oxford University Press, 1977), 127.

10. Ibid., 127–28.

11. See Horwitz, *The Transformation of American Law: 1780–1860*, 31–40.

12. Cited in William Nelson, *Americanization of the Common Law: The Impact of Change on Massachusetts Society, 1760–1830* (Cambridge: Harvard University Press, 1975), 121.

13. Horwitz, *The Transformation of American Law: 1780–1860*, 32.

14. Ibid., 35.

15. Ibid.

16. See, for example, *Palmer v. Mulligan*, 3 Cai. R. 307 (1805); *Platt v. Johnson*, 15 Johns. 213 (1818).

17. *Palmer v. Mulligan*, 3 Cai. R. 307 (1805).

18. Ibid.

19. *Platt v. Johnson* (1818).

20. *Panton v. Holland*, 17 John. 92, 94 (1819).

21. Horwitz, *The Transformation of American Law: 1780–1860*, 40.

22. Quoted in ibid., 8.

23. Lon L. Fuller, "Human Interaction and the Law," in Robert Paul Wolff, ed., *The Rule of Law* (New York: Simon and Schuster, 1971), 176. See also Melvin Aron Eisenberg, *The Nature of the Common Law* (Cambridge: Harvard University Press, 1988).

24. Quoted in Wolff, *The Rule of Law*, 117.

25. Lon L. Fuller, "Human Interaction and the Law," in Wolff, ed., *The Rule of Law*, 189.

26. Elaine Scarry, *The Body in Pain: The Making and Unmaking of the World* (New York: Oxford University Press, 1985), 153.

27. Holmes, *The Common Law*, 77.

28. Wolff, ed., *The Rule of Law*, 173.

29. Ibid., 190.

30. Holmes, *The Common Law*, quoted in Charles O. Gregory, Harry Kalven Jr., Richard Epstein, *Cases and Materials on Tort* (Boston: Little, Brown and Company, 1977), 68.

31. While Ian Hacking has shown that probability, as we understand it, first emerged in the 1660s, he has also shown that it was not associated with what was normal or customary until the 1820s. With the "avalanche of printed numbers" about birth, mortality, and disease that took hold in the first half of the nineteenth century and that later in the century came to include data about crime and suicide, the normal became a simple matter of prediction. Statistical regularities gave rise to the laws of chance which figured prominently in the law of negligence later in the nineteenth century.

32. Thomas, *Cross-Examinations*, 21.

33. John P. McWilliams Jr., *Political Justice in a Republic: James Fenimore Cooper's America* (Berkeley: University of California Press, 1972), 119.

34. Cooper himself was embroiled in a number of legal disputes over the title to property; foremost among them was the Three-Mile Point controversy. Cooper's father, himself a judge, had legal title to a narrow strip of land near Otsego Lake in New York called Three-Mile Point. During the judge's lifetime, and for some time afterward, townspeople used the land for recreational purposes with the permission of the Cooper family. Over the years, however, public use had resulted in the destruction of some of the land and structures on it. When James Fenimore Cooper became the executor of his father's will, he distributed a hand-bill prohibiting public use. A public uproar followed which included the publication of libelous comments about Cooper and his books in the local newspapers. Cooper sued. The broad contours of the dispute became the subject of one of Cooper's later novels, *Home as Found* (1838). See the discussion of this novel in Eric Sundquist, *Home as Found: Authority and Genealogy in Nineteenth-Century American Literature* (Baltimore: Johns Hopkins University Press, 1979). See also Cooper, *The Letters and Journals of James Fenimore Cooper*, ed. James F. Beard.

35. See, for example, William P. Kelly, *Plotting America's Past* (Carbondale: Southern Illinois University Press, 1983); McWilliams, *Political Justice in a Republic*; Thomas, *Cross Examinations*.

Chapter Three
Negligence before the Mast

1. Henry Flanders, *A Treatise on Maritime Law* (Boston: Little, Brown and Company, 1852).

2. The memoir, originally published in 1843, was not Cooper's own but that of an old shipmate of his by the name of Ned Myers. Cooper transcribed and

edited it, and it appeared under his name. See James Fenimore Cooper, *Ned Myers; Or, A Life Before the Mast* (Annapolis: Naval Institute Press, 1989). Subsequent cites appear in the text.

3. These are, in chronological order: *The Pilot* (1824); *The Red Rover* (1827); *The Water-Witch* (1830); *Homeward Bound* (1838); *Mercedes of Castile* (1840); *The Wing-and-Wing* (1842); *The Two Admirals* (1842); *Afloat and Ashore* and *Miles Wallingford* (double novel, 1844); *Jack Tier* (1848); and *The Sea Lions* (1849).

4. According to one account, Cooper also met with English press gangs and pirates during this turbulent voyage. See Thomas Philbrick, *James Fenimore Cooper and the Development of the American Sea Fiction* (Cambridge: Harvard University Press, 1961), 42.

5. By the time Cooper began to write, Smollett had already written *Roderick Random* (1748), *Peregrine Pickle* (1751), and *The Adventures of Sir Launcelot Greaves* (1760–61), all of which included some naval characters and settings. More of a direct influence on Cooper was Scott's more recent attempt at nautical fiction with *The Pirate* (1822).

6. See Horwitz, *The Transformation of American Law: 1780–1860*, 88.

7. As a technical matter, most ship collisions were adjudicated not in common law courts, but in admiralty courts called into being by the Constitution. (Article III, Section 2 gives jurisdiction of maritime matters to the federal courts for the resolution of all cases pertaining to the sea.) Yet the difference in jurisdiction had little bearing on the development of the negligence concept and the substantive principles of fault and carelessness remained essentially the same in both. On the strength of this similarity, one early ship collision case argued that common law jurisdiction over marine torts should be concurrent with that of admiralty.

8. Horwitz, *The Transformation of American Law: 1780–1860*, 88 n.141.

9. Nathan Dane, 73 *A General Abridgement and Digest of American Law* 35 (1824).

10. So powerful was the older understanding that it lingered long after the more modern notion of negligence was first articulated. For example, in his pathbreaking treatise, *A General Abridgement*, Dane draws on both meanings of negligence at different times.

11. I am indebted to the analysis provided by Horwitz here. See Horwitz, *The Transformation of American Law: 1780–1860*, 88.

12. Benjamin Oliver Jr., *Forms of Practice; Or American Precedents* 619 (1828).

13. *The Whaleman's Shipping List and Merchant Transcript*, May 4, 1847, V (8), 1.

14. The rules for filing Protests and an explanation of their purpose were included in most contemporary seamen's manuals. See, for example, Frederic W. Sawyer, *The Merchant's and Shipmaster's Guide, in Relation to Their Rights, Duties and Liabilities* (Boston: Benjamin Loring & Co., 1840), 139.

15. *Case of the Ship Stephania of New Bedford*, Matthew Fisher, Master (Records of The Old Dartmouth Historical Society, New Bedford, Mass.).

16. One could argue that the prudent and subdued hero had his origins in the ancient Greek epics, if not earlier.

17. James Walce provides a historically relevant and rich discussion of the novel in his *Early Cooper and His Audience* (New York: Columbia University Press, 1986), 67–77.

18. James Fenimore Cooper, *Precaution* (New York: D. Appleton and Company, 1873), 188.

19. See, for example, George E. Hastings, "How Cooper Became a Novelist," *American Literature* (1940), 12:20–51.

20. In *Persuasion*, it is young Louisa Musgrove who experiences the near-fatal accident in falling from a high wall. See Jane Austen, *Persuasion* (Harmondsworth: Penguin Books, Inc., 1965), chap. 12.

21. Ibid., 254.

22. James Fenimore Cooper, *The Pilot: A Tale of the Sea* (Albany: State University of New York Press, 1986), 39. My emphasis. Subsequent cites appear in the text.

23. According to notes he made in preparation for the novel, Cooper based the portrait of the pilot on the legendary figure of John Paul Jones, an important, although to Cooper's mind, sadly neglected hero in America's war for independence.

24. See Kay Seymour House, "Historical Introduction," *The Pilot* (Albany: State University of New York Press, 1986), xxi–xxv.

25. James Fenimore Cooper, *The Red Rover, A Tale* (New York: The Library of America, 1991), 599. Subsequent cites appear in the text.

26. James Fenimore Cooper, *The Water-Witch, or The Skimmer of the Seas* (Boston: Houghton, Osgood and Company, 1880), 358–59.

27. Edgar Allan Poe, "MS. Found in a Bottle," in *The Complete Tales & Poems* (New York: Vintage Books, 1975), 119. Subsequent cites appear in the text.

28. Edgar Allan Poe, *The Narrative of Arthur Gordon Pym* in *Selected Writings of Edgar Allan Poe*, ed. Edward Davidson (Boston: Houghton, Mifflin and Company, 1956), 257.

29. See Wai Chee Dimock, *Empire for Liberty: Melville and the Poetics of Individualism* (Princeton: Princeton University Press, 1989), 114–15.

30. Herman Melville, *Moby Dick* (New York: W. W. Norton & Company, 1967), 103. Subsequent cites appear in the text.

31. For a brilliant accounting of the general conflict embodied by these two main characters, see Sacvan Bercovitch, *The American Jeremiad* (Madison: The University of Wisconsin Press, 1978), 192–23.

32. See Thomas, *Cross-Examinations*, 234.

33. These included Richard Henry Dana Jr. and Charles Sumner.

34. James Fenimore Cooper, "Proceedings of the Naval Court Martial in the Case of Alexander Slidell Mackenzie . . . to which is appended An Elaborate Review by James Fenimore Cooper" (New York: Henry G. Langley, 1844), 272. Subsequent cites appear in the text. For other materials pertinent to the case, see Harrison Hayford, ed., *The Somers Mutiny Affair* (Englewood Cliffs, N.J.: Prentice-Hall, Inc., 1959).

35. Charles Sumner also did. Before examining the evidence in his *North American Review* article on the *Somers* case itself, Sumner, for example, provides

a long history of famous British mutinies, including those of the *Bounty*, *Nore*, and *Spithead* in the hope that "[i]t may teach us further, that the commander cannot be too wakeful in his care to preserve his ship. . . ." Charles Sumner, "The Mutiny of the Somers," *North American Review*, LVII (July, 1843), 197.

36. Richard Henry Dana Jr., quoted in Charles Francis Adams, *Richard Henry Dana: A Biography*, I (Boston: Houghton, Mifflin and Company, 1891), 56. Subsequent cites appear in the text.

37. Thomas's argument revolves around the idea of a procedural violation that is nevertheless condoned. See Thomas, *Cross-Examinations*, 214.

38. Herman Melville, *Billy Budd, Foretopman* in *Selected Tales and Poems*, ed. Richard Chase (New York: Holt, Rinehart and Winston, Inc., 1950), 355.

39. Holmes, *The Common Law*, 111.

40. Richard Henry Dana Jr., *Two Years Before the Mast, A Personal Narrative* (New York: Penguin Books, 1964), 97. Subsequent cites appear in the text.

41. Richard Henry Dana Jr., *The Seaman's Friend* (Boston: Thomas Groom & Co., 1851, rpt. by Scholars' Facsimiles & Reprints, 1979), iii. Subsequent cites appear in the text.

42. In 1854, as counsel to a steamship owner accused of negligently colliding with a sailing ship, Dana found himself in the enviable position of being able not only to reiterate existing standards for collision, but to rewrite them to make them even more specific. In this case, known simply as *The Osprey*, 1 Sprague 245 (1854), Dana argued for a new rule that distinguished between sailing vessels and steamers and that reconstituted the requirements for their behavior. Dana persuaded the court that since the steamer had superior capabilities, it should be required to get out of the way while the sailing vessel held its course, rather than requiring both vessels to turn to their right.

43. Its impact is indicated, among other things, by the fact that it was adopted by an Act of Congress in 1890 as part of international law. Dana records his sense of personal triumph in the case in Richard Henry Dana Jr., *The Journal of Richard Henry Dana, Jr., Vol. II*, ed. Robert F. Lucid (Cambridge: Harvard University Press, 1968), 662–63.

44. In admiralty law, this quality is referred to as "good" or "prudent seamanship" and is synonymous with the qualities invoked by negligence law. See Grant Gilmore and Charles Black, *The Law of Admiralty* (Mineola, N.Y.: Foundation Press, 1975), 509.

45. There were scores of popular nautical short story writers in this period (some who started writing before Dana, but a majority of whom wrote after him), whose works are not, for reasons of scope, mentioned here. See, for example, John Codman (alias Captain Ringbolt), *Sailors' Life and Sailors' Yarns* (New York: C. S. Francis & Co., 1847); William Leggett, *Naval Stories* (New York: Carvill, 1834); William Leggett, *Tales and Sketches of a Country Schoolmaster* (New York: Harper, 1829); John Gould, *Forecastle Yarns*, ed. Edward Gould (Baltimore: Taylor, 1845); Nathaniel Ames, *An Old Sailor's Yarns* (New York: Dearborn, 1835).

46. T. S. Arthur, "The Shipwreck," in *HairBreadth Escapes or Perilous Incidents in the Lives of Sailors and Travelers in Japan, Cuba, East Indies, Etc.,*

Etc. (New York: Worthington Co., 1889), 150. Subsequent cites appear in the text.

47. John Sherburne Sleeper (alias Hawser Martingale), "The Unlucky Ship, or Ned Spanker's Story," in *Tales of the Ocean and Essays for the Forecastle* (Boston: G. W. Cottrell, 1857), 202. Subsequent cites appear in the text.

48. John Sherburne Sleeper (alias Hawser Martingale), "The Drunken Captain, or Ned Rollins's Story," in *Tales of the Ocean and Essays for the Forecastle* (Boston: G. W. Cottrell, 1857), 104. Subsequent cites appear in the text.

Chapter Four
"Nobody to Blame"

1. Frank Norris, "The Mechanics of Fiction," in *The Responsibilities of the Novelist* (New York: Greenwood Press, 1968), 152–53.

2. Mark Twain and Charles Dudley Warner, *The Gilded Age: A Tale of Today* (New York: New American Library, 1980), 47. Subsequent cites appear in the text.

3. The "nobody" to which Twain refers here and in which I am interested in this chapter bears some resemblance to the eighteenth-century phenomenon of nobodies delineated by Catherine Gallagher in her recent book, *Nobody's Story: The Vanishing Acts of Women Writers in the Marketplace, 1670–1820* (Berkeley: University of California Press, 1994). But where Gallagher seems interested in the extent to which the fictional and authorial persona of "nobody" made possible a writerly and readerly identification, I focus more on the late nineteenth-century use of the concept by those who wished to avoid being identified.

4. Karl Marx, *Capital* (New York: Random House, Inc., 1906), 412.

5. Ibid. My emphasis.

6. Thomas Hardy, *Tess of the d'Urbervilles* (New York: W. W. Norton & Co, 1965), 269.

7. Susan Gillman, *Dark Twins: Imposture and Identity in Mark Twain's America* (Chicago: University of Chicago Press, 1989), 5.

8. It is tempting to think of Twain as among the first to imply, if only indirectly, that the legal understanding of identity might benefit from looking to the more diverse and fully amplified understanding of human subjectivity in, for example, literature. The so-called humanizing effects of literature on the law have long been touted by scholars. However, in response to this tradition, a countertradition has asserted itself that provides a more skeptical view of the literary representation of subjectivity itself, reminding us that the literary subject has often been not the "everyman," but the voice of the prosperous middle classes.

9. Louis C. Hunter, *Steamboats on the Western Rivers* (Cambridge: Harvard University Press, 1949), 300–301.

10. Ibid.

11. Ibid., 302.

12. Mark Twain, *Life on the Mississippi* (New York: Penguin Books, 1984), 189. Subsequent cites appear in the text.

13. Mark Twain, *Mark Twain's Letters*, eds. Edgar Marquess Branch,

Michael B. Frank, Kenneth M. Sanderson (Berkeley: University of California Press, 1988), I, 358.

14. Horwitz, *By the Law of Nature*, 100.

15. Ibid., 102.

16. Reports varied wildly. See Twain, *Mark Twain's Letters*, I, 83n. 5.

17. Rumors at the time suggested that Dorris had been named to protect the ship's owners who had, among other things, failed to have defects in the boilers repaired. Others, including some on the commission, felt that the separation of the hull that resulted from the *Pennsylvania*'s race with the *Duke* not long before the accident, was the more likely cause of the explosion. See the account in Edgar Marquess Branch, *Men Call Me Lucky: Mark Twain and the Pennsylvania* (Oxford, Ohio: Friends of the Library Society, Miami University, 1985), 8: 45–47.

18. "Capt. Kinefelter," Daily Memphis *Avalanche*, 20 August 1858, 3.

19. "Steamboat Anti-Liquor Law," Memphis *Daily Appeal*, 23 June 1858, 2. For additional accounts of the controversy surrounding Dorris, see also "Who Was to Blame?" Natchez *Daily Courier*, 23 June 1858, 2; "Alleged Cause of the Explosion of the Pennsylvania," Memphis *Daily Appeal*, 19 June 1858, 2; "The Explosion of the Pennsylvania," Memphis *Daily Morning Bulletin*, 22 June 1858, 1.

20. Albert Paine, *Mark Twain: A Biography*, I (New York: Harper & Brothers, 1912), 143.

21. Bernard DeVoto, *Mark Twain's America* (Boston: Houghton Mifflin Company, 1967), 103–4.

22. In a footnote in *The Gilded Age*, Twain himself notes that the account of the disaster is taken from real life. That it was based on his brother's death is commonly acknowledged by Twain scholars. For the most comprehensive accounts of the actual events and their transformation into fiction, see Branch, *Men Call Me Lucky: Mark Twain and the Pennsylvania*; Michael H. Marleau, "'The Crash of Timbers Continued—The Deck Swayed under Me': Samuel L. Clemens, Eyewitness to the Race and Collision between the *Pennsylvania* and *Vicksburg*," *Mark Twain Journal* 28 (1990): 1–36.

23. See Twain, *Mark Twain's Letters*, II, 80—85.

24. The dream, which apparently occurred shortly before the *Pennsylvania* disaster, involved a vision of Henry, Twain's brother, lying in a metallic coffin, dressed in a suit of his brother's, with a bouquet of white roses resting on his chest. See Forrest G. Robinson, "Why I Killed My Brother: An Essay on Mark Twain," *Literature and Psychology* 30 (1980), 174.

25. Ibid., 171.

26. Hunter, *Steamboats on the Western Rivers*, 289.

27. See, for example, *Dunlap v. Steamboat Reliance*, 2 Fed Rep 249 (1880); *Spear v. Philadelphia, Wilmington & Baltimore Railroad Co. et al*, 119 Pa. St. 61 (1888). In still other cases a more moderate view held that where there was clear evidence of human wrongdoing, as in the case of a race between two steamboats, like that between the *Boreas* and the *Amaranth*, the disaster was attributable to human negligence.

28. Hunter, *Steamboats on the Western Rivers*, 290.

29. Twain wrote several accounts of earthquakes for this and other newspapers. See Mark Twain, *Early Tales and Sketches*, ed. Edgar Branch and Robert H. Hirst, vol. 1, 1851–64 (Berkeley: University of California Press, 1979), 289–310.

30. 4 *Ruling Case Law* (*RCL*) 709, ed. William M. McKinney, vol. 4 (1914).

31. Ibid., 708.

32. Ibid., 713–14.

33. For instance when the boiler of the eastern steamboat, *Enterprise*, blew up near Charleston, South Carolina, in 1816, some held that a bolt of lightning had brought the explosion on. See Hunter, 284n. 29.

34. *Ryan v. New York Central R. Co.*, 35 N.Y. 210 (1866).

35. *Wood v. Pennsylvania R. Co.*, 61 F.2d 767 (1896).

36. *Baltimore City Passenger R. Co. v. Kemp*, 61 Md. 74 (1884).

37. *Springer v. Pacific Fruit Exchange*, 92 Cal. App. 732, 268 P. 951 (1928).

38. *Purcell v. St. Paul City R. Co.*, 48 Minn. 134, 50 N.W. 1034 (1892).

39. *Ramsey v. Carolina-Tennessee Power Co.*, 195 N.C. 788, 143 S.E. 861 (1928).

40. For the connection between the two men, see Philip P. Weiner, *Evolution and the Founders of Pragmatism* (Cambridge: Harvard University Press, 1949), 152–56.

41. Nicholas St. John Green, *Essays and Notes on the Law of Tort and Crime* (Menasha, Wis.: George Banta Publishing Co., 1933), 11. Subsequent cites appear in the text.

42. Holmes, *The Common Law*, 1.

43. Quoted in Horwitz, "The Doctrine of Objective Causation," in *The Politics of Law: A Progressive Critique*, ed. David Kairys (New York: Pantheon Books, 1983), 204.

44. Ibid.

45. Ibid.

46. William Graham Sumner, "The Shifting of Responsibility," in *Essays of William Graham Sumner*, II, ed. Albert Keller and Maurice Davie Sumner (New Haven: Yale University Press, rpt. Archon Books, 1969), 263.

47. Indeed, a concern with responsibility surfaced earlier as well. Not yet defined as a problem of responsibility, as such, the notion emerged in some of the nautical novels and stories that concerned me in the previous chapter.

48. Norris, "The Mechanics of Fiction," in *The Responsibilities of the Novelist*, 152.

49. Dimock, *Residues of Justice*, 168.

50. Ibid., 172.

51. See Gillman, *Dark Twins: Imposture and Identity in Mark Twain's America*, 5.

52. Eric Sundquist, *To Wake the Nations: Race in the Making of American Literature* (Cambridge: Harvard University Press, 1993), 225–70.

53. See Myra Jehlen, "Reading Gender in The Adventures of Huckleberry

Finn," in Gerald Graff, James Phelan, eds., *The Adventures of Huckleberry Finn: A Case Study in a Critical Controversy* (Boston: Bedford St. Martin's, 1995).

54. See Randall Knoper, *Acting Naturally: Mark Twain in the Culture of Performance* (Berkeley: University of California Press, 1995).

55. See Bruce Michelson, *Mark Twain on the Loose: A Comic Writer and the American Self* (Amherst: University of Massachusetts Press, 1995).

56. Brook Thomas, "Tragedies of Race, Training, Birth, and Communities of Competent Pudd'nheads," *American Literary History*, vol. 1, no. 4, 1989, 773. In this piece Thomas focuses on the negative attributes of the notion of training in *Pudd'nhead Wilson* as a symptom of nineteenth-century thought that turned for better or for worse to the authority of professional, collective opinion for its determination of such things as race.

57. See Mark Seltzer, *Bodies and Machines* (New York: Routledge, 1992), 17.

58. Mark Twain, *A Connecticut Yankee in King Arthur's Court* (New York: New American Library, 1963), 53. Subsequent cites appear in the text.

59. Hunter, *Steamboats on the Western Rivers*, 314.

60. White, *Tort Law in America: An Intellectual History*, 149.

61. Holmes, *The Common Law*, 94.

62. Twain was sympathetic to the laboring poor, but his sympathies, as Louis Budd remarks, never went "beyond orthodox limits." Budd makes the point that Twain was more attuned to the plight of the "Old World 'commoner'" than to the "captives of New York City sweatshops." Louis J. Budd, *Mark Twain: Social Philosopher* (Bloomington: Indiana University Press, 1962), 136–37.

63. Ibid., 138.

64. While it is clear that Twain felt pressed to take advantage of money-making ventures, and even relished them at times, it is equally clear that he saw them as a vice. As further evidence of his bifurcated view of Twain, Justin Kaplan writes that "the writer Mark Twain saw omens of disaster long before the promoter Mark Twain, who all his life believed that he was lucky. . . ." Justin Kaplan, *Mr. Clemens and Mark Twain* (New York: Simon and Schuster, 1966), 281.

65. For a description of Twain's obsession with the Paige typesetter, see ibid., 281–88.

66. Although it was a collaborative effort, *The Gilded Age* was written in relatively discrete sections. The stories of Col. Sellars, the Hawkinses, and Laura, were exclusively Twain's. For a complete breakdown of the writing, see Bryant Morey French, *Mark Twain and the Gilded Age: The Book that Named an Era* (Dallas: Southern Methodist University Press, 1965), 60–61.

67. See Hunter, *Steamboats on the Western Rivers*, 364.

68. The first accident insurance company in the United States was the Franklin Health Assurance Co. of Massachusetts, founded in 1850, which was followed in 1863 by the Travelers Insurance Co., established by James G. Batterson. R. W. Osler, *Guide to Accident & Sickness Insurance* (Indianapolis: The Rough Notes Company, Inc., 1952), 144–45.

69. See Daniel J. Boorstin, *The Americans: The Democratic Experience* (New York: Random House, 1973), 175. Few studies devote as much time to the origins

of the accident insurance industry as they do to that of life insurance. The best of these is *Morals and Markets: The Development of Life Insurance in the United States* (New York: Columbia University Press, 1979). For a brief description of the legal implications of the nineteenth-century insurance industry, see Lawrence M. Friedman, *A History of American Law* (New York: Simon and Schuster, 1985), 545.

70. For the importance of insurance in Twain's Hartford, see Kenneth R. Andrews, *Nook Farm: Mark Twain's Hartford Circle* (Cambridge: Harvard University Press, 1950), 118.

71. For Twain's account of this financial debacle, see Mark Twain, *The Autobiography of Mark Twain*, ed. Charles Neider (New York: HarperCollins, 1959), 231.

72. By today's standards, nineteenth-century insurance settlements were not high, but their very existence seemed inflationary to victims who had grown accustomed to no compensation at all. See White, *Tort Law in America*, 148–49.

73. In addition to this speech, Twain wrote many letters condemning the insurance industry, including one to Charles Cole Hine, the editor of the monthly *Insurance Monitor*, who had asked Twain to contribute an article. "I've got plenty of money & plenty of credit—& so I won't write about your wicked & dreadful insurance business till my gas bills go to protest & the milk-man ceases to toot his matutinal horn before the gates of Yours Truly & Defiantly, Mark Twain," Twain wrote. Twain, *Mark Twain's Letters*, IV, 69.

74. Mark Twain, *The Complete Works of Mark Twain: Mark Twain's Speeches* (New York: Harper & Brothers, 1923), 81.

75. See Friedman, *A History of American Law*, 269 ff.

76. Ibid., 546.

77. Quoted in Maxwell Geismar, *Mark Twain: An American Prophet* (Boston: Houghton Mifflin, 1970), 456.

78. See Andrews, *Nook Farm*, 119.

79. Mark Twain, "Accident Insurance—Etc.," in *Mark Twain's Speeches* (New York: Harper & Brothers, 1923), 222–23.

80. Ibid., 224.

81. Holmes, *The Common Law*, 96.

82. Mark Twain, "Abner L. Jackson (About to Be) Deceased," in *Mark Twain's Fables of Man*, ed. John S. Tuckey (Berkeley: University of California Press, 1972). Subsequent cites appear in the text. I am grateful to Professor Lee Krauth for bringing this story and "The International Lightning Trust" to my attention.

83. Twain had fun with the subject of lightning and the causal confusion it could generate in yet another story, "Mrs. McWilliams and the Lightning." In this story, the eponymous Mrs. McWilliams mistakes the sound of distant cannon announcing Garfield's election for a thunderstorm and proceeds to lock herself up in the bedroom closet for fear that she and the house, which does not have a lightning rod, will be struck.

84. Mark Twain, "The International Lightning Trust," in *Mark Twain's Fables of Man*, 86. Subsequent cites appear in the text.

Chapter Five
The Law of the Good Samaritan

1. *Buch v. Amory Manufacturing Co.*, 69 N.H. 257, 44 Atl. 809, 811 (1897).

2. Stephen Crane, *The Monster* in *The Complete Short Stories of Stephen Crane*, ed. Thomas A. Gullason (Garden City: Doubleday and Company, Inc., 1963), 448. My emphasis. Subsequent cites appear in the text.

3. See, for example, *Bohn V. Havemeyer*, 114 N.Y. 296 (1889); *Ogley v. Miles*, 139 N.Y. 458 (1893); *Jackson v. Standard Oil Co.*, 98 Ga. 749 (1896); *Buch v. Amory Manufacturing Co.*, 69 N.H. 257, 44 Atl. 809 (1897); *Allen v. Hixson*, 11 Ga. 460, 36 Southeastern Rptr. 810 (1900); *Union Pac. Ry. Co. v. Cappier*, 72 Pac. Rptr. 281 (1903).

4. *Plessy v. Ferguson*, 163 U.S. 537 (1896).

5. Morton J. Horwitz, *The Transformation of American Law: 1780–1860*, 253.

6. Oliver Wendell Holmes, quoted in *Liability and Responsibility: Essays in Law and Morals*, eds. R. G. Frey and Christopher W. Morris (Cambridge: Cambridge University Press, 1991), 41.

7. Francis Hilliard, *Law of Remedies for Torts* (Boston: Little, Brown, 1873), quoted in Horwitz, *The Transformation of American Law: 1870–1960*, 113.

8. The Supreme Court of New Hampshire overthrew the doctrine of punitive damages in 1873. The Supreme Court of Colorado followed in 1884.

9. Even in the absence of such dicta, however, the good Samaritan cases bespeak the horrors of idly standing by, of failing to come to the rescue. In their analysis of the language of judicial opinions in general, Richard Weisberg and Jean-Pierre Barricelli point out how one judge's concerted effort to appear dispassionate on the subject of the good Samaritan law backfired, provoking its legal audience to take the opposite view. See Richard Weisberg and Jean-Pierre Barricelli, "Literature and Law," in *Interrelations of Literature*, ed. Jean-Pierre Barricelli and Joseph Gibaldi (New York: The Modern Language Association, 1982), 165–68.

10. *Buch v. Amory Manufacturing Co.*, 811.

11. *Union Pac. Ry Co. v. Cappier*, 72 Pac. Rptr. 281 (1903).

12. Ibid., 283.

13. Thomas Babington Macaulay, quoted in Joel Feinberg, *Harm to Others: The Moral Limits of the Criminal Law* (New York: Oxford University Press, 1984), 152.

14. Richard Trammel, "Saving Life and Taking Life," in *Killing and Letting Die* (Englewood Cliffs, N.J.: Prentice-Hall, Inc., 1980), 168. See also Michael Menlowe and Alexander McCall Smith, eds., *The Duty to Rescue: The Jurisprudence of Aid* (Aldershot, UK: Dartmouth Publishing Company, 1993).

15. Feinberg, *Harm to Others*, 170. As a result, Feinberg adds, positive duties are most equitably and effectively managed if they are "split up in advance through the sharing of burdens and the assigning of special tasks" 170–71.

16. See Francis Bohlen, "The Moral Duty to Aid Others as a Basis of Tort Liability," *56 University of Pennsylvania Law Review* 217 (1908), 220.

17. James Barr Ames, "Law and Morals," 22 *Harvard Law Review* 97. See also Feinberg, *Harm to Others*, 130–50. In his ongoing effort to dispel the myths that support the law's position on good Samaritanism, Feinberg points out that the law's definition of benefit is overly broad. The law, he explains, understands the term "benefit" in a generic sense in which it is technically a move to affect a person's interest in a favorable way. The problem with this standard is that it too easily conflates efforts to advance a person's interest beyond "the baseline of its normal condition" with efforts merely to prevent a person's "interest-curve" from taking a sharp decline from the norm. The difference, Feinberg offers, is like that between giving someone an outright gift—a hundred dollars, a gold watch—and thus making that person better off than he or she was before the gift versus saving someone's life and thus restoring that person to a *status quo ante*. On this model, the gift is an act of benevolent generosity of the kind that cannot properly be compelled, while the preservation of life is a benefit in the technical sense only and one that cannot logically be excluded from the reaches of the law.

18. As Lee Clark Mitchell points out, even the narrator is implicated in the racism of the story. See "Face, Race, and Disfiguration in Stephen Crane's *The Monster*," *Critical Inquiry* 17 (Autumn 1990), 187.

19. For a sense of the centrality of this consensus-forming strategy to American culture as a whole, see Sacvan Bercovitch, *The American Jeremiad* (Madison: University of Wisconsin Press, 1978). See also Bercovitch, *The Rites of Assent*, 50–51, 190–91.

20. Joseph R. Gusfield, *Symbolic Crusade: Status Politics and the American Temperance Movement* (Urbana: University of Illinois Press, 1963), 5. As the title of the book suggests, Gusfield is concerned specifically with the temperance movement, but his point about the class implications of moral reform in the nineteenth century have relevance across the board.

21. It is important to note in the context of any discussion about good Samaritanism that while Darwin's notion of a "struggle for existence" tended to dominate nineteenth- and early twentieth-century thought, counter-theories did exist. For a theory of intraspecies harmony and altruism, see, for example, Petr Kropotkin, *Mutual Aid: A Factor of Evolution* (Boston: Extending Horizons Books, rpt. of 1914 edition).

22. Horwitz, *The Transformation of American Law: 1870–1960*, 124. For an opposing view, see Rabin, "The Historical Development of the Fault Principle: A Reinterpretation," in *Perspectives on Tort Law*, ed. Robert Rabin.

23. Holmes, *The Common Law*, 95.

24. For an explanation of Holmes's subtle manipulation of morality, see G. Edward White, *Justice Oliver Wendell Holmes* (New York: Oxford University Press, 1993), 259, 264, and Horwitz, *The Transformation of American Law: 1870–1960*, 125.

25. The incident is recounted in R. W. Stallman, *Stephen Crane* (New York: George Braziller, 1968), 218–32.

26. Crane, New York *Journal* (September 20, 1896), 17–18.

27. Quoted in Stallman, *Stephen Crane*, 221.

28. For a reading of the incident that emphasizes Crane's own complicity in

the class warfare, especially through his sentimentalization of the figure of the prostitute, see Christopher Wilson, "Stephen Crane and the Police," *American Quarterly* 48 (June 1996).

29. There were, of course, exceptions to this rule. Women, for example, were far more willing to provide hands-on relief for the needy. See Lori D. Ginzberg, *Women and the Work of Benevolence* (New Haven: Yale University Press, 1990).

30. See Stuart M. Blumin, *The Emergence of the Middle Class* (Cambridge: Cambridge University Press, 1989), 194–95.

31. For a brilliant discussion of the many important ways in which Howells's work is concerned with risk and the economy, see Wai Chee Dimock, *Residues of Justice: Literature, Law, Philosophy*, 158–81.

32. William Dean Howells, *A Hazard of New Fortunes* (New York: Oxford University Press, 1990), 384. Subsequent cites appear in the text.

33. Although it makes no direct mention of industrial accidents, Rebecca Harding Davis's novel, *Life in the Iron Mills* (1861), raises the problem of employers' neglect of the workers as well.

34. Elizabeth Stuart Phelps, *The Silent Partner* (New York: The Feminist Press, 1983).

35. Elizabeth Stuart Phelps, "The Tenth of January," in *The Silent Partner* and "The Tenth of January" (New York: The Feminist Press, 1983), 339. Subsequent cites appear in the text.

36. For an enlightening discussion of the operation of these doctrines in the antebellum period, see Brook Thomas's discussion of their relevance to Melville's "Bartleby, The Scrivener," and "The Paradise of Bachelors and the Tartarus of Maids," in *Cross-Examinations*, 167 ff.

37. It should be noted that the doctrine of the assumption of risk is both a tort and a contract doctrine. The tort rationale was predicated on the fiction that employees would become more vigilant and thus protect each other while the contract rationale was predicated on the fiction that the employees were free to contract with an employer for a certain job, and thus able voluntarily to "assume" its benefits and liabilities.

38. Karl Marx, *Capital*, 466.

39. Willa Cather, "Behind the Singer Tower," *24 Stories* (New York: Penguin Books, 1993). Subsequent cites appear in the text.

40. *Sann v. H.W. Johns Mfg. Co.*, 16 App. Div. 252, 144 N.Y. Supp. 641 (1897).

41. *Allen v. Hixson*, 11 Ga. 460, 36 Southeastern Rptr. 810 (1900).

42. *Saylor v. Parsons*, 98 N.W. 500 (1904).

43. *Lamson v. American Axe & Tool Co.*, 177 Mass. 144 (1900).

44. Quoted in Mark Tushnet, *The American Law of Slavery, 1810–1860* (Princeton: Princeton University Press, 1981), 184–85.

45. *Buckley v. The Gutta Percha and Rubber Manufacturing Co.*, 113 N.Y. 540 (1889).

46. See, for example, *Finnerty v. Prentice*, 75 N.Y. 615 (1878); *Hickey v. Taafe*, 99 N.Y. 204 (1885); *White v. Whitemann Lithographic Co.*, 131 N.Y. 631 (1892).

47. Although foreign-born workers comprised more than half the workforce by the late nineteenth century, they were paid far less than their white counterparts. In a work published in 1917 on the conditions of labor in the United States, W. Jett Lauck reported that the average weekly earnings of a native-born male of a native-born white father were $14.37, while the earnings of the foreign-born were $11.92. Moreover, Lauck reports that newer immigrants (Croatians, Poles, Russians, Italians) earned even less than older ones (English, Germans, Irish). See W. Jett Lauck and Edgar Sydenstricker, *Conditions of Labor in American Industries* (New York: Funk & Wagnalls Co., 1917), 38.

48. The figure of the clumsy, blundering black is a staple in the fiction of regional humorists like George Washington Harris, but it also emerges in the fiction of Stowe, Twain, and Melville, among others.

49. For a wonderful survey of the different uses of physical caricatures in minstrelsy, see Robert C. Toll, *Blacking Up: The Minstrel Show in Nineteenth-Century America* (New York: Oxford University Press, 1974).

50. See, for example, David R. Roediger, *The Wages of Whiteness: Race and the Making of the American Working Class* (London: Verso, 1991), 116.

51. Toll, *Blacking Up*, 69.

52. George Lipsitz, *Time Passages: Collective Memory and American Popular Culture* quoted in Roediger, *The Wages of Whiteness*, 116. Lipsitz is referring to antebellum minstrelsy, but the characterization holds true for postbellum minstrelsy as well.

53. One also thinks immediately of the self-sacrificing Jim in Twain's *Huckleberry Finn*.

54. David Halliburton, *The Color of the Sky: A Study of Stephen Crane* (Cambridge: Cambridge University Press, 1989), 184.

55. The nominal symbolism also makes Twelve into an image of the Apostles as well as that of a jury.

56. Halliburton, *The Color of the Sky*, 200.

57. Just as Halliburton is not the only critic to think Trescott will continue offering aid, I am not the only one to think he will and must stop the arrangement. Michael Fried, for example, notes that there is an "intimation—it seems more than just a bare possibility—that Johnson will now have to be abandoned. . . . See Fried, *Realism, Writing, Disfiguration* (Chicago: University of Chicago Press, 1987), 142.

58. Charles W. Chesnutt, *The Marrow of Tradition* (Ann Arbor: University of Michigan Press, 1969), 318. Subsequent cites appear in the text.

59. *Hurley v. Eddingfield*, 59 Northeastern Reporter 1058 (1901).

60. Charles W. Chesnutt, "The Averted Strike," in *The Short Fiction of Charles W. Chesnutt* (Washington, D.C.: Howard University Press, 1981), 385. Subsequent cites appear in the text.

61. Charles W. Chesnutt, *The Colonel's Dream* (New York: Doubleday, Page & Co., 1905, rpt. by Mnemosyne Publishing, Co., 1969), 256–67. Subsequent cites appear in the text.

62. Charles W. Chesnutt, "Stryker's Waterloo," in *The Short Fiction of Charles W. Chesnutt*, 365. Subsequent cites appear in the text.

Chapter Six
Stop, Look, and Listen

1. Frank H. Spearman, "The Million-Dollar Freight Train, *McClure's Magazine* XIV (February 1900), 380–86. Subsequent cites appear in the text.

2. *Palsgraf v. Long Island R.R. Co.*, 248 N.Y. 339, 162 N.E. 99 (1928). Subsequent cites appear in the text.

3. Reuben Lucius Goldberg (1883–1970) was famous for satirizing the effects of technology in his cartoons. For a delightful compendium of his work, see Philip Garner, *Rube Goldberg: A Retrospective* (New York: The Putnam Publishing Group, 1983).

4. For a fascinating perspective on the controversies stirred by the case, see John T. Noonan Jr., *Persons and Masks of the Law: Cardozo, Holmes, Jefferson, and Wythe as Makers of the Masks* (New York: Farrar, Straus and Giroux, 1976), 111–51.

5. Thomas Haskell, *The Emergence of Professional Social Science* (Urbana: University of Illinois Press, 1977), 40.

6. This fiction was an especially popular choice with men and boys of the working classes. So successful and popular was this fiction that it spawned a journal, *The Railroad Man's Magazine*, that featured novel-length railroad stories as well as nonfiction articles about all aspects of life on the railroad's right-of-way. But the influence of the fiction and of railroad mania in general was felt in other classes as well, as stories about railroad signaling were often found in the pages of middle- and upper-class periodicals, such as *Scribner's*, *Harper's*, and William Dean Howells's prestigious *Atlantic Monthly*.

7. For an illuminating history and analysis of the safety bicycle, see Wiebe E. Bijker, *Of Bicycles, Bakelites, and Bulbs: Toward a Theory of Sociotechnical Change* (Cambridge, MA: MIT Press, 1997), 19–100.

8. Of course, Jean Baudrillard may be right in arguing that in positing an equivalence between a signifier and a signified, the sign excludes ambivalence and thus falsely imposes meaning. But my interest in this chapter is in the pattern of meaning that the sign imposes, whether it is ideologically mystifying or not. See Jean Baudrillard, *For a Critique of the Political Economy of the Sign*, trans. Charles Levin (Telos Press, 1981), 148, 160.

9. In some ways, signs and signals are synonymous with the law. The legal scholar Peter Goodrich writes: "The question of law remains which mechanisms of reference or which visual insignia best mark and remind the subject of its obligations or best hold it to law." Peter Goodrich, *Oedipus Lex: Psychoanalysis, History, Law* (Berkeley: University of California Press, 1995), 43.

10. For a thorough history of the automobile, see John B. Rae, *The Road and the Car in American Life* (Cambridge: MIT Press, 1971).

11. Thus, while the following analysis concentrates on the varieties of railroad signaling as the standard-bearer for modern signaling as a whole, it attends as well to the uses of signaling for cars, and other vehicular traffic, such as interurbans, streetcars, and trolleys.

12. For more detailed information about this and many of the other devices

mentioned in this section, see Marshall M. Kirkman, *The Science of Railways* (New York: The World Railway Publishing Company, 1900), 244–301. See also John Armstrong, *All About Signals* (Kalmbach Publishing Co., 1957).

13. For an enlightening description of the interlocking system, see Armstrong, *All About Signals*, 17–21.

14. Cited in John R. Stilgoe, *Metropolitan Corridor: Railroads and the American Scene* (New Haven: Yale University Press, 1983), 153.

15. Frank V. Whiting, "Stop, Look, Listen," *The Outlook*, August 23, 1913, 929. Subsequent cites appear in the text.

16. Rex Stuart, "People Act as If They *Wanted* to Be Killed," *The American Magazine* September 1921, 126.

17. Stilgoe uses the term in *Metropolitan Corridor*, 167.

18. Many of the safety posters are depicted and discussed in *Railway Age Gazette*. This one appears in *Railway Age Gazette*, June 2, 1916, 1193.

19. The American Railway Association continued this campaign throughout the 1920s and 1930s. Many of these posters were reprinted by the Norfolk Southern Corporation in 1992. I am grateful to the railroad signaling historian Robert McKnight for making me aware of this safety campaign and for sending me copies of many of these posters.

20. In addition to the actual sign, many posters from the period reiterated this warning. In particular, one issued by the Georgia Railroad in 1920 featuring a car, a train, and a pedestrian all converging on a railroad crossing, read: "When you approach a Railroad Crossing every heartbeat may bring you nearer eternity—unless you Stop, Look, and Listen." Reprinted by Norfolk Southern Corporation, 1992.

21. Holmes, *The Common Law*, 108.

22. *Baltimore & Ohio R. Co. v. Goodman*, 275 U.S. 66 (1927). Subsequent cites appear in the text.

23. See Armstrong, *All About Signals*, 10.

24. Charles Edward Russell, "Speed," *Hampton-Columbian Magazine* 27, October 1911, 430.

25. *Pokora v. Wabash Railroad Company*, 292 U.S. 98 (1934). Earlier cases that took issue with the case include *Torgeson v. Missouri-K.T.R.R.*, 124 Kan 798, 262 P. 564 (1928) where the court held that it was "safer to approach the crossing slowly and drive straight across, than to stop and get out." Subsequent cites appear in the text.

26. See Cecelia Tichi, *Shifting Gears* (Chapel Hill: University of North Carolina Press, 1987), 137–40, for the suggestion that while Adams deplored much about the machine-age world, he upheld many of the values of the engineer.

27. For a wonderful description of how comprehensive a change Taylor's ideas were for the culture at large, see Martha Banta, *Taylored Lives* (Chicago: University of Chicago Press, 1993).

28. For the stories of "Head-On" Joe Connolly and W. G. Crush, see B. A. Botkin and Alvin F. Harlow, eds., *A Treasury of Railroad Folklore* (New York: Crown Publishers, 1953), 354–56.

29. The Lionel catalogue for 1929, published in 1928, quoted in Stilgoe, *Metropolitan Corridor*, 137.

30. Archibald Williams, *The Marvel of Railways* (London: Seeley, Service & Co., 1924), 174.

31. Ibid, my emphasis, 175.

32. Ibid.

33. E. A. Ross, *Social Control* (New York: The Macmillan Company, 1914), 110. I am grateful to Professor Priscilla Wald for this reference.

34. Russell, "Speed," 454, my emphasis. Specifically, Russell is speaking of the stress found among engineers.

35. See, for example, Kirkman, *The Science of Railways*, 224–44.

36. George M. Stratton, "Railway Disasters at Night," *The Century Magazine*, LXXIV, May 1907, 119.

37. Kirkman, *The Science of Railways*, 495.

38. James O. Fagan, *Confessions of a Railroad Signalman* (Boston: Houghton, Mifflin Co., 1908), 128–29. Subsequent cites appear in the text.

39. Harold Titus, "A Little Action," reprinted in Frank P. Donovan Jr., and Robert Selph Henry, eds. *Headlights and Markers: An Anthology of Railroad Stories* (New York: Creative Age Press, Inc., 1946). Subsequent cites appear in the text.

40. Frank L. Packard, "The Night Operator," reprinted in Frank P. Donovan Jr., and Robert Selph Henry, eds., *Headlights and Markers*. Subsequent cites appear in the text.

41. Of course, there were stories in which such tensions surfaced for characters who were not employed as signalers. For example, the story of a hard-nosed division superintendent who is torn between his love for his fiancee and his love for the hustle and bustle of his life and duties in the railroad yards, the popular Hollywood film, *Danger Lights* (1930), depicts such a rivalry without reference to signaling.

42. Herbert D. Ward, "The Semaphore," *Scribner's Magazine*, XIV, December 1893. Subsequent cites appear in the text.

43. Wadsworth Camp, "The Signal Tower," reprinted in Edward J. O'Brien, ed., *The Best Short Stories of 1920* (Boston: Small, Maynard & Company, 1920). Subsequent cites appear in the text.

44. Frank Condon, "When the Light Turned," *The Railroad Man's Magazine*, IV, November 1907, 345.

45. Interestingly, the elements of sensory (mis)perception noted above, including the self-doubt and the phantasmic quality of the lights perceived by the engineer in this last story, became, in stories that further developed this theme, elements of *extra*-sensory (mis)perception. Indeed, color blindness, inclement weather, and poor visibility at night all contributed to an aura of inexplicability that pervaded the accident narrative and resulted in the frequent transformation of illegible or inadequate signs into hallucinations and ghosts. For examples of railroad ghost stories, see Charles Dickens's "The Signalman," Frank Spearman's "The Despatcher's Story," Cy Warman's "Ghost Train Illusion," and the legend of President Lincoln's ghost train reported in collections of railroad folklore.

46. Johnston McCulley, "Richard Hughes—Railroad Detective," *The Railroad Man's Magazine*, vol. V, no. 4 May 1908, 604–5. For the suggestion that

bad lighting is at the heart of other ghostly tales in this genre, see also John R. Stilgoe, "Sounders and Silence: Some Isolated Train-Order Stations in Fiction," *Railroad History*, no. 157, Autumn 1987, 49.

47. Francis Lynde, *Scientific Sprague* (New York: A. L. Burt Company, 1912). Subsequent cites appear in the text.

48. Cy Warman, "The Mysterious Message," in *The Express Messenger and Other Tales of the Rail* (New York: Charles Scribner's Sons, 1897). Subsequent cites appear in the text.

49. Indeed, the story that best exemplifies this kind of signal failure is a detective story—more accurately, a detective novel that was one in a series of juvenile railroad novels by the enormously popular author Allen Chapman. In *Ralph, the Train Dispatcher, or the Mystery of the Pay Car* (1911), the eponymous Ralph, who works his way up through the ranks of the railroad just as Horatio Alger's Dick does on the street, learns not only to dispatch trains but to decipher the misleading messages of a group of disgruntled ex-employees that is interrupting and subverting the railroad's official telegraphs in order to abscond with a large sum of money on the pay car.

50. For the clearest explanation of the importance of the *Palsgraf* decision with respect to the future of causation and of Green's importance on it, see G. Edward White, *Tort Law in America*, 100 ff.

Chapter Seven
Epilogue

1. Jonathan Harr, *A Civil Action* (New York: Random House, Inc., 1996).

2. Charles Reznikoff, *Testimony: The United States (1885–1915) recitative*, vol. II (Santa Barbara: Black Sparrow Press, 1978), 95. I am grateful to Professor Sidney Goldfarb for calling my attention to Reznikoff's work.

3. Siegfried Giedion, *Mechanization Takes Command* (New York: Oxford University Press, 1948).

4. *Escola v. Coca Cola Bottling Co. of Fresno*, 24 Cal. 2D 453, 150 P.2d 436 (1944). Subsequent cites appear in the text. Technically speaking, *Escola* was the second reported case about a defective product. It followed *Macpherson v. Buick Motor Co.*, 217 N.Y. 382, 11 N.E. 1050 (1916). However, *Macpherson* (a case concerning a defective automobile wheel), though extremely significant, stands for the proposition that there need be "no privity of contract" between a consumer and a negligent manufacturer in order to assign liability to the manufacturer. While *Macpherson* may have paved the way for the application of strict liability in cases of product injury, then, *Escola* is still the first case to do so.

5. J. D. Salinger, "Uncle Wiggily in Connecticut," in *Nine Stories* (Boston: Little Brown and Company, 1968), 32. Subsequent cites appear in the text.

6. *Barnard v. Kellogg*, 77 U.S. (10 Wall) 383, 388–89, 19 L.Ed. 987 (1870).

7. Stephen King, "The Sun Dog," in *Four Past Midnight* (New York: Penguin Books, 1991), 603. Subsequent cites appear in the text.

8. Igor Kopytoff, "The Cultural Biography of Things: Commoditization as Process," in *The Social Life of Things: Commodities in Cultural Perspective*, ed., Arjun Appadurai (New York: Cambridge University Press, 1986), 64.

9. Ralph Nader, *Unsafe at Any Speed: The Designed-in Dangers of the American Automobile* (New York: Grossman Publishers, 1965), 8–9.

10. Stephen King, "Trucks," in *Night Shift* (New York: New American Library, 1979), 142. Subsequent cites appear in the text.

11. In the movie *Maximum Overdrive*, which is based on "Trucks" and directed by Stephen King, the girl's simple affirmation of a hierarchy between man and machine based on the production process becomes a haunting refrain.

12. Stephen King, *Christine* (New York: Penguin Books, 1983), 251. Subsequent cites appear in the text.

13. See, for example, *Heider v. Employers Mutual Liability Ins. Co.*, 231 So. 2D 438 (La. App. 1970).

14. The court in this case made a definite distinction between asbestosis and cancer, a distinction that remains somewhat obscure.

15. *Jackson v. Johns-Manville Sales Corporation*, 781 F.2d 394 (1986), my emphasis.

16. Don DeLillo, *White Noise* (New York: Penguin Books, 1984), 131. Subsequent cites appear in the text.

17. John Cole, The Evolving Case-Control Study, 32 *J. Chronic Dis.* 15 (1979).

18. *Miller v. National Cabinet Company*, 8 N.Y.2d 277, 204 N.Y.S.2d 129, 168 N.E.2d 811 (1960). Originally the widow was so unaware of the etiology of her husband's death that she based her first claim for benefits on a back injury her husband had sustained at work while moving a piano.

19. In re *"Agent Orange" Product Liability Litigation*, 597, F. Supp. 740, aff'd 818 F.2d 145 (2d Cir. 1987).

20. Ultimately, the famous and interminable litigation on Agent Orange did not so much resolve the problem of toxicity and disease as sidestep it, holding for policy reasons alone that the veterans of the war should be compensated for their injuries. "Whether their hurt can be traced to Agent Orange or whether they are merely 'casually unfortunate,'" the court wrote, "is beside the point in the broader context of the nation's obligations to Vietnam veterans and their families," See ibid.

21. *Loerch v. Abbott Laboratories*, Hennepin County District Court, Minnesota, 1988.

22. It is known, for instance, that an estimated 200,000 American workers will die before the end of the twentieth century from forty or more years of exposure to asbestos, and that the Chernobyl accident may result in 30,000 to 250,000 deaths from cancer in the former Soviet Republics. Figures cited in Richard H. Gaskins, *Environmental Accidents: Personal Injury and Public Responsibility* (Philadelphia: Temple University Press, 1989), 16.

Index

NAN GOODMAN has a Ph.D. in English and American Literature from Harvard and a J.D. from Stanford. She has taught at the University of Colorado Law School and is an Assistant Professor of English at the University of Colorado at Boulder.